Democracy and
Possessive Individualism

SUNY Series in
Political Theory:
Contemporary Issues

Philip Green, Editor

Democracy and Possessive Individualism

The Intellectual Legacy of
C. B. Macpherson

edited by
Joseph H. Carens

State University of New York Press

Published by
State University of New York Press, Albany

© 1993 State University of New York

For information, address the State University of New York Press
State University Plaza, Albany, N.Y. 12246

Production by Bernadine Dawes
Marketing by Terry Swierzowski

Library of Congress Cataloging-in-Publication Data

Democracy and possessive individualism: the intellectual legacy of
C. B. Macpherson / edited by Joseph H. Carens.
        p. cm. — (SUNY series in political theory. Contemporary
issues)
    Includes index.
    ISBN 0-7914-1457-4 (hc : alk. paper). — ISBN 0-7914-1458-2 (pb :
alk. paper)
    1. Macpherson, C. B. (Crawford Brough), 1911- . 2. Democracy.
3. Individualism. 4. Liberalism. I. Carens, Joseph H.
II. Series.
JC423.D4398 1993
  321.8–dc20
                                                92-17915
                                              CIP

1 2 3 4 5 6 7 8 9 10

Carens, Joseph H. Democracy and
Possessive Individualism

To the memory of
Christian Bay

Contents

Acknowledgments

The papers in this volume were presented originally at a memorial conference for C. B. Macpherson held at the University of Toronto in October 1989. The conference marked the conclusion of the centenary celebrations of the Department of Political Science and inaugurated the biannual C. B. Macpherson Memorial Lecture Series sponsored by the University of Toronto Faculty Association. I acknowledge with gratitude the financial support provided for the conference by the Social Sciences and Humanities Research Council of Canada and several sponsors from within the University of Toronto: the Office of the Vice President/Research, the Department of Political Science, the Faculty Association, the Office of the President, the Department of Philosophy, the Faculty of Arts and Sciences, and the Graduate School.

In organizing the conference, and subsequently arranging for publication of the papers, I received help from many people. I cannot name them all, but I would like to express my appreciation publicly to at least some.

Late in the book's production process, I faced a difficult and painful problem: how to respond, if at all, to Mihailo Marković's political role in contemporary Serbia. (I have discussed this in a note immediately preceding Marković's article in the book.) In thinking about this issue, I was aided immensely by conversations with many people. Some helped me to find my way along the path I ultimately pursued. Others disagreed with that path but helped me to reflect more deeply. I talked with all of the contributors at least briefly and, in some cases, at length. In addition, I had extensive conversations with Ed Andrew, Ronnie Beiner, Seyla Benhabib, Richard Bernstein, Val Bunce, Ellen Comisso, Frank Cunningham, Phil Green, Amy Gutmann, Alkis Kontos, Will Kymlicka, Brian Langille, Clay Morgan, Julie Mostov, Cliff Orwin, Tom Pangle, Arthur Ripstein, Marion Smiley, Dennis Thompson, David Welch, and Melissa Williams. I owe special thanks to Jennifer Nedelsky for her time, support, and counsel in connection with this problem.

My other debts concern matters more routine for this sort of enterprise, but the debts are no less real for that. Bob Fenn shared with me the responsibility for organizing the conference. Vera Melnyk's administrative skills made it possible to have a conference. Ilone Eurchuk, Hyla Levy, and Marian Reed typed countless letters, lists, proposals, and papers before and after the conference. Marian bore the main responsibility for these tasks and deserves special thanks for the work she has done on this project over the last few years. Four of my colleagues chaired panels at the conference and provided support and advice both before and after the event: Ronnie Beiner, Frank Cunningham, Alkis Kontos, and Jennifer Nedelsky.

David Braybrooke, Amy Gutmann, and Nan Keohane gave comments at the conference but did not have the time to expand these into papers. Sheldon Wolin gave a paper but had committed it elsewhere for publication. Although their written work does not appear in this volume, all four of them made important contributions to the success of the conference.

Disliking administrative work as I do, I would never have undertaken to organize the conference in the first place if Marsha Chandler, then chair of the department and now Dean of Arts and Sciences, had not emphasized the importance of the enterprise to the department. Perhaps I would not have undertaken it even then had she been less committed to my taking it up. Having induced me to accept, she elicited much of the financial support from other sources within the university— including one crucial grant when it looked as if the whole project might collapse because of insufficient funds—and in other ways provided the resources needed to make the conference work well.

While I found the administrative work a burden, the connections I made with the participants more than compensated me for my efforts. In addition to learning a lot, I made new friends and strengthened ties with old ones.

I have only one regret. Christian Bay, a long-time colleague of C. B. Macpherson, had been scheduled to chair one of the sessions. However, illness prevented him from doing so and claimed his life several months later. We all miss his gentle yet critical spirit. This book is dedicated to his memory.

I never met C. B. Macpherson. By the time I arrived at the University of Toronto in 1985, he was already too ill for the sort of public or social occasion at which that might have been possible. But I teach in the department in which Macpherson taught from 1935 until 1977, with only a brief interruption during World War II. It is a department that, by long tradition, treats political theory as central to political science and embraces a wide range of political views. This enlightened approach—which makes the University of Toronto such a wonderful place to teach political science, and especially political theory—is not due solely to Macpherson. The continuation of the tradition so long after his retirement testifies to a wider collective wisdom. But Macpherson probably contributed more than any other individual to establishing that tradition and to sinking its roots so deeply. That is a part of his legacy for which I am particularly grateful.

Chapter 1
Possessive Individualism and Democratic Theory: Macpherson's Legacy

Joseph H. Carens

> The fox knows many tricks, the hedgehog only one. One good one.
> —Archilochus

By his own account, C. B. Macpherson was more a hedgehog than a fox. In the preface to his last book, Macpherson observed wryly, "Although the papers range widely in subject matter, the critic who remarked that I never write about anything except possessive individualism will here find no need to retract."[1] Macpherson used the concept of possessive individualism as a lens through which to view critically the familiar concepts and categories of liberal political theory: human nature, rationality, power, freedom, justice, equality, democracy, state, property, participation, pluralism, and human rights. Still, it is an overstatement to say that Macpherson wrote only of possessive individualism—unless one includes in that concept its opposite, the "creative

I wish to thank Jennifer Nedelsky, Ed Andrew, Frank Cunningham, and Alkis Kontos for comments on a previous draft of this essay. The epigram by Archilochus is from a fragment that appears in *Greek Lyrics,* 2d ed., trans. Richard Lattimore (Chicago: University of Chicago Press, 1960), 17. Isaiah Berlin's famous essay on Tolstoy (*The Hedgehog and the Fox* [London: Weidenfeld and Nicolson, 1953]) has so shaped contemporary perceptions of the contrast between the hedgehog and the fox that it is easy to overlook the fact that Archilochus himself was celebrating the hedgehog.

and cooperative individualism"[2] that can only be achieved in a genuinely democratic society. Macpherson's positive goal was to retrieve a richer, deeper understanding of democracy from the distortions and limitations imposed on it by possessive individualism, both in theory and in practice. Thus, possessive individualism and democracy constitute the two poles of Macpherson's intellectual project: the critical and the constructive.

AN OVERVIEW OF MACPHERSON'S ACCOUNT
OF POSSESSIVE INDIVIDUALISM

The centrality of individualism to liberalism had not gone unremarked prior to Macpherson's work. His distinctive contribution was to explore how a certain conception of property ownership had shaped liberal thinking about individualism. Beginning with Hobbes, Macpherson argued, one finds a tradition of political theory in which ownership is constitutive of individuality, freedom, and equality.[3] To be an individual is to be an owner—in the first instance, an owner of one's own person and capacities, but also of what one acquires through the use of one's capacities. To be free is to be an owner. Freedom is defined in terms of independence from others, and one is independent only when one has the right to use one's property, including one's abilities, as one chooses. Even equality is linked to ownership, because being an owner of one's own person and capacities is a status that every individual can enjoy equally.

In the political theory of possessive individualism society is presumed to consist of relations among independent owners, and the primary task of government is to protect owners against illegitimate incursions upon their property and to maintain conditions of orderly exchange. The notion of ownership here draws upon an understanding of property as private and exclusive, entailing the right of owners to exclude others and to use or dispose of their property as they choose.[4] This version of individualism is ultimately justified on the grounds that it is congruent with human nature, for human beings are portrayed as bundles of appetites that are, in principle, unlimited and not subject to rational scrutiny. A social world organized around individuals as owners will, it is said, maximize the satisfaction of such desires.

The concern for democracy comes late in this tradition—only in the nineteenth century—and it is grafted onto these possessive roots.

Democracy is conceptualized merely as a means of choosing one's governors, and this is justified as an extension of the principle that individual owners should be free to make choices about how best to pursue their individual interests, assuming that the basic system of property ownership is not itself in question.[5]

This is, in brief, the conception of human nature and society that Macpherson called "possessive individualism." He argued that it had shaped liberal political theory from Hobbes to the present, despite changes in language and doctrine, and that it remained dominant in the late twentieth century despite the emergence of an alternative version of liberal individualism that he traced primarily to J. S. Mill.

According to Macpherson, possessive individualism is fundamentally flawed for two reasons. First, it generates an impoverished view of life, making acquisition and consumption central and obscuring deeper human purposes and capacities. Wordsworth's famous complaint— "Getting and spending we lay waste our powers"—nicely captures one dimension of Macpherson's objection to possessive individualism. The possessive view of life distorts the democratic ideal, which Macpherson described as a commitment to "provide the conditions for the full and free development of the essential human capacities of all the members of the society."[6] According to Macpherson, possessive individualism reduces this lofty goal to the maximization of utilities.

Second, possessive individualism holds out a false promise. Most people cannot really enjoy even the impoverished individuality, freedom, and equality that possessive individualism ostensibly offers to all, because a system based on private property and so-called free exchange inevitably generates a concentration of ownership of all the means of production except labor. Most people are compelled to sell their labor to gain access to the means of life. They are free and equal individuals in name only. In reality, they are subordinate to the owners of capital, who are able to use the power that ownership brings to control those without capital and to extract benefits from them. The original meaning of democracy, Macpherson argued, was rule on behalf of the common people or the formerly oppressed. The possessive individualist version of democracy denies and conceals the oppression and class domination inherent in a society based upon private—and unequal—property. It ignores the obstacles to effective popular political participation that such a society creates.

Despite these flaws, possessive individualism is not a mistake, at least not in any simple sense. Macpherson argued that possessive individual-

3

ism held sway in political theory precisely because it grew out of and reflected (as well as concealed) the realities of liberal society. Human beings are not, by nature, possessive individuals, but this is the sort of human being that capitalism requires and, to a large extent, produces.

Of the many provocative and important features of this account of possessive individualism, let me highlight three that figure prominently in the essays in this volume: the unity of the liberal tradition, the relation of the economic and the political, and the place of difference in the democratic ideal. I will not defend Macpherson, but merely explicate and clarify his views on these topics so that the issues at stake in this volume may be seen in clearer focus.

First, there is the question of the unity of the liberal tradition. Viewed through the lens of possessive individualism, the differences between liberal theorists seem less important than their similarities. For example, Macpherson treated talk of natural right and natural law among liberals as a facade for an underlying utilitarian structure of thought. His reading made Locke much closer to Hobbes than most previous interpreters had thought, and Bentham closer to both. In his words, "Bentham built on Hobbes."[7] All this is highly controversial. In the eyes of many critics, Macpherson's reading of liberal theorists neglected important differences of social circumstance, political purpose, and intellectual context.

Macpherson's unifying reconstruction of the liberal tradition rests, in my view, upon three methodological presuppositions, only the first of which he identified as such. At the beginning of *Possessive Individualism,* Macpherson argued that the possessive individualist conceptions of human nature and society that liberal theorists share often operate as background assumptions in the theories themselves, with different elements being more explicit in some authors than in others.[8] These assumptions help to account for contradictions and gaps in an author's argument, in the sense that they reveal how an author could have failed to notice the contradictions or gaps. Macpherson used this approach to account for various puzzles about the authors whom he discusses in *Possessive Individualism,* such as Locke's having two conflicting pictures of the state of nature.[9]

He employed the same approach in later works. For example, according to Macpherson, Bentham put forward a concept of utility that was formally open to any sort of satisfaction but unduly emphasized material satisfactions to the point of insisting that only satisfactions that could be measured by money really counted. Bentham was committed to the egalitarian principle that everyone should count for one and no one for more than one, but he accepted, and even defended, social and economic inequalities that he himself had shown to be incompatible with that principle. Bentham moved without any plausible justification from general claims about the importance of security to an absolute defense of existing property rights.[10] All these unexplained and logically indefensible moves in Bentham's arguments could only be accounted for, Macpherson argued, by the hypothesis that Bentham's thought had been shaped by possessive individualist assumptions of which he was not himself fully aware.

In addition to this claim about the importance of shared background assumptions in the interpretation of a tradition of political theory, Macpherson's case for the unity of the liberal tradition rested upon two other methodological premises that he himself did not treat as explicitly as the preceding. First, Macpherson assumed that there is a logic to social developments that can be captured and revealed in political theory. What made Hobbes a great theorist was his capacity to identify the underlying logic of capitalist society at a time when it was just beginning to unfold. Macpherson did not claim that there had been no significant changes in society since the seventeenth century. On the contrary, he described Harrington as "a more realistic analyst" of the seventeenth century than Hobbes.[11] Harrington's theory was also informed by possessive assumptions, but he did not pursue their implications as relentlessly as Hobbes. As a result, Harrington was able to be more faithful to the complexity of the society in which he lived, a society which was not yet fully bourgeois. But Hobbes explored the logic of liberalism more fully. He abstracted more from the surface realities of his own time and penetrated more deeply to the underlying reality of what was implicit and what was to come. This underlying logic is what ties the liberal tradition together and gives Hobbes an enduring relevance today.

Second, what matters most in understanding a political theory is not the intention of the author, but rather how a theory actually supports or challenges prevailing (or emerging) social relations and social institutions. Two examples illustrate this approach. In one of his last essays, Macpherson suggested that Hobbes's theory objectively supported the emerging capitalist order by providing an understanding of human nature and society that made bourgeois social relations appear legitimate, even though Hobbes himself was quite hostile to the capitalists of his day and was not writing with the aim of supporting them.[12] The other example is the Levellers who, prior to Macpherson, had generally been regarded as radical democrats. Macpherson argued that the Levellers made individual freedom central to their political thought and property central to their conception of individual freedom. They failed to see the limiting implications of these conceptions, and, as a result, they "paved the way, unwittingly, for Locke and the Whig tradition."[13] In both these cases—and many others—Macpherson derived the unity of the liberal tradition not from the intentions of the authors or the understandings of their contemporaries, but from what he took to be the underlying implications of their views.

I turn now to the question of the relation between the economic and the political. Macpherson's account of possessive individualism offered, above all, a critique of class domination, private property, and economic inequality. He emphasized the similarities between economic and political power, and the dependence of the latter upon the former. Did he unduly subordinate the political to the economic, neglecting the distinctiveness of political institutions and political life?

Macpherson's own answer to this question could be inferred from his discussion of two sets of predecessors: developmental idealists such as T. H. Green, Barker, and MacIver, and empirical realists such as Schumpeter, Dahl, and Verba. The former put forward an understanding of human nature that emphasized human self-realization through conscious and creative activity rather than acquisition and consumption. They saw democratic political participation through shared deliberation about the common good as an essential element in this conscious and creative activity, and one that all citizens could enjoy. Macpherson embraced these ideals but argued that the developmental idealists had neglected or been naïve about the way in which the economic organization of society would either block or make possible the realization of these ideals. "The theorists of the first half of the twentieth century increasingly lost sight of class and exploitation. They generally wrote as if democracy itself, at least a democracy that embraced the regulatory and welfare state, could do most of what could be done, and most of what needed to be done, to bring a good society."[14] He offered a related objection to that branch of developmental idealism that emphasized "the multiplicity and moral value of group life."[15] Macpherson did not repudiate this sort of pluralism in principle, but argued that the focus on the diversity of group life had concealed and left in the shadows the more fundamental problem of class.

By neglecting the distance between their vision of the good society and the way liberal democratic institutions actually and inevitably worked in a capitalist society, the developmental idealists made themselves vulnerable to the charge that they were unrealistic. But those who made this charge, the empirical realists, suffered from their own lack of realism.[16] On the one hand, they were more accurate than the idealists in describing much of the political behavior in liberal democracies. They presented a picture of democracy as a system of elites competing for the votes of an ill-informed and uninvolved citizenry, and of pluralism as groups pursuing their own narrow interests rather than the public good. But they did not ask *why* individuals and groups behaved in such narrowly self-interested ways, thus suggesting that this was simply the inevitable outcome of human nature rather than the product of capitalist organization and culture. Similarly, they emphasized the differences between economic and political power while neglecting the more important similarities of purpose and effect. The empirical realists had nothing to say about how economic and political power cohere as extractive power to the advantage of one class over another. Thus, their emphasis on the difference between the economic and the political served to legitimate the system even while they were acknowledging some aspects of its elitism and nonresponsiveness. In sum, for Macpherson, the failures of both the developmental idealists and the empirical realists showed the dangers of trying to discuss the political in abstraction from the economic, or indeed of accepting such a distinction at face value.

Finally, there is the issue of how human differences fit into a democratic ideal. In one famous section of *Democratic Theory,* Macpherson asserted that his theory of democracy assumed "the nonopposition of essentially human capacities," that is, that in a truly democratic society each member of society would be able to develop his or her capacities without preventing others from developing theirs.[17] At one point he described this as an "assumption of potential substantial harmony."[18] Macpherson himself characterized this assumption as "staggering" at first sight, but argued that it was a necessary postulate of any "fully democratic theory."[19]

As I see it, Macpherson was not talking here about the possibilities of abundance or about the absence of all conflicts, but rather about the necessary presupposition of any claim that it is possible to have a society that is not based on domination and subordination. If one rejects this assumption and asserts instead that the fundamental goods of some groups and individuals will conflict with those of others even in the best society we can hope to achieve, then one must accept the claim—not unknown in the history of political thought—that happiness for some inevitably depends upon the misery of others.

AN OVERVIEW OF THE BOOK

In exploring the implications of Macpherson's intellectual project for political theory today, the essays in this book take up the three topics I have just discussed, as well as several closely related ones. All of the essays address Macpherson's problems, concerns, and arguments, although some of them focus exclusively on responding to Macpherson while others use him more as a point of departure. Some of the authors are more sympathetic to Macpherson than are others, but none is uncritical. Above all, they pay tribute to Macpherson by taking his ideas seriously even as they try to challenge or transcend them.

James Tully focuses on Macpherson's account of early modern British political thought. He celebrates the importance of Macpherson's possessive individualism thesis while providing a magisterial survey of recent scholarship that calls that thesis into question. According to Tully, this new scholarship shows that the writers of the early modern period were concerned with the problems of creating, maintaining, and justifying a stable political order rather than with the problems of an emerging capitalism. The scholarship identifies at least three distinct—and somewhat conflicting—lines of thought in responding to these problems of political order.

First, there is the juristic tradition. This tradition did indeed make considerable use of a concept of self-ownership, but it was a juridical and moral concept rather than an economic one. It emphasized self-preservation rather than acquisition, and it derived from Grotius rather than Hobbes. Second, there was the seventeenth-century literature on questions of political economy. It adopted a mercantilist rather than a market perspective, presupposing that economic affairs should be organized and regulated to preserve and strengthen the state. This literature treated the individual as a "repository of productive capacities" to be used by and for the state through the manipulation of rewards and punishments. This is a concept of the individual quite different from both the juristic and the Macphersonian possessive concepts. The third discursive tradition to which Tully points is civic humanism or republicanism, which can be traced from the Italian Renaissance to the late eighteenth century. This tradition made property central, but tied it to an ideal of citizenship and civic virtue. It was this republican tradition, not the juristic one, that eventually reflected upon and legitimated market capitalism. However, it did this in the eighteenth century (not the seventeenth), and through discussions of "commercial society" (a more complex phenomenon than "market society") it produced deep criticisms as well as defenses of this new form of society.

On the whole, Tully concludes, the scholarship about these three discursive traditions shows that Macpherson's analysis fails to take adequate account of the intellectual and social context of early modern thought and of the diversity among the writers of this period. Nevertheless, Tully says, Macpherson's work still stands as a model of original and provocative questioning of the history of political thought.

Like Tully, Louise Marcil-Lacoste focuses on Macpherson's work on the seventeenth century, but she limits her concern to Macpherson's discussion of Hobbes and she is far more sanguine than Tully about the enduring validity of Macpherson's work. Indeed, Marcil-Lacoste basically accepts Macpherson's analysis and seeks to extend it by doing for equality what Macpherson has done for liberty. Just as Macpherson has shown how the Hobbesian understanding of individual freedom was informed and distorted by unarticulated possessive assumptions that shaped the liberal tradition and continue to constrain our thinking about freedom today, so Marcil-Lacoste argues that the concept of equality in Hobbes is shaped by negative possessive assumptions that drastically limit its capacity to serve as a positive social value and that inform discussions of equality down to the present day. She shows how Hobbes's treatment of the passions, of felicity, and of obligation all presuppose inequality and yet provide the context for his discussion of natural equality. Thus, in Hobbes, equality can only be understood negatively, as a form of egoism. Equality is indissolubly linked to inequality. By exposing these negative presuppositions, Marcil-Lacoste hopes to retrieve a richer, more positive understanding of equality from the constraints imposed by Hobbes's seventeenth-century conceptual prison.

The conventional view of Bentham portrays him as the author of an abstract, atomistic, and narrowly rationalistic version of utilitarianism. It is a position that fits well with Macpherson's suggestion that he represents the logical final development of the political theory of

9

possessive individualism that Hobbes had introduced. Nancy Rosenblum presents another Bentham, one who paved the way for romanticism and who was more expressive and sensitive than most critics since J. S. Mill have thought him to be. She ties her critique of Macpherson's view of Bentham to larger debates about individualism and holism and about the relation between ontology and politics.

According to Rosenblum, Macpherson (and other holists) are mistaken in describing Bentham's individualism as abstract, atomistic, and narrowly rationalistic. Bentham's own sensibility, she argues, was shaped more by horror of pain than calculation of gain. Far from seeing the individual as independent of society, Bentham emphasized the importance of socialization and social connections in human life. For that reason, he made securing expectations a central theme of his work. Furthermore, Bentham's individualism did not inevitably entail a commitment to capitalism. That is the mistake of supposing that ontology determines politics. Bentham's primary political purpose was not, in fact, to offer an apology for capitalism but to expose the ways in which those with more power inflict pain on those with less and to offer proposals to reduce this oppression. When he defended private property, he did so in the name of securing expectations against an abstract, absolute, and unrealizable egalitarianism whose pursuit would cause great suffering.

John Keane's essay provides a bridge between the previous three essays, which start from Macpherson's reading of the past, and the subsequent ones, which take up Macpherson's view of the democratic present and future. He begins with a defense of Macpherson's method of interpretation, which he sees as a "deliberately selective" retrieval of those aspects of the liberal and democratic tradition that are most relevant to the task of democratizing the present. Keane thus poses a challenge to the critiques of Tully and Rosenblum, and provides a somewhat different account of Macpherson's method from my own.

The rest of Keane's essay in turn celebrates and criticizes Macpherson's vision of democracy, introducing a number of themes that are pursued by other authors. Keane endorses Macpherson's claims that democracy should be more than the selection of political elites and that capitalist property rights are incompatible with the democratic goal of equal human fulfillment. He argues, however, that Macpherson's democratic ideal rests on problematic assumptions about the objectivity of truth and goodness, and especially about the desirability of a democratic society as a vehicle for human self-realization. According to Keane, these assumptions are incompatible with ethical pluralism and stand in tension with democratic procedures. Like Tully, Keane argues that Macpherson's reading of the liberal tradition neglects that tradition's concern for limiting the power of the state and reconciling the freedom of individuals and groups within civil society with the requirements of political order, a concern that Keane says contemporary democrats ought to share. Like Rosenblum, Keane links Macpherson to the expressivist tradition with its assumption of collective harmony and criticizes him for neglecting issues of institutionalization, such as the question of what place market exchanges and conflict-resolving mechanisms might have in a postliberal democratic society. Finally, Keane claims that Macpherson's vision is informed by an unwarranted optimism about technological progress and mastery of nature as a solution to the problems of scarcity and environmental degradation. Keane says that Macpherson fails to appreciate the ways in which democracy is threatened by these problems, and yet offers the best way of dealing with them.

While Keane emphasizes the importance of differences in democracy, Virginia Held asks us to pay attention to one particular form of difference—gender—and to consider how Macpherson's work, especially his treatment of freedom, looks in the light of contemporary feminist insights and concerns. In contrast to Keane, she endorses the emphasis that Macpherson placed on substantive rather than procedural democracy and shares his optimism about the compatibility of human developmental powers. She also agrees with his claim that freedom requires access to the means of life and labor. But she argues that Macpherson's critique of liberal freedom does not go far enough in seeing what is needed for women to develop their full human capacities.

From a feminist perspective, the internal obstacles to self-development go much deeper than Macpherson acknowledges. As an example, Held points to the way women in our society are taught to feel an incapacitating shame, a form of oppression neither captured by Macpherson's categories nor cured by the changes he proposes. False images and distorted feelings are forms of disempowerment that women suffer *as women,* not just as members of a noncapitalist class. The gendered division of labor within the household—psychic as well as physical—places unequal and unfair demands on women. In all these ways, Held draws attention to the way in which feminism has challenged conventional distinctions between public and private, making relevant to political theory matters that have been treated as issues of personal psychology. Furthermore, Macpherson's conception of human

11

development remains deeply individualistic, even if it is not narrowly possessive. Feminists emphasize relations among human beings, especially relations of trust, care, and shared enjoyment. Feminist theory treats as central the question of how social institutions and cultural practices foster (or discourage) such relations, thus challenging a conception of the person and public life that isolates such concerns as "private."

Jane Mansbridge draws our attention primarily not to what Macpherson said, but to what he did not say and to what this silence obscures. In this, she adopts a form of critique that Macpherson himself used against the developmental liberals. She applauds Macpherson's effort to broaden the meaning of democracy and to bring to light the tension between democratic ideals and the patterns of domination produced by capitalism, but like Keane she argues that Macpherson neglected crucial political concerns that would endure even in a more egalitarian society and that we must somehow address today. First, she says, Macpherson writes only about coercive power as a form of domination in the context of relations among unequals. But coercive—indeed, extractive—power may be necessary even in an egalitarian society. Democratic theory must address questions about the legitimacy and limits of such power. We cannot assume that power among equals would be unnecessary or, if necessary, unproblematic. Second, she argues that Macpherson's emphasis on social relations rather than political ones led him to say little about how political participation would contribute to human development, as opposed to his frequent discussion of the importance of access to the means of production. Finally, she suggests that Macpherson has little to contribute to our understanding of the problem of deliberation in a democracy, attributing his neglect of this issue to his assumption of the harmony of human interests in a fully democratic society.

Chantal Mouffe shares Mansbridge's view that the political is distinctive and important, but she approaches the political in a very different way. She begins by endorsing Macpherson's basic project, which she sees as an attempt to develop "the radical potential of the liberal-democratic ideal," but then criticizes Macpherson by contrasting his position with that of Norberto Bobbio, another liberal-democratic socialist. Bobbio, she says, is more committed both to liberal-democratic institutions and to pluralism than Macpherson, and both of these liberal commitments are ones that contemporary radical democrats should share.

The importance of liberalism for democracy is revealed, Mouffe argues, by Carl Schmitt, who sees the two as antagonistic. Schmitt argues that democracy requires homogeneity among citizens, and that this democratic homogeneity conflicts with the liberal ideal of the moral equality of all human beings and with the pluralism that flows from that ideal. According to Schmitt, the rationalism, universalism, and individualism of liberalism are incompatible with the political. For Schmitt, Mouffe says, the political is "concerned with the relations of friend and enemy. It deals with the creation of a 'we' opposed to a 'them'. Its subject matter is conflict and antagonism and these indicate precisely the limits of rational consensus." Mouffe argues that we should learn from Schmitt's analysis of the political even while rejecting his denial of pluralism and his attempt to separate liberalism and democracy. Contemporary theories like those of Rawls and Habermas do entail a rationalist denial of the political. We must recognize, instead, that liberty and equality are not universal truths but the values of a particular kind of regime: liberal democracy. We must also recognize that these values are in tension with each other, that their meanings are contested, and that widespread acceptance of particular interpretations of their meanings can be established only temporarily and only through struggle. Political philosophers like Macpherson contribute to the struggle to establish a radical interpretation of liberal democracy.

William Connolly pursues the issues of harmony, conflict, and difference in the context of his own quest for a radical interpretation of democracy. Connolly starts by reviewing the four models of democracy discussed by Macpherson in *The Life and Times of Liberal Democracy,* paying particular attention to his critique of class inequality as an obstacle to the democratic ideal of the equal development of human capacities. Connolly agrees that the reduction of inequality is an essential prerequisite for democratic practice, although he argues that the degree of equalization needed for effective democratic citizenship can be achieved through progressive taxation and an emphasis on inclusive, rather than exclusive, modes of consumption.

Connolly's main challenge to Macpherson focuses on Macpherson's ideal of human development. Connolly is concerned that this ideal entails the assumption that there is a true identity to the self that can be realized once the right institutional framework is established. This is an assumption that, Connolly says, fits with the normalizing tendency of modern societies to treat particular socially constructed identities as natural standards and to insinuate these standards into the psyches of all members of society. By contrast, Connolly cherishes the potential which democracy offers for calling identities into question. Like Mouffe—and perhaps even more than she—Connolly places conflict and contestation at the center of his democratic ideal. "Because democracy contains the possibility of heightening the experience of contingency, it is through democratic engagement that the care for difference can be cultivated and embodied in the agonism of politics."

Care for difference is only one pole of Connolly's democratic project. At the other pole lies the characteristic democratic concern with consent as the basis for legitimate collective action. Connolly worries that some forms of democratic theory "lend too much legitimacy to the drives to unity and consensus." Thus, he treats the presence of consensus as a sign of probable closures and concealments in need of politicization. However, he does not want to legitimate any form of nonconsensual politics, and so he regards the absence of consensus as a reason for democratic criticism. This is the "ambiguity of politics" that is crucial to democratic practice. And despite his worries about the suppression of difference, Connolly wants to preserve a constructive, not merely critical, form of democracy—namely, the possibility of using democratic means to organize collective action for general goals.

If Connolly offers a deconstructionist critique of some aspects of Macpherson's thought, Ernesto Laclau reads others as a form of proto-deconstructionism. Drawing in particular on *The Real World of Democracy*, Laclau argues that Macpherson made the theory of democracy radically contextual by revealing the contingent character of the links between liberalism and democracy, and by showing that there were other ways, both traditional and modern, of conceiving democracy besides those dominant in liberal discourse.

Laclau seeks to extend that radical contextualization. He argues that, in the modern world, at the very time that democracy is gaining universal acceptance as a criterion of political legitimacy, the meaning of *democracy* has become more and more indeterminate. There are many ways of conceiving of the oppressed masses in the modern world. Both Shiite fundamentalism and various forms of European totalitarianism present themselves as democratic discourses in this sense. Indeed, there is "a plurality of underdogs" whose struggles may conflict with, as well as complement, one another. If one tries to avoid this indeterminacy in the meaning of democracy by defining it narrowly as control of the representatives by those whom they represent, the same problem simply reemerges in another form, because the representatives play a crucial role in constructing the interests, the will, and even the identity of the represented. Thus, the universal acceptance of democracy means that democratic terms such as *liberty* and *equality* have become empty signifiers. What counts as democratic, who is included or excluded by that definition, how freedom and equality are interpreted—in short, the meaning of democracy itself—must always be constructed in a particular context. It follows that this construction can and will be contested.

Several of the authors in this work stress the importance of considering the institutionalization of democratic ideals and— especially in light of recent developments in Eastern Europe—of rethinking Macpherson's critique of markets. This is precisely what Mihailo Marković undertakes in his essay. (Marković's own role in some of the developments in Serbia led me to consider whether it was appropriate to keep his article in this volume. I discuss this issue in a note immediately preceding Marković's article.) Marković begins by drawing attention to the ongoing relevance of Macpherson's critique to the political economy of contemporary liberal democratic societies. His major focus, however, is on Eastern European socialism. Marković argues that the attempt to transform private property into truly social property has failed, both in highly centralized, Soviet-style planning systems (in which the state—or more precisely, the bureaucratized Party elite—became the effective owner of most property) and in Yugoslavia (where decentralization left no one with the responsibilities of ownership). In both, the result was waste and corruption. However, Marković argues that privatization of property is no solution for these economies for two reasons. First, private property brings its own characteristic problems and abuses. Second, there is so much social property in these economies that privatization is not a feasible option. Instead, the solution lies in a new form of social property in which the responsibilities of ownership are assigned to democratic representatives, market prices are used to allocate property among alternative uses, and laws regulating property protect against abuse and usurpation.

After briefly reviewing recent political developments in Eastern Europe, Marković explores some possible models of democracy for socialist societies. The best model of democracy would not only reject one-party rule but would challenge party rule itself as inadequately democratic even when it is the outcome of freely contested elections in a multiparty system. What is needed is a deeper form of self-government in which citizens have more effective control over their elected

15

representatives, and in which the scope of democratic control is extended to the economy through a participatory system of self-management that would move from workers' councils at the local level to a branch of the legislature responsible for economic management.

Given the emphasis that several authors in this volume have placed upon historical context and the contestability of concepts, William Leiss's essay provides an appropriately challenging conclusion, since it calls into question Macpherson's basic problematic (and that of most of the other authors) from what might be called a radical neo-Hegelian ecological perspective. Leiss argues that Macpherson understood his own work from the perspective of philosophical history. He saw the epoch in which he lived as determined, above all, by the conflict between capitalism and socialism. He also saw his political theory as a contribution to the progressive resolution of that struggle. Macpherson was right about his epoch, Leiss says, but that age is now at an end. The three types of democracy that Macpherson identified—Western liberal, socialist, and national liberation—have all been exhausted as creative political forces, and their ideals have been unmasked as illusions. A historical compromise between capitalism and socialism has been achieved. While concrete struggles for democracy and justice are still necessary, no new political forms will emerge from those struggles. Indeed, we can now see that what the protagonists of this dying epoch shared was more fundamental than what divided them. Capitalists and socialists alike were committed to the pursuit of technological mastery over nature. The global environmental crises generated by this pursuit will define the new epoch that is now emerging, and will set the agenda for the next stage of human development—that is, "to find adequate political forms to yield an appropriate representation of the relation between humanity and nature."

CONCLUSION

One way to characterize all of C. B. Macpherson's writings is to say that he embraced the highest aspirations of the liberal-democratic tradition, while insisting that the tradition had failed deeply to meet those aspirations, that it could not do so on its own terms, and that it could not even provide the intellectual resources to think adequately about those aspirations and how they might be realized. Macpherson pursued an intellectual inquiry that he thought required both a deep continuity with the liberal-democratic tradition and a radical departure from it. His quest was to advance our thinking about the highest goals of liberal democracy and about ways of bringing those goals closer to fruition. That quest is his legacy to us.

The authors of this volume take up that legacy. In one way or another, they all pursue the same quest, and they all build on Macpherson even when they challenge him and depart from his ideas to emphasize the importance of new critical perspectives. This enterprise is rendered all the more urgent by the collapse of state socialism. Now, more than ever, what is needed is critical reflection about Western liberalism and democracy by those who are committed, as Macpherson was, to retrieving the best of the tradition and to developing its unrealized possibilities. The essays in this volume contribute to that project.

NOTES

1. C. B. Macpherson, *The Rise and Fall of Economic Justice and Other Papers* (Oxford: Oxford University Press, 1985), hereafter cited as *RFEJ.*

2. The phrase is taken from a review of Macpherson's *Democratic Theory* by Alasdair MacIntyre in the *Canadian Journal of Philosophy* 6, no. 2 (June 1976): 177-81 at 178. Macpherson himself endorsed the term as a description of his project on p. 198 of the same issue.

3. The summary of possessive individualism in the next few paragraphs is taken in particular from C. B. Macpherson, *The Political Theory of Possessive Individualism: Hobbes to Locke* (Oxford: Clarendon Press, 1962), 3, hereafter cited as *PI,* and from C. B. Macpherson, *Democratic Theory: Essays in Retrieval* (Oxford: Clarendon Press, 1973), 192-94 and 199, hereafter cited as *DT.*

4. Macpherson contrasted this private and exclusive property with traditional views emphasizing the constraints of justice and social duty upon the use of property and concepts of common property with rights of access for all. See especially *DI,* 120-40.

5. For the view of democracy summarized in this and the following paragraph, see *DI,* C. B. Macpherson, *The Real World of Democracy* (Oxford: Clarendon Press, 1966), hereafter cited as *RWD;* and C. B. Macpherson, *The Life and Times of Liberal Democracy* (Oxford: Oxford University Press, 1977), hereafter cited as *LTLD.*

6. *RWD,* 37.

7. *PI,* 3. See also p. 270.

8. Ibid., 4-8.

9. Ibid., 238-47.

10. *LTLD,* 27-33.

11. *PI,* 193.

12. *RFEJ,* 136.

13. *PI,* 158. Ironically, Macpherson himself has been criticized on grounds quite similar to those on which he based his criticism of the Levellers. In an essay entitled "Human Rights as Property Rights," Macpherson suggested that human rights claims be put forward as claims about property rights in order to enable the immense prestige of property to work for them rather than against them (*RFEJ,* 84). However, Jennifer Nedelsky has argued that this strategy (which Macpherson is not alone in endorsing) ignores the limits implicit in the conception of property as it has evolved in Anglo-American culture. It overestimates the capacity of reformers to make the concept of property serve egalitarian ends despite its long historical association with inequality. It also underestimates the power of the concept of property to limit and distort egalitarian reforms that attempt to employ it. See Jennifer Nedelsky, *Private Property and the Limits of American Constitutionalism* (Chicago: University of Chicago Press, 1991).

14. *LTLD,* 70.

15. *DT,* 201.

16. For Macpherson's discussion of the empirical realists, see especially *LTLD,* 77-92, and *DT,* 77-80.

17. *DT,* 54-55.

18. Ibid.

19. Ibid.

Chapter 2
The Possessive Individualism Thesis:
A Reconsideration in the Light
of Recent Scholarship

James Tully

C. B. Macpherson's thesis of possessive individualism has played a role in contemporary political thought similar to the role of Max Weber's thesis of the Protestant ethic and the spirit of capitalism. Initially a challenge to the received wisdom, it soon became the reigning orthodoxy, and then it was subjected to intense and sustained criticism. The problems with the thesis that this scrutiny brought to light were sufficient to cause many scholars of early modern English political thought to become skeptical of it, and many of its supporters argue, as Gordon Schochet has recently done, that Macpherson was right for the wrong reasons.[1] Accordingly, scholarship has moved in two directions. First, the research concerned with the relations between early modern political thought and capitalist relations of production has become considerably more technical, both historically and analytically, than Macpherson's original argument.[2] Second, scholars have moved on to study different questions. The thesis of possessive individualism now stands partly aside from and tangential to the central concerns and debates in this area. Nonetheless, like the Weber thesis, it has not only

At the conference, before presenting the paper printed here I offered an appreciation of C. B. Macpherson's monumental contribution to the development of political theory in Canada.

had a substantive influence on how we think of the history of the present, but it also continues to be an important object of comparison and contrast when we reflect critically on early modern political thought and our relationship to it. If we think of its role, therefore, as a constant provocation to critical research and reflection on the history of the present, rather than as a dogma whose worth is measured by the number of adherents, then it is one of the most challenging and successful hypotheses to be advanced in the history of European political thought over the last thirty years.

My aim here is to review the major criticisms that caused some scholars to dissent from the possessive individualism thesis, and to present an overview of current research in the field. I do this in the following steps: First, I review the political problem of the postwar period that Macpherson sought to illuminate by means of his thesis. Then, I lay out the various parts of the thesis and briefly summarize those criticisms brought against the thesis which themselves have managed to survive critical scrutiny. In the following section, I turn to current work in the field—first, to the flowering of specialized studies of early modern English political thought, and then to three lines of research that occupy the ground once held by the Macpherson thesis.[3] These are the work on republicanism or civic humanism initiated by John Pocock, on the "arts of government" begun by Michel Foucault, and on juristic political thought and institutions by Richard Tuck and Istvan Hont. This work shows us that early modern English political thought is more complex and addressed to a wider range of political problems than the thesis of possessive individualism led us to believe. We now have a richer and more nuanced account of the variety of ways in which Europeans reflected on the emergence of markets and how they sought to explain, challenge, and justify them. In addition, this scholarship has opened up a form of reflection on the seventeenth century which is not determined by the question of the rise of capitalism, yet which was, in fact, recommended by Macpherson as a line of research years ago.

THE "TWENTIETH-CENTURY DILEMMA" AND A NEW PROBLEM

As Macpherson saw it in 1962, liberal democratic political theory faced a dilemma. It was impossible in the twentieth century to generate a valid theory of political obligation for societies that are both liberal-democratic and market societies.[4] For there to be a valid theory of obligation for such societies, two conditions must be met. First, the members of the society must "see themselves, or [be] capable of seeing themselves, as equal in some respect more fundamental than all the respects in which they are unequal" (272). Second, there must be "a cohesion of self-interests, among all those who have a voice in choosing the government, sufficient to offset the centrifugal forces of a possessive market society" (273). In the "heyday of the market society"—from the seventeenth century to the middle of the nineteenth century—the equality condition was met by the apparent equality of subordination to the laws of the market, and the cohesion-of-interests condition was met by the restriction of political power to a cohesive possessing class. The emergence of class-conscious industrial work forces with the franchise in the later nineteenth century undermined both the belief in the equal subordination to the market and the cohesion of interests, and thereby rendered invalid the liberal theory of obligation that had been based on these conditions.

Because modern societies are still market societies, he continued, the assumptions of possessive individualism continue to be factually accurate. That is,

> The individual in market society *is* human as proprietor of his own person. However much he may wish it to be otherwise, his humanity does depend on his freedom from any but self-interested contractual relations with others. His society does consist of a series of market relations. (275)

This premise is, as he puts it, "factually accurate" yet "morally offensive." So, the dilemma is: "Either we reject possessive individualist assumptions, in which case our theory is unrealistic, or we retain them, in which case we cannot get a valid theory of obligation" (275). Thus, we can see that what he hoped to do in advancing the thesis of possessive individualism was to show that, with the emergence of industrial working classes, liberal theory could not provide "a valid theory of political obligation to a liberal democratic state in a possessive market society" (275).

As we might expect, he goes on to entertain one practical route out of the dilemma—namely, to abandon the actual relations of a possessive market society while retaining liberal political institutions. This, by definition, would solve the problem of cohesion, since the centrifugal forces were said to be caused by market relations. Nonetheless, he goes on to claim that this socialist alternative would not solve the problem of equality. This is surprising, since in his later works an equality of nonpossessive, productive, and expressive individualism is advanced on a democratic-socialist base. Instead, this early text takes a completely unexpected turn in the last pages.

He says that the question of whether or not we need to change the actual possessive market relations is now of "secondary importance" because there has been an additional change in modern societies. This is the introduction of atomic warfare. Now, the destruction of every individual on the planet is a real possibility and this has "created a new equality of insecurity among individuals" (276). This new Hobbesian equality of insecurity itself provides the basis for a new theory of obligation, not to a nation-state but to a "wider political authority." The possibility of global destruction has caused the problems of possessive individualism to shrink and they now can "be brought to manageable proportions" (277). Thus

> the self-interested individual, whatever his possessions, and whatever his attachments to a possessive market society, can see that the relations of the market society must yield to the overriding requirement that, in [Richard] Overton's words, which now acquire a new significance, "humane society, cohabitation or being, ... above earthly things must be maintained." (277)

Overcoming existing market relations—the transition to socialism—is accordingly not the first priority. Rather, the task of liberal-democratic political theory is to develop a theory of obligation to "a wider political authority" based on the equality of insecurity brought about by the change in the technology of warfare, and then to investigate how market relations are connected to the primarily political-military framework. Once this has been ascertained, one could ask how far market relations, as well as military relations, "must yield" within a theory of obligation based on humanity's interest in security rather than in acquisition. Such a theory, which he saw as amending Hobbes "more clearly than he was by Locke," would require careful attention to the changes wrought by the new mode of warfare (277).

This challenge to set aside debate on the transition to socialism and to face straightforwardly the new problem posed by atomic weapons was rarely taken up by his followers or his critics. They continued to let the problematic of capitalism versus socialism set the terms of their reflection on seventeenth-century political thought. Indeed, one of the ironies of contemporary political thought is that Macpherson's best critic, John Dunn, was one of the few to take up precisely this issue of political obligation in the nuclear age.[5] However, after a period of sustained testing of the thesis of possessive individualism from within the conventions of the contemporary problematic of socialism versus capitalism, political theorists have freed themselves from this problematic, which has tended to dominate our scholarship since the war and which has been held in place by the division of the world into capitalist and socialist states. These scholars have shifted their attention to the political and military dimensions of early modern political thought and action. This research has thus begun to furnish us with histories of the foundations of our contemporary political-military predicament and, thereby, to put us in a position to take up the question Macpherson recommended to us long ago.

THESIS AND CRITICISMS

I'll teach you differences.
—Kent, *King Lear,* 1.4.88-89

Macpherson summarized the thesis of possessive individualism as follows:

(1) Man, the individual, is seen as absolute natural proprietor of his own capacities, owing nothing to society for them. Man's essence is freedom to use his capacities in search of satisfactions. This freedom is limited properly only by some principle of utility or utilitarian natural law which forbids harming others. Freedom therefore is restricted to, and comes to be identified with, domination over things, not domination over men. The clearest form of domination over things is the relation of ownership or possession. Freedom is therefore possession. Everyone is free, for everyone possesses at least his own capacities. (2) Society is seen, not (as it had been) as a system of relations of domination and subordination between men and classes held together by reciprocal rights and duties, but as a lot of free equal individuals related to each other through their possessions, that is, related as owners of their own capacities and what they have produced and accumulated by the use of their capacities. The relation of exchange (the market relation) is seen as the fundamental relation of society. Finally (3) political society is seen

as a rational device for the protection of property, including capacities; even life and liberty are considered as possessions, rather than as social rights with correlative duties.[6]

He claimed that this conception of "man"[7] as "an infinitely desirous consumer of utilities," of society as a set of market relations, and of government as a mechanism to protect the property each individual has in his person, capacity to labor, and contracts can be found in the writings of Thomas Hobbes, the Levellers, James Harrington, John Locke, David Hume, Edmund Burke, Jeremy Bentham, and James Mill.[8] These authors developed this shared set of beliefs in response to and as the legitimation of a "possessive market society," which Macpherson carefully defined by means of a model. He claimed such a society had emerged in England by the 1640s. This ideology replaced an earlier "traditional" view that was neither possessive nor individualist. Finally, the shared beliefs of these writers make up a single tradition of political thought called "English liberalism" or "English utilitarian liberalism."

The major criticisms of this thesis up to 1981 were summarized by David Miller in a well-known article in *Political Studies* in 1982.[9] I assume that these are reasonably familiar to most readers, and therefore that I do not need to repeat them here. Miller concluded his summary by saying, "It is not easy, on the basis of these critical observations, to develop an ideological model of comparable power to Macpherson's which can then be applied to each of our subjects [that is, authors]." This is certainly true. Not only did the critics show that these authors—with the important exception of Bentham—were not endorsing unlimited acquisition of property in a capitalist society, but also that each of the authors was addressing slightly different problems within a variety of political vocabularies or languages. Where Macpherson saw one continuous tradition over two centuries, his critics have seen a motley or plurality of political problems and responses and also a variety of different uses of similar concepts. The emphasis has been on *difference*, not sameness, as it has been throughout the human sciences in recent years. Having disaggregated Macpherson's synthesis and shown the diversity of political thought and action of the early modern period it causes us to overlook, later scholars have not attempted to erect a new synthesis that would, after all, as a new form of reflection, simply obscure again the diversity and ambiguity of use of early modern political thought that we have so painstakingly sought to recover.

However, to build a bridge to these three lines of research that I wish to discuss, let us recall some of the common threads of criticism that Miller mentioned in 1982. From Hobbes to Locke, unlimited consumption was not considered rational or morally permissible. By the late eighteenth century, Europeans may have been faced by the possibility of a society given over to unlimited consumption, but this does not seem to be a concern of writers in the earlier period. When property rights were defended, it was against attacks from absolute monarchs or "degenerative" representative bodies. These rights were limited by government and correlated with obligations to the destitute. The word "property" had a broader reference than it carries today. It included personal rights, especially religious and civil liberties. Although no one argued against commerce, manufacturing, or agricultural improvement per se, no one had a vision of a full-scale commercial or capitalist society. Macpherson's model of a "possessive market society" misrepresents the political economy in the texts as well as what we know of the English "economy" in the seventeenth century. Moreover, the thesis of possessive individualism misidentifies the primary problems that these theorists were addressing. They were not concerned with justifying unlimited accumulation in a market society, but with more basic political problems of political order, preservation, state-building, obedience, and liberty in a situation of insecurity brought on by a century of civil wars, religious wars, the Thirty Years' War, and the European wars of the latter half of the seventeenth century.

Initially, of course, these criticisms were advanced within the framework presupposed by the thesis of possessive individualism—that is, that these texts were responses to problems thrown up by the emergence of capitalist relations. In general, the criticisms were simply that the authors were not endorsing market relations as fully as Macpherson claimed, or that England was not as far along the road to capitalism as he claimed. However, the cumulative effect of these criticisms was to call into question the background picture which both Macpherson and his critics shared. It now looked as if we had imposed a form of representation on the period, and that our debates within it simply reinforced this framework, causing us to misunderstand the texts. As Wittgenstein famously described this type of philosophical problem, "A *picture* held us captive. And we could not get outside it, for it lay in our language and language seemed to repeat it to us inexorably."[10] It was in the late 1970s, within this period of skepticism about the appropriateness of the background picture of the period held by Macpherson and his critics, that new lines of research were initiated. The works in this period—by

25

JAMES TULLY

Quentin Skinner on Hobbes, Richard Tuck on Hobbes and the Levellers, John Pocock on Harrington, John Dunn and Mark Goldie on Locke, and Keith Tribe on economic discourse—all criticized and set aside the central questions of Macpherson and his critics.[11] They took up the *political* problems that the earlier critics had identified as central to the theorists of the period. At the same time, Michel Foucault published his study of early modern forms of power, bodies of knowledge, and types of subjectivity. Carole Pateman began to probe gender relations in early modern English political thought, and Carolyn Merchant presented a provocative study of attitudes toward ecology and women in seventeenth-century political thought.[12] There is, of course, no doubt that Macpherson welcomed this plurality of approaches, even though it both displaced and disaggregated the synthetic picture on which his thesis rested. Let us now survey this literature using the thesis of possessive individualism as an object of comparison in order to draw three contrasts.

THE IMPORTANCE OF POLITICAL POWER

One common feature of current work on seventeenth-century English and European political thought has been the claim that the central problem of the period is the nature of political (not economic) power.[13] How had the representative bodies and absolute monarchies acquired political power? How do the people, individually and collectively, stand in relation to it as subjects or citizens? How can it be exercised without causing civil war? What is the "true original, extent, and end of civil government"? As Locke put it in the *Two Treatises*,

> The great question which in all ages has disturbed mankind, and brought on them the greatest part of those mischiefs which have ruined cities, depopulated countries, and disordered the peace of the world, has been, not whether there be power in the world, nor whence it came, but who should have it. (1.106)

One way in which this problem was conceptualized was to think of the people as individuals who have rights over their powers to defend themselves and to preserve themselves, and then to conceptualize the relation between governors and governed as the delegation or alienation of these powers to the ruler under certain conditions. It is within this

26

context of explaining the nature of political power that the concept of man possessing rights over his person and capacities was used by a number of juristic political philosophers.[14] Macpherson famously underscored the importance of a concept of self-proprietorship in Hobbes, the Levellers, and Locke, but he set this in the economic context of a possessive market society. Let us examine the contrast.

The first and basic premise of possessive individualism, from which the thesis takes its name, is that man is proprietor of his own person and capacities. This is taken by Macpherson to be an economic conception of the self—a concept of an individual who possesses rights of ownership over his person and capacities that he exercises through contractual relations on a market free of the authoritative allocation of work and in which the capacity to labor is alienated for a period of time in exchange for a wage. The psychological motive which moves the possessive individual is an infinite desire to consume, acquire, or seek to satisfy utilities.[15]

The first part of this concept—that of jural self-possession or self-ownership—is neither necessary nor sufficient to liberalism. In contemporary liberalism, for example, John Rawls, in the most influential liberal theory of the postwar period, holds that a person has a contingent relation to his or her own abilities, as the mere repository of them, and that one's abilities are the "common assets" of the community.[16] (I will return to this repository conception later.) Jeremy Bentham, too, thought it was "nonsense upon stilts" to speak of persons having rights over themselves, and he chastised the drafters of the *Declaration of the Rights of Man and Citizen* for introducing this language.[17] Conversely, G. A. Cohen has argued in a number of recent articles that socialists should accept the basic political premise of self-ownership—that individuals have rights over their persons and capacities—and then show that partial egalitarian conclusions can be drawn from it.[18] In this he echoes, as Richard Ashcraft and Christopher Lasch have shown, early nineteenth-century English and American radicals who argued that the best way to defeat the claims of capital was to defend the rights of labor over their persons and capacities.[19]

My preliminary point here is that a similar concept can be used in various—and, indeed, contradictory—ways in different political contexts. How then was the concept of self-proprietorship used in the seventeenth century?

It is certainly true that the concept of self-proprietorship plays a central role in the writings of some of the Levellers and in Locke's *Two*

Treatises of Government, as Macpherson claimed. However, its conventional and long-standing Roman law use was not economic. To say that a man was master or proprietor of himself was to define him in opposition to a slave, who was, by definition, under the will of his master. Thus it had the double register of signaling that one was master of oneself in the sense of being able to govern oneself ethically, in the neo-Stoic texts, and of exercising some form of jurisdiction over the self free from the control of others. This was taken in two directions. In the absolutist tradition, if "men" have rights of ownership over themselves, then, because rights are alienable, they are able to alienate these rights completely to another. Thus it is possible to argue that individuals alienate their selves completely to an absolute monarch, without limitation, and thus stand to the sovereign as slave to master. We see Rousseau arguing against this theory in the *Contrat social.*[20] The second way in which this strong theory of self-ownership was used was to justify the slave trade, on the assumption that blacks freely alienated their rights over themselves in a contractual relation with European slave traders.

These "alienation" theorists were opposed by what are called "delegation" theorists. They wished to defend a limited form of constitutional monarchy, and thus interpreted self-ownership in a slightly different way. Although an individual, in contrast to a slave, has rights over the self and its capacities, these rights are limited, and some are inalienable. Thus, one could never contract into complete subjection to a sovereign nor be without a right to defend oneself if attacked by a tyrant. This is the context in which the notion of an "inalienable right" is first used.[21] As Keith Thomas pointed out, the difficulties the Levellers had with extending the franchise to servants were not with wage labor, as Macpherson assumed, but rather with servants being under the will of another and thus not their own masters.[22]

The primary use of the concept of rights over the self in the seventeenth century is in the constitution of government and the relation of subjection to it. The framework in which this is discussed by both Hobbes and Locke is laid down by Hugo Grotius in *The Laws of War and Peace* (1625). Grotius wrote in the wake of seventy years of religious wars, and in the midst of a wave of civil wars and the Thirty Years' War. This catastrophe led to a widespread skeptical crisis which began in the "rule of faith" controversy and spread to the moral and natural sciences. Grotius was faced with constructing a political theory for a Europe that had a plurality of religions and no unifying political authority above the individual states.[23] He argued that despite their religious and moral differences, all Europeans desire self-preservation. States established for this purpose alone, and not for enforcing higher-order religious beliefs, would secure the obedience of all subjects and bring peace. He put this basic agreement on the principle of self-preservation in the terms of self-ownership *(suum)*. Each man has a natural right to defend himself from attack and a natural right to preserve himself by acquiring things necessary for subsistence. A natural duty to abstain from that which belongs to another correlates with the two rights. This constitutes the *suum*—that which is properly one's own. Governments are established by alienating the rights of self-defense to the sovereign and by agreeing to the regulation of the right of preserving oneself in the interest of peace and order.

This is a juridical concept of self-ownership. However, the concept is moral, political, and military, not economic. It is not concerned with the alienation of labor power but with political power or the power of self-defense. The individual, as well as the state, is concerned with preservation, not consumption. Labor power appears here as the means to preserve oneself, not as something that facilitates utility satisfaction, and it is regulated by government for the sake of preservation. This Grotian framework plays a powerful role in English political thought throughout the century.[24]

Hobbes was concerned with the same problems as Grotius—that is, how to build a strong state that subjects would obey in the face of civil war caused by religious diversity. What Macpherson saw as economic competition among self-interested consumers in Hobbes's state of war is now seen as competition for power to protect oneself in the English Civil War.[25] Hobbes does not strengthen Grotius's concept of self-possession, nor does he put it to economic uses. He reduces it to an impracticable right to preserve oneself that is alienated to a sovereign in all cases except when one's life is directly threatened. The sovereign regulates labor and trade in order to preserve the population and to strengthen the state in relation to other European states.[26]

The Levellers use a concept of self-ownership, not to legitimate market exchanges but rather to justify the right to resist constituted authority (first the king and then Parliament) in the terms of a natural right to self-defense. The proprietorship model is used in this way by the Parliamentary side throughout the English Civil War and later in the Exclusion Crisis and the Glorious Revolution.[27]

Turning now to Locke, it is clear that he wrote within this general Grotian framework, although, of course, he made a number of important innovations within it. In Locke's theory, individuals are said to have the right to defend themselves and others, and the right to acquire by means of labor things necessary for preservation. These two rights correlate with duties to others. The power one has to defend oneself and others is the origin of political power. This is conditionally delegated to governors when political society is established. If government abuses this power, it devolves back to the people individually, who exercise it in an armed struggle to defend themselves against their governors. Further, the right which one has to preserve oneself by labor is given up to be regulated and limited by government for the sake of preservation. Gopal Sreenivasan has argued persuasively that this limit is never transcended.[28]

As the work of Richard Ashcraft, Julian Franklin, and Mark Goldie shows, Locke wrote this to justify armed resistance by a group of radical Whigs against Charles II and his policy of religious uniformity. Locke certainly argued that the government infringement of property constituted a justification for revolt, but by "property" he meant the civil and religious rights of Dissenters and their possessions, which were confiscated during the great persecutions of the Restoration. Here government was exercising a wider range of political power than the people had conditionally entrusted to them. It was treating political subjects as if they were slaves, as in the alienation theory, rather than as persons with a range of inalienable rights over their persons, capacities, and possessions.[29]

Max Weber once wrote that you could take the conceptual scheme developed by Marx to explain the historical appropriation and alienation of labor power from workers to the capitalist class and apply it just as well to the historical appropriation and alienation of political power from the people and local lords (the "private bearers of executive power") to the institutionalized concentration of political power in the modern world. "The whole process is a complete parallel to the development of the capitalist enterprise through gradual expropriation of the independent producers."[30] As I have sought to suggest, the irony of this statement is that the conceptual scheme was first developed to explain political power and state formation and then, from Smith to Marx, transferred to labor power. In *The Political Theory of Possessive Individualism,* Macpherson took for granted the application of this conceptual scheme to labor power and projected it back onto the texts of Hobbes, the Levellers, and Locke. In so doing, he overlooked what is central to these texts: the analysis of political power. As Keith Tribe pointed out, this scheme, which presupposes that labor power is alienated or delegated to a capitalist class, caused Macpherson to misinterpret the role of labor power as well. The problem is not how labor power is exchanged with a master (which is not seen as problematic at all). Rather, as we saw earlier, the problem of labor power is how it is given over to be "regulated" by government for the sake of preservation.[31]

MERCANTILISM AND THE UTILIZABLE INDIVIDUAL

The second contrast I wish to draw is between Macpherson's argument that seventeenth-century England was a possessive market society which theorists from Hobbes to Locke wrote to legitimate, and the current view that seventeenth-century political economy is better understood as a "mercantile system," to use Adam Smith's phrase.[32] On this view, labor power, property relations, and trade are regulated by political power or government in order to preserve and strengthen the state. The state, in turn, is considered to be locked in a zero-sum, balance-of-power system of military and commercial rivalry with other European states over the conquest, colonization, and exploitation of the non-European world. In order to strengthen the state and increase its wealth, it was considered necessary to promote, regulate, and coordinate the productive activities of the population by means of law. The improvement of the productivity of labor required not only legal and administrative regulation, but also the development of knowledge of the "history of trades," of demography, and of the conditions of work, and, thus, the beginnings of political economy, statistics, comparative political science, and demographics. Laborers, in order to be trained to work or to fight, have to be cared for in their health, manners, and education, and directed to productive labor, which is integrated into the mercantile strategies of the "welfare-warfare" state, to use Lawrence Stone's apt phrase.[33]

As we have seen, labor power is conceptualized as a means to preservation, and it is regulated by political power to this end in both the state of nature and political society. Both Hobbes and Locke picture laboring activity as regulated and "limited" by the government.[34] The key term they use to describe and legitimate this political economy is "improvement," and they contrast this ethos of European improvement

JAMES TULLY

with Amerindian hunting and gathering society, not with feudalism. Indeed, the emphasis on labor, cultivation, and improvement is the standard justification of the dispossession of Amerindians.[35]

Moreover, the way in which the laboring individual is conceptualized in the political economy literature from Montchrétien to William Petty is very different from the concept of an individual with rights over his person and capacities in the *Two Treatises*. The individual is taken to be a mere repository of productive capacities that could be trained into mechanical abilities by the repetition of simple operations. This concept of the utilizable self is given expression in Locke's immensely influential *An Essay Concerning Human Understanding* and applied in his 1697 *Report to the Board of Trade* on the reform of the workhouse system.

At the center of his analysis is the premise that an individual is "only as white paper or wax to be moulded or fashioned as one pleases."[36] Since individuals desire to avoid pain or punishment or to seek reward or pleasure, they can be led to engage in mental or physical behavior by the application of punishments and rewards. As a result of the continual repetition and practice of any complex behavior, suitably broken down into operational parts, the individual becomes accustomed and habituated to it, eventually finding pleasure in it.[37] One system of rewards and punishments that Locke proposes to apply in order to reform the "relaxation of discipline and the corruption of manners," to uproot the vice of idleness, and to implant the virtue of industry is the use of bodily rewards and punishments in the workhouse system. His proposal for reform of the national system of workhouses was praised until the Webbs's day as a model for reforming and habituating children and adults to labor. As Locke's 1793 editors remarked,

> Mr. Locke appears to be convinced that rewards and punishments, and the mixing of habits of industry with principles of religious duties, were the surest means of effecting that reformation of the manners of the people, which, in those days, was judged essential to the strength and safety of the nation.[38]

This malleable individual was also said to have an overriding interest in, or love of, self, as Macpherson correctly noted. However, this self-referring motivation—whether Augustinian, Epicurean, or neo-Stoic in inspiration—was not to be taken to be an interest in the satisfaction or maximization of market or economic utilities. Rather, it was believed to be an interest in avoiding punishment and gaining reward. The typical forms of punishment were eternal damnation, violent death, starvation, or, among republicans, dishonor. The typical rewards were salvation, preservation, power, honor, and reputation.

Michel Foucault studied the dispersion of techniques of discipline and habituation in the workhouse, schools, armies, and administrative institutions. In his lectures on *raison d'État,* he argued that these techniques and types of rationality were linked to state-building and later to the formation of an array of "arts of government" of individuals and populations. With perhaps a reference to the Macpherson thesis, he concluded that

> the main characteristic of our modern rationality . . . is neither the constitution of the state . . . nor the rise of bourgeois individualism. I won't even say that it is a constant effort to integrate individuals into the political totality. I think that the main characteristic of our political rationality is the fact that this integration of the individuals in a community or in a totality results from a constant correlation between an increasing individualization and the reinforcement of this totality.[39]

William McNeill's study of military discipline and the rise of a permanent military-commercial complex, Marc Raeff's study of the "well-ordered state" in Germany and Russia, and Michael Ignatieff's study of eighteenth-century England all followed in the early 1980s. Neal Wood discussed Locke's analysis of techniques of habituation, and Sidney Pollard showed how the experimentation on child labor in the workhouse system laid the basis for factory discipline and scientific management.[40]

One of the necessary features of Macpherson's possessive market society is "no authoritative allocation of work."[41] This more recent work shows that seventeenth-century theory and practice failed to approximate this condition. Quite the opposite. In Locke's plan for the workhouse system, the majority of the laboring population remains under the jurisdiction of the workhouse authorities from the ages of three to fifty-five. Whether successive Boards of Trade recommended more or less regulation, or whether their policies aimed at constituting individuals or collectivities of various kinds, they understood these as tactics within an overall strategy of regulation and reform.[42]

The rediscovery of the concept of the individual as a passive repository of abilities, open to manipulation and use, in political economy and proposals for labor reform renders problematic our understanding of the genesis of capitalist wage labor. With the separation of the worker from the means of production, the owner (the capitalist) came to control the production process. It is clear from Dugald Stewart and Adam Smith onward that the capitalist inherited the concept of the worker as a repository of abilities.[43] However, this is incompatible with the laborer having any type of rights or proprietorship over his person and capacities, as he does in the *Two Treatises*. The laborer in the capitalist wage contract must totally alienate the rights he has over his capacities in the workplace. Therefore, the wage relationship under capitalism must consist in the junction of the alienation conception of rights associated with absolutism and slavery, which I mentioned earlier, and the conception of the laborer as a repository of capacities.[44]

The concept of the individual as proprietor and master of his own labor in the nonabsolutist tradition in which Locke wrote is incompatible with wage labor under capitalism, since the laborer could not alienate his sovereignty over his abilities. Rather, he sells a complete "service" to a master, as in the precapitalist putting-out system.[45] This explains, therefore, how both civic humanists and Lockean jurists, from Adam Ferguson to Henri Storch, could use the concept of sovereignty or rights over one's abilities to combat—rather than to justify—the degradation of labor in the capitalist division of labor.

COMMERCIAL SOCIETY AND THE SELF-INTERESTED INDIVIDUAL

Perhaps the biggest challenge to the political theory of possessive individualism has come from historians working on "civic humanist" or republican forms of political thought. John Pocock's monumental reconstruction of republicanism or civic humanism is at the center of this enterprise. He first challenged Macpherson's interpretation of Harrington.[46] Pocock argued that *Oceana* is a contribution to a tradition of republican political thought running from the Italian Renaissance to the late eighteenth century. In this tradition, property is conceptualized differently than in the juristic tradition that we have been considering. Landed property provides the independence necessary for citizenship, and citizenship consists in developing and exercising civic virtue through political participation in service—especially military service—to the public good. In this manner, one comes to develop what is of utmost value: a civic personality. Accordingly, the distribution of property is of primary importance. It determines the form of government and the access to public office. In attempting to explain Harrington's theory in the terms of the possessive market model, Macpherson overlooked this distinctive form of political analysis.

Pocock's work is part of a larger project to recover republican modes of political thought and action across Europe from the sixteenth century to the French and American revolutions. Scholars such as Gordon Wood, Nannerl Keohane, Eco Haitsma-Mulier, Carol Blum, Richard Tuck, and Quentin Skinner[47] have underlined not only the importance of republican language in the early modern period, in contradistinction to the juristic language of Hobbes and Locke, but also the variety of political uses to which it was put. Thus this complements the way in which historians of juristic political thought have brought to light the contradictory ideological uses of the terms of possessive individualism, which Macpherson assumed were used solely to legitimate the rise of capitalism. In addition, these scholars have sought to probe how juristic and republican thinkers responded to the development of the analysis of politics in the terms of interests and reasons of states, which I mentioned in the previous section.[48]

Historians influenced by the "Pocockian Moment" have turned their attention to eighteenth-century English, Scottish, French, and German political economy. The upshot of this work has been to suggest that Hobbes, Locke, and possessive individualism are largely *irrelevant* to the ways in which market societies—capitalism—were reflected upon, criticized, and legitimated.[49] The reflection on capitalism occurred in the eighteenth century in a discussion centered on the concept of a "commercial society" and in terms different from, and often opposed to, those of Hobbes and Locke. Consequently, it is this complex and distinctive eighteenth-century vocabulary that was gradually woven into the daily practices of capitalism and came to be partly constitutive of it. Let me summarize some of the features of this third challenge to possessive individualism.

First, with the establishment of the Bank of England in 1696 and the introduction of public credit and debt (mainly to finance foreign wars), a new type of moveable, nonlanded property appeared. It was conceptualized in the republican language as a "monied interest," the "corruption" of public life and the loss of citizen virtue. The language of republicanism continued to be central to both the criticism and legitimation of market relations in the eighteenth-century, challenging and even displacing juristic modes of analysis.

The transition to a distinctively commercial society was complemented in England—and all of Europe, according to Theodore Robb—with a widely shared perception of political stability and steady economic growth. The earlier conventional stance that politics is the art of basic state-formation and preservation in conditions of insecurity was now taken as solved. Theorists could thus turn to the question of sustained economic growth, the causes of the wealth of nations, and even to the regulative idea—at the end of the century—of a consumer society. In this context the modern notion of progress began to be applied, calling into question the variety of concepts of a limit in seventeenth-century republicanism, neo-Stoicism, natural law, and political economy.[50]

One of the dominant questions of eighteenth-century Scottish and English political thought was, What is the explanation of the apparently self-sustaining growth of commercial societies? The first response was to argue that Europe had progressed through four historical stages of society, each individuated by its unique mode of production, from hunting and gathering to its present "commercial" or "civilized" stage. Locke's history of property in the *Two Treatises* was interpreted in this scheme, and his Scottish commentators, from Gersham Carmichael on, redescribed the natural law tradition of Grotius, Pufendorf, and Locke in these new terms.[51]

The most striking feature of a commercial society was taken to be the self-sustaining character of its basic institutions. Writers as diverse as Mandeville, Hume, Smith, Ferguson, Condorcet, and Sieyès attributed this characteristic to the "division of labor" and "specialization." By virtue of being caught up in the practices of division of labor in economic, political, and military life, individuals were constrained to behave in ways which—willy-nilly and unintentionally—led to the overall improvement and growth of these societies. In addition, individuals constrained to act in this way would gradually become "polished," "disciplined," "civilized," and "pacific." If behavior within the causal constraints of divisions of labor within commercial society explained the growth of European society, then the regulation and governance of every area of life in the seventeenth century could be seen as unnecessary. Mandeville can be read as advancing precisely this observation.[52]

As a result, the kind of regulation in detail typical of seventeenth-century reform was criticized and repudiated. It was associated with enlightened absolutism in France, from Richelieu and Colbert to Linguet and Louis XVI, and with the mercantile system in England. Smith, Condorcet, Bentham, and Sieyès all argued that modern commercial societies with representative political institutions and the division of labor were far too complex to know and to govern in this way. Indeed, they argued that the attempt to exercise this type of control failed and stifled improvement. Rather, progress and the wealth of nations are the unplanned consequences of leaving individuals more or less alone to pursue their enlightened self-interest in divisions of labor in commercial society. They disagreed over how much coordination and invigilation was required of the autonomous "processes" in which humankind found itself constrained to work and live, but they all agreed on the existence and permeability of the processes themselves.

As we can see in hindsight, these later thinkers simply took for granted the organized forms of thought (the scientific disciplines) and the political, economic, and technical institutions that the seventeenth-century theorists and state-builders had constructed. These appeared now to be quasi-autonomous and tending in a progressive direction without an overall director. The political act that symbolized this transition from early modern to modern thought was the execution of Louis XVI. The absolute monarch, who stood above the law, was replaced by the republic, in which everyone was subject to the laws of politics, economics, science, and the division of labor, and moved forward by this very subjection.

Individuals caught up in the dependency relations of the market, which rewarded economically rational behavior and punished irrational behavior, would gradually become enlightened. Their selfish pursuit of unlimited wants would bring about the greatest good of the greatest number. As markets spread around the globe, governments would become economically interdependent and war would no longer be in their interest. Citizens, experiencing the cost and destructiveness of war, and thinking only of their self-interest, would curb military spending and adventurism through a free press and representative government. Thus—as Kant was able to sum up this line of thought in *An Idea for a Universal History from a Cosmopolitan Point of View*—supposing humans to be devils, the unintended consequences of their unsocial sociability in commercial societies were leading them to material progress and international peace.[53]

Does the thesis of possessive individualism apply, therefore, to late-eighteenth-century Scottish political economy? First, it would have to be rewritten to take into account these features I have mentioned, because they continue to be constitutive of our liberal political theory. Most important of these is the assumption that there is an independent economic realm in which work is allocated in accordance with the law of supply and demand. Therefore, the authoritative allocation of work by government is not required. Macpherson claimed that this feature was present in seventeenth-century theory and practice, whereas eighteenth-century theorists thought this was unique to their own era, and present-day scholars tend to support this view. Furthermore, if we think of liberalism as a practice of government in which we question if there is "too much government" and test policy against its effects on the independent economy, then liberalism is a tradition which emerged in the eighteenth, not the seventeenth, century.[54]

Second, these writers were ambivalent about the achievements of commercial society. The basis of their ambivalence, as Pocock had argued, was the charge, advanced by neo-Harrington republicans, that the division of labor, specialization, and dependency would lead to the loss of "civic virtue," the disintegration of a manly and unified civic personality, and to a soft or "effeminate" character. The apologists argued, not without hesitation and nostalgia, that commercial society brought about progress, civility, polish, sociability, and manners, thereby superseding the rude and militaristic eras of civic virtue that the republicans sought anachronistically to revive. Thus, the debate over early modern capitalism was conducted in distinct vocabularies different from those of Hobbes and Locke. Defenders and critics of commercial society also questioned and criticized class structure, the degree of political participation, the subordination of women, the degradation of the individual, and especially the rise of standing armies and interstate war.[55] Even writers such as Smith, who endorsed commercial society, did not justify unlimited accumulation. Private property was limited by the needs of the destitute on the one hand and by the needs of the modern state on the other.[56] Most of these writers were also aware of the sociological and historical conditions that gave rise to and sustained the self-interested and possessive individual. Moreover, to concentrate on the "individualism" of these writings is, as Foucault has argued, to overlook the other side of the analysis—that is, the attempt to explain and to govern the "population" as a whole, which was seen as a distinct domain with its own regularities and requisite policies of regulation and administration.[57]

Finally, it is misleading to see this body of thought focused on nothing but a "market society." These writers saw commercial societies as divided—composed of an economic realm and a political-civil realm of representative institutions, a public sphere, a range of civil and religious liberties, and a problematic military complex. As Habermas, Foucault, Fontana, Landes, and others have stressed, these divisions of "man," "woman," "citizen," and "soldier" were as problematic for Hutcheson, Hume, Montesquieu, Voltaire, Rousseau, Sieyès, Kant, and Constant as they were later for Hegel and Marx, and for us today.[58]

As we saw in the first part of this chapter, Macpherson wished to preserve liberal political and civil institutions while altering the market relations that thwart our participation in and expansion of them. However, the original thesis of possessive individualism does not contain an analysis of the history of these institutions in English political thought or practice. He went on in his later writings to investigate aspects of civil and political society in English political thought, and to recommend research into military-economic relations. In so doing, he was following in the footsteps of the great critical thinkers of the eighteenth and nineteenth centuries, yet also passing on to us his own distinctive contribution to this tradition that still forms the horizon of our political thought—even for those who wish to question and deconstruct the tradition itself. Macpherson's original and thought-provoking questioning within this two-hundred-year tradition of critical reflection on the history of the present is his true intellectual legacy.

NOTES

1. "Macpherson was almost right—but not at all for the right reasons." Gordon Schochet, "Radical Politics and Ashcraft's Treatise on Locke," *Journal of the History of Ideas* 50, no. 3 (July-Sept. 1989): 491-510, 508. See also Neal Wood, *John Locke and Agrarian Capitalism* (Berkeley: University of California Press, 1986). He argues that capitalism in England arose in the agrarian sector, and he abandons Macpherson's model of a possessive market society (which had the virtue of being testable) for the description of capitalism growing from and evolving out of seeds in the seventeenth century.

2. See Alan Ryan, *Property* (Minneapolis: University of Minnesota Press, 1987); Andrew Reeve, *Property* (Atlantic Highlands, N.J.: Humanities Press, 1986); Jeremy Waldron, *The Right to Private Property* (Oxford: Clarendon Press, 1989); James Grunebaum, *Private Ownership* (London: Routledge and Kegan Paul, 1987); Gopal Sreenivasan, "The Limits of Private Rights in Property," B.Phil. diss.,

Oxford University, 1988; Stephen Buckle, *The Natural History of Property* (Oxford: Basil Blackwell, 1990).

3. There is also a large body of feminist and ecological scholarship which I do not discuss because it does not challenge the Macpherson thesis as directly as the other three, and it is discussed in the other papers of the conference.

4. C. B. Macpherson, *The Political Theory of Possessive Individualism* (Oxford: Oxford University Press, 1962). All page references noted in the text are to this edition.

5. John Dunn, "Political Obligations and Political Possibilities," in *Political Obligation in Its Historical Context* (Cambridge: Cambridge University Press, 1980), 241-301, and "The Future of Political Philosophy in the West," in *Rethinking Modern Political Theory* (Cambridge: Cambridge University Press, 1985), 171-90.

6. C. B. Macpherson, "The Deceptive Task of Political Theory," in *Democratic Theory* (Oxford: Oxford University Press, 1975 [1973]), 195-207, 199. Compare Macpherson, *The Political Theory of Possessive Individualism*, 3.

7. Macpherson uses *man* throughout all editions. I have followed this in presenting his views. See the comments in C. Pateman and T. Brennan, "Mere Auxiliaries to the Commonwealth: Women and the Origins of Liberalism," *Political Studies* 27, no. 2 (1979): 183-200, on the absence of gender analysis in Macpherson's thesis.

8. Political thought from Hobbes to Locke is treated in *The Political Theory of Possessive Individualism.* For Hume, see "The Economic Penetration of Political Theory: Some Hypotheses," *Journal of the History of Ideas* 39 (1978): 101-18. For Burke, see *Burke* (Oxford: Oxford University Press, 1980). For Bentham and Mill, see *The Life and Times of Liberal Democracy* (Oxford: Oxford University Press, 1977); and, further, *Property: Mainstream and Critical Positions* (Toronto: University of Toronto Press, 1978).

9. David Miller, "The Macpherson Version," *Political Studies* 30, no. 1 (1982): 125.

10. Ludwig Wittgenstein, *Philosophical Investigations,* trans. G. E. M. Anscombe (Oxford: Basil Blackwell, 1988), r. 115.

11. Quentin Skinner, "The Ideological Context of Hobbes's Political Thought," *Historical Journal* 9 (1966): 286-317, and "Conquest and Consent: Thomas Hobbes and the Engagement Controversy," in *The Interregnum,* ed. G. E. Aylmer (London: Macmillan, 1974), 79-98, and "The Limits of Historical Explanation," *Philosophy* 41 (1966): 199-215. John Pocock, ed., *The Political Works of James Harrington* (Cambridge: Cambridge University Press, 1977), and *The Machiavellian Moment* (Princeton: Princeton University Press, 1975). Richard Tuck, *Natural Rights Theories: Their Origins and Development* (Cambridge: Cambridge University Press, 1979). John Dunn, *The Political Thought of John Locke* (Cambridge: Cambridge University Press, 1969). Mark Goldie, "The Roots of True Whiggism: 1688-1694," *History of Political Thought* 1, no. 2 (1980): 195-236. Keith Tribe, *Land, Labour, and Economic Discourse* (London: Routledge and Kegan Paul, 1978).

See the overview in John Pocock, "The Varieties of Whiggism from Exclusion to Reform," in *Virtue, Commerce, and History* (Cambridge: Cambridge University Press, 1985), 215–311.

12. Michel Foucault, *Surveiller et punir* (Paris: Éditions Gallimard, 1975); C. Pateman and T. Brennan, "Mere Auxiliaries to the Commonwealth"; and Carolyn Merchant, *The Death of Nature: Women, Ecology, and the Scientific Revolution* (San Francisco: Harper and Row, 1981).

13. I have discussed the theme of this section more fully in John Locke, *A Letter Concerning Toleration*, ed. James Tully (Indianapolis: Hackett, 1983), 1–17, and in James Tully, *An Approach to Political Philosophy: Locke in Contexts* (Cambridge: Cambridge University Press, 1993), chaps. 1 and 8.

14. For the historical background to this juristic way of thinking about political power, see Quentin Skinner, *The Foundations of Modern Political Thought* (Cambridge, Cambridge University Press), 2:113–349, and Richard Tuck, *Natural Rights Theories*.

15. See the lengthy passage quoted in the text at 23–24. Compare Macpherson, *The Political Theory of Possessive Individualism*, 53–61.

16. John Rawls, *A Theory of Justice* (Oxford: Oxford University Press, 1971), 179.

17. See Jeremy Waldron, *Nonsense Upon Stilts* (London: Methuen, 1987), 19–77.

18. G. A. Cohen, "Socialist Equality and Capitalist Freedom," in *Work, Markets and Social Justice*, ed. Jon Elster (Oxford: Oxford University Press, 1986).

19. Christopher Lasch, "The Sociology of Liberty in Recent Historical Writing," paper delivered at the Seminar on Republicanism at the University of Rochester, Rochester, N.Y., 1988. Richard Ashcraft, "A Victorian Working Class View of Liberalism and the Moral Life," in *Liberalism and the Moral Life*, ed. Nancy Rosenblum (Cambridge: Harvard University Press, 1989).

20. Jean-Jacques Rousseau, *Contrat social*, ed. R. Grimsely (Oxford: Oxford University Press, 1974), 1:iv.

21. See Tuck, *Natural Rights Theories*, 52–54, 101–42; and James Tully, *A Discourse on Property* (Cambridge: Cambridge University Press, 1980), 104–16.

22. Keith Thomas, "The Levellers and the Franchise," in *The Interregnum*, ed. G. E. Aylmer (London: Macmillan, 1974).

23. See Richard Popkin, *The History of Skepticism from Erasmus to Spinoza* (Berkeley: University of California, 1979) for the skeptical crisis. For Grotius in this context, see Richard Tuck, "The Modern Theory of Natural Law," in *The Languages of Political Theory in Early Modern Europe*, ed. A. Padgen (Cambridge: Cambridge University Press, 1987), 99–123; Richard Tuck, *Philosophy and the State in Europe: 1550–1650* (Cambridge: Cambridge University Press, 1992); and James Tully, introduction to *On the Duty of Man and Citizen*, by Samuel Pufendorf, edited by J. Tully (Cambridge: Cambridge University Press, 1991).

24. Richard Tuck, *Natural Rights Theories*, 58–174; Knud Haakonseen, "Hugo

Grotius and the History of Political Thought," *Political Theory* 13 (1985): 239-65; and Stephen Buckle, *The Natural History of Property.*

25. David Johnston, *The Rhetoric of Leviathan* (Princeton: Princeton University Press, 1986); Deborah Baumgold, *Hobbes's Political Theory* (Cambridge: Cambridge University Press, 1987); Richard Tuck, *Hobbes* (Oxford: Oxford University Press, 1989); and S. A. Lloyd, *Mind over Matter: Hobbes's Political Philosophy* (Cambridge: Cambridge University Press, 1990).

26. Thomas Hobbes, *Leviathan*, ed. C. B. Macpherson (Harmondsworth: Penguin, 1968), 261-74, 294-302, 728.

27. Richard Tuck, *Natural Rights Theories*, 143-56; Julian Franklin, *John Locke and the Theory of Sovereignty* (Cambridge: Cambridge University Press, 1978); and David Wootton, ed., *Divine Right and Democracy* (Harmondsworth: Penguin, 1986), 22-58.

28. John Locke, *Two Treatises*, secs. 7, 129, 130. This framework of Locke's theory was brought out in the late 1970s and 1980 by Franklin in *John Locke*, Tuck in *Natural Rights Theories*, and Tully in *A Discourse on Property*. It has been enriched, improved, and corrected by Richard Ashcraft in *Revolutionary Politics and Locke's Two Treatises of Government* (Princeton: Princeton University Press, 1986) and *Locke's Two Treatises of Government* (London: Unwin Hyman, 1987). The study of Locke on property by Gopal Sreenivasan, "The Limits of Private Rights in Property" surveys the major studies of Locke on property from Macpherson to Jeremy Waldron and finds Locke's concept of property to be essentially limited.

29. I discuss this in detail in chaps. 1 and 2 of Tully, *An Approach to Political Philosophy.*

30. Max Weber, "Politics as a Vocation," in *From Max Weber*, ed. Gerth and Mills (New York: Oxford University Press, 1978), 79-129, 82.

31. Keith Tribe, *Land, Labour, and Economic Discourse*, 51, and chap. 1 of Tully, *An Approach to Political Philosophy.*

32. I have discussed the theme of this section more fully in chaps. 6 and 7 of Tully, *An Approach to Political Philosophy.*

33. Eli Heckscher, *Mercantilism*, 2d ed., trans. M. Shapiro, 2 vols. (London: Allen and Unwin, 1955); Lawrence A. Harper, *The English Navigation Laws* (New York: Columbia University Press, 1939); and John Coleman, ed., *Revisions in Mercantilism* (London: Methuen, 1969).

34. Hobbes, *Leviathan*, 297-98, 367-68; Locke, *Two Treatises*, secs. 3, 31, 37, 38, 42, 50, 120, 130.

35. Hobbes, *Leviathan*, 301-2; Locke, *Two Treatises*, vol. 2, secs. 30, 41, 42, 43. William Cronon, *Changes in the Land* (New York: Hill and Wang, 1983); and chaps. 5 and 11 of Tully, *An Approach to Political Philosophy.*

36. John Locke, *The Educational Writings*, ed. James Axtell (Cambridge: Cambridge University Press 1968), 325.

37. John Locke, *An Essay Concerning Human Understanding,* ed. Peter Nidditch (Oxford: Oxford University Press, 1975), 2:21.69-70.

38. John Locke, preface to *A Report to the Board of Trade* (London: 1793 [1697]

39. Michel Foucault, "The Political Technology of Individuals," in *Technologies of the Self,* ed. Luther Martin et al. (Amherst: University of Massachusetts Press, 1988), 145-63, 161-62. See also "Governmentality," in *Theoretical Practice* (Summer 1979), 5-21; "Politics and Reason," in *Michel Foucault: Politics, Philosophy, Culture,* ed. Lawrence Kritzman (New York: Routledge, 1988), 57-86.

40. William McNeill, *The Pursuit of Power* (Chicago: University of Chicago Press, 1982), 117-44; Marc Raeff, *The Well-Ordered Police State* (New Haven: Yale University Press, 1983); Michael Ignatieff, *A Just Measure of Pain* (New York: Pantheon, 1978); Neal Wood, *The Politics of Locke's Philosophy* (Berkeley: University of California Press, 1983); and Sidney Pollard, *The Genesis of Scientific Management* (Cambridge: Harvard University Press, 1965). See also Paul Slack, *Poverty and Policy in Tudor and Stuart England* (London: Longman, 1988), and the interesting discussion in Charles Taylor, *Sources of the Self* (Cambridge: Harvard University Press, 1989), pt. 3.

41. C. B. Macpherson, *The Political Theory of Possessive Individualism,* 53.

42. See the reform proposals in F. M. Eden, *The State of the Poor,* 3 vols. (London: 1797).

43. Dugald Stewart, *Lectures on Political Economy,"* in *The Collected Works,* ed. W. Hamilton (1855), 8:318; Adam Smith, *An Inquiry into the Nature and Causes of the Wealth of Nations,* ed. R. H. Campbell (Oxford: Clarendon Press, 1976), vol. 2, V.i.f.50, 781-82. See chap. 7 of Tully, *An Approach to Political Philosophy.*

44. Compare Marx's definition of capitalist wage labor in Karl Marx, *Capital,* trans. Ben Fowkes (New York: Vintage Books, 1977), 1:480.

45. John Locke, *Two Treatises of Government,* sec. 85.

46. John Pocock, *The Political Works of James Harrington,* 43-76. Pocock's republican studies include *The Machiavellian Moment* (1975) and *Virtue, Commerce, and History* (1985); see especially "Authority and Property: The Question of Liberal Origins," 51-73 and "The Mobility of Property and the Rise of Eighteenth-Century Sociology," 103-25. For criticisms of Pocock's work, see Ian Shapiro, *Political Criticism* (Berkeley: University of California Press, 1990), 166-206.

47. Gordon Wood, *The Creation of the American Republic* (Chapel Hill: University of North Carolina Press, 1969); Nannerl Keohane, *Philosophy and the State in France* (Princeton: Princeton University Press, 1980); Eco Haitsma-Mulier, *The Myth of Venice and Dutch Republican Thought* (Assen: Van Gorcum, 1980); Carol Blum: *Rousseau and the Republic of Virtue* (Chicago: University of Chicago Press, 1986); Richard Tuck, *Philosophy and the State in Europe: 1550-1650* (Cambridge: Cambridge University Press, 1992); Quentin Skinner, *The*

JAMES TULLY

Foundations of Modern Political Thought, vol. 1: *The Renaissance,* Quentin
Skinner, "The Idea of Negative Liberty: Historical and Philosophical Perspectives," in *Philosophy in History,* ed. Richard Rorty (Cambridge: Cambridge University Press, 1984), 193-225.

48. See Anthony Pagden, ed., *The Languages of Political Theory in Early Modern Europe,* 1987.

49. See Istvan Hont and Michael Ignatieff, eds., *Wealth and Virtue* (Cambridge: Cambridge University Press, 1983), especially John Dunn, "From Applied Theology to Social Analysis: The Break between John Locke and the Scottish Enlightenment," 119-325. But see chap. 11 of Tully, *An Approach to Political Philosophy,* for some continuities.

50. See chap. 7 of Tully, *An Approach to Political Philosophy.*

51. See James Moore, "Locke and the Scottish Jurists," in *Conference for the Study of Political Thought* (Washington, D.C., 1980, unpublished); James Moore and Michael Silverthorne, "Gershom Carmichael and the Natural Jurisprudence Tradition in Eighteenth-Century Scotland," in *Wealth and Virtue,* ed. Hont and Ignatieff, 73-88; Istvan Hont, "The Language of Sociability and Commerce," in *The Languages of Political Theory,* ed. A. Pagden, 253-77; and chap. 11 of Tully, *An Approach to Political Philosophy.*

52. Bernard Mandeville, *The Fable of the Bees,* 2 vols. (London, 1727).

53. Immanuel Kant, "Idea for a Universal History from a Cosmopolitan Point of View," in *Kant Selections,* ed. Lewis White Beck (New York: Macmillan, 1988), 413-27.

54. Michel Foucault, *Résumé des cours 1970-1982* (Paris: Juliard, 1989), 114.

55. For Enlightenment views of women, see Sylvania Tomaselli, "The Enlightenment Debate on Women," *History Workshop Journal,* 1985, 101-23; Joan Landes, *Women and the Public Sphere in the Age of the French Revolution* (Ithaca, N.Y.: Cornell University Press, 1988). For the critical response to war and preparation for war, see F. H. Hinsley, *Power and the Pursuit of Peace,* 2d ed. (Cambridge: Cambridge University Press, 1985). Pocock has always stressed the ambivalence to commerce and specialization among eighteenth-century writers.

56. Hont and Ignatieff, "Needs and Justice in the Wealth of Nations," in *Wealth and Virtue,* 1-44.

57. Michel Foucault, "Governmentality."

58. See the *International Conference on Republican Thought and Practice,* organized by Bianca Fontana, Pasquale Pasquino, and François Furet (Cambridge and Paris, Oct.-Dec. 1989). Also Jurgen Habermas, *Strukturwandel der Offentlichkeit* (Neuwied: Luchterhand, 1962); Michel Foucault, *Surveiller et punir,* Joan Landes, *Woman and the Public Sphere,* John Pocock, "Virtue, Rights, and Manner," in *Virtue, Commerce, and History,* 37-51; and Bianca Fontana, ed., *Constant's Political Writings* (Cambridge: Cambridge University Press, 1989), 1-42.

Chapter 3
Equality as Egoism

Louise Marcil-Lacoste

Amidst the prodigious diversity of notions of equality that have been delineated since the eighteenth century, the association of envy with views favoring equality is a recurrent thesis which has many of the features of what Macpherson called a "social assumption." More frequently mentioned than theorized, and more frequently asserted than demonstrated, the association is generally vindicated as a consensus concerning the limits of equality as a value, not to mention egalitarianism as a pitfall.

According to this view, the search for equality—either in its radical form, termed "egalitarianism," or even in its moderate forms, calling for "more" equality—does not proceed from reason or moral sense, let alone an intuitive sense of justice. Rather, it proceeds from envy as a clear case of psychological rationalization. Thus, the quest for equality derives from a bitter contemplation of others' better fortune, qualities, or positions, and ultimately what Ayn Rand has termed the "hatred of the good for being the good." In other words, once generalized as the basic passion of all human beings, envy makes equality indistinguishable from egoism in its generalized form.[1]

From a Macphersonian perspective, it is easy to understand this account of equality as the necessary consequence of possessive individualism. If the human being considered universally is a proprietor, and if to be human means either to have possessions or to strive for them, then envy of possessions will be regarded as a major characteristic of relationships between human beings. Envy is the pathological version in nonproprietors of the human feature they are said to share with proprietors, or something entirely focused on possessions. It follows that the attempt to pass from inequality to equality is doomed, leading at most to the alternation of proprietors. Thus, egoism is not only what makes all human beings equal, but is also the manner in which possessive individualism morally disqualifies even the search for other forms of human relations.

Underlying this representation of equality there is, however, an important assumption that I call "negative equality," which can be summarized in the following dual thesis: Equality is a fact about human nature; what all human beings share is some negative attribute related to the human condition. Human beings are thus fundamentally equal—all exposed, nay condemned, to errors, sufferings, and evils, they find their ultimate resemblance in the prime equalizer: death. By means of negative equality, equality is thus asserted as a fact about human limitations rather than as a right about justice in human relationships. Furthermore, by means of negative equality, the human condition is not only condensed into a fatal destination, but the issue of equality is also reduced to a negative calculus in which only the negative features of the human condition are to be compared and weighed. Thus, behind equality as egoism, there is a momentous assumption that negative equality is the ultimate standard or the only possible form of equality between human beings.

Because Thomas Hobbes is at once the most obvious candidate for the origin of the thesis relating equality to egoism and Macpherson's own paradigm for consistent possessivity, the analysis of the role of equality in his deduction from the state of nature is offered here as a test case. However antisocial Hobbes's natural man turns out to be, he is not, as Macpherson rightly insisted, a nonsocial man.[2] The precise question to address is the role played by equality in his deduction from the state of nature, and my suggestion is that it is not because human beings are defined as egoists that equality is proclaimed impossible. Rather, it is because equality is deemed unthinkable except as a negative concept that human beings are characterized as egoists. Because of this negative assumption, equality and inequality become interchangeable terms.[3] Revealing clues to this reading occur in what Macpherson has cited as Hobbes's sole explicit statements on social relations—that is, those passages taken from the *Leviathan* where the "two-stage logical abstraction" marks the transition from the state of nature to the civil state.[4] In what follows, we shall focus on five such clues.[5]

NEGATIVE CONCEPTION OF DESIRE

In chapter 6 of the *Leviathan,* Hobbes proposes his Galilean resolution of natural passions into terms of desire (endeavor toward something) and aversion (endeavor away from something). This culminates in his celebrated assertion that "whatsoever is the object of any man's appetite or desire, that is it which he for his part calleth good." In this chapter, Hobbes insisted on the impossibility of all men desiring the same thing. He writes, "Because the constitution of man's body is in continual mutation, it is impossible that all the same things should always cause in him the same appetites and aversions; much less can all men consent in the desire of almost any one and the same object."[6]

This inference—one's desire being inconstant, one cannot desire at all times the same object and all cannot desire at any time the same object—is a consistent application to appetites of *Nosce teipsum,* the main philosophical rule stated in the opening pages of the *Leviathan.* Mocking the assumption that *read thyself* could exhibit wisdom by proceeding from "uncharitable censures of one another behind their backs," Hobbes presented it as a way to see the similitude of the thoughts and passions of all men. He explained, "For the similitude of the thoughts and passions of one man, to the thoughts and passions of another, whoever looketh into himself, and considered what he doth, when he does *think, opine, reason, hope, fear &c.* and upon what grounds; he shall thereby read and know, what are the thoughts and passions of all other men upon the like occasions."[7]

A crucial qualification was added—namely, that this similitude is not to be expected in the object of human desires. Hobbes writes, "I say the similitude of *passions,* which are the same in all men, desire, *fear, hope, & c.;* not the similitude of the *objects* of the passions, which are the things *desired, feared, hoped, & c."* [8] From this it follows not only that no universalization of any object of human desire is possible, but that there is nothing simply and absolutely good or evil, nor any common rule of good and evil to be taken from "the nature of the objects themselves."[9] Pleasure (or delight) is then "the appearance or sense of Good," while molestation (or displeasure) is "the appearance or sense of Evil."[10] In chapter 6, Hobbes's main concern is to show that appearances extend to the "expectation of consequences," that is, beyond the actual presence of an object.[11] This thesis is further systematized by defining desire itself in a negative manner—that is, as "the absence of the object."[12]

However complex the domain of appetites and aversions—especially if in reading oneself, one does not attempt to "read in himself this or that particular man; but mankind"[13]—Hobbes's rejection of the possibility of a *summum bonum* because of the impossibility of generalizing any object of desire is a significant step in the direction of negative equality.[14] Equality cannot be expected to stand for the thesis that men are equal in that they desire the same thing. Nor can it be expected that equality could be later analyzed in terms of the object of human desire. This negative definition of human desire already paves the way toward the asymmetry between desire and aversion—that is, toward the *summum malum* that will occur in the final step of the deduction.[15]

INEQUALITY AS DESIRE

The second clue to Hobbes's assumptions occurs again in the sixth chapter, in the manner that his logical definitions of appetites are construed. Indeed, although their precise role is not fully spelled out, many forms of inequalities define natural passions. In Hobbes's logical definitions, which include those of close to forty appetites, inequality plays a key role in at least ten of them. Moreover, Hobbes's further inferences show that the passions determined by inequality are the most important in the logic of his system.[16] All those passions fall within the category of "pleasures of the mind," a domain that Hobbes will later describe as the one where the greatest equality among human beings obtains. Pleasures of the mind obviously include "desire of riches" or covetousness ("a name always used in signification of blame; because men contending for them, are *displeased* with one another attaining them") and "desire of office," precedence, or ambition (a name "used also in the *worse* sense, for the reason before mentioned").[17]

Inequality is also central to the "joy arising from the imagination of man's own power and ability, [which] is that exultation of the mind which is called GLORYING: but if grounded on the flattery of others; or only supposed by himself, for delight in the consequences of it, is called VAIN-GLORY."[18] What is implicitly denounced by vainglory (otherwise called "pride") is the false estimation of one's own power, not the role of inequality in the logic of human passions. This is confirmed with the symmetrical passion to glorying, "dejection of mind," the grief arising from want of power, also defined in the same chapter.[19]

Inequality is also present in Hobbes's definition of jealousy as a degree of complexity added to the passion of love.[20] "*Love* of one singularly, with desire to be singularly beloved" becomes jealousy when this desire is attended "with fear that love is not mutual." This definition is revealing because the "passion of love"—here contradistinguished from "love of persons for society" (kindness) and from "love of persons for pleasing the sense only" (natural lust and luxury)—stands for love inasmuch as the passion is reciprocated, or what may be called the issue of equality as it applies to the relationship between two persons.

What must be underscored is that jealousy is predicated on the expected failure of equality.[21] It is the kind of passion that arises when, between two individuals, the reciprocity of love does not obtain or, more precisely, when there is no assurance that it does.[22] Jealousy, in other words, spells out the fear that is involved in mutuality as the object of desire, thereby showing that the desire of equality between two persons inevitably gives rise to suspicion. It is only suspicion, rather than love, that can be generalized, because perpetual mutation and inconstancy are the basic features of human desires.[23]

More revealing still is Hobbes's definition of envy as a negative feature added to emulation—that is, the only passion whose definition explicitly includes a reference to equality. Envy is categorized as a passion between two persons, but it differs from jealousy for, in Hobbes's terms, jealousy applies to persons, while envy applies to "wealth, honour, or other good."[24] Moreover, love (to which jealousy is related) supposes the presence of the object, whereas emulation and envy (as desires) suppose the absence of the object. Hobbes states, "*Grief* for the success of a competitor in wealth, honour, or other good, if it be joined with the endeavour to enforce our own abilities to equal or exceed him, is called EMULATION, but joined with endeavour to supplant or hinder a competitor, ENVY."[25]

The discussion of emulation and envy then systematically proceed in a negative manner.[26] Arising from grief for the success of a competitor, the endeavor to enforce one's own abilities puts the attempts to "equal him" and "to exceed him" on a par.[27] This competitive endeavor culminates in a foremost aggressive feature, that is, envy itself where the attempt to supplant a competitor clearly evokes death, if not sudden killing, as the logical conclusion of this passion. This potentiality is indeed developed in Hobbes's further inferences, especially in chapter 8, where the logical extension of pride in anger, rage, and fury—as well as the logical extension of jealousy in rage—are clearly asserted.[28] Also, whereas Hobbes's treatment of jealousy refers to the fear that equality of passion does not obtain, his treatment of envy offers no ground to causeless fears. It is clearly predicated upon a situation in which the sharing of goods does not obtain. This paves the way toward the final step of the argument where the idea that such a sharing cannot logically obtain will be derived from the impossibility of equality between two persons, when any two men happen to desire the same thing which cannot be enjoyed in common.[29]

Hobbes goes on to offer an account of laughter ("sudden glory") as the "apprehension of some *deformed* thing in another, by comparison whereof they suddenly applaud themselves," a natural passion, Hobbes thinks, most often found among those "who are conscious of the fewest abilities in themselves," because they are "forced to keep themselves in their own favor, by observing the imperfections of other men."[30] In contrast, "weeping" (or sudden dejection) is a passion caused "by such accidents, as suddenly take away some vehement hope or some prop of their power." Hobbes adds incidentally that weeping is more incipient in those who "rely principally on helps external, such as are women and children."[31] But, he insists, laughter and weeping being sudden motions, "no man laughs at old jests; or weeps for an old calamity." Supposing the inequalities embedded in the logic of human passions to be of the latter kind (for instance, the condition of women), custom would "take away weeping," including, one would surmise, for the unequal.[32]

The key role which inequalities play in Hobbes's definition of human passions, together with the centrality of the passions determined by inequalities in the logic of his system, shows how crucial his assumptions about equality are to his understanding of human desire. This is further confirmed in Hobbes's following chapters. In chapter 8, the very definition of virtue stands as the condensation of all the inequalities at work in the definitions of natural passions. When Hobbes writes that "VIRTUE generally, in all sorts of subjects, is somewhat that is value for *eminence;* and consisteth in comparison," his explanation is limpid. "For if all things were equal in all men, nothing would be prized."[33] Similarly, the whole of chapter 10 is specifically devoted to those passions determined by inequalities, this time and appropriately in the context of power. "Natural power" is then defined as "*the eminence* of the faculties of body, or mind, or as *extraordinary* strength, forme, prudence, arts, eloquence, liberality, and nobility." From this it follows— for here the worth of a man is defined as "his price"—that dominion, victory, good fortune, riches, and the like are *honorable*, whereas servitude, ill fortune, poverty, and similar conditions are *dishonorable.*[34] As for instrumental powers, they are the means and instruments to acquire more, such as riches, reputations, or friends. They are, Hobbes remarks, "the secret working of God, which men call Good Luck."[35] They are not, one should notice, the secret working of inequalities.

What must be underscored is that, together with the logic of passions, powers already stand as the social (although not yet civil) specifications of passions defined by inequalities. They are the systematization of inequality as desire to the extent that inequalities play a key role in determining, by more specific passions, the general definition of desire as the absence of the object.

FELICITY AS POWER

As a conclusion to the definitions of passions offered in chapter 6 and focusing on "the forms of speech" by which the passions are expressed, Hobbes says: "Continual success in obtaining those things which a man from time to time desireth, that is to say, continual prospering, is that men call FELICITY."[36] He insists, "I mean felicity of this life," emphasizing the transitory character of felicity, because "there is no such thing as perpetual tranquillity of mind, while we live here; because life itself is but motion and can never be without desire, nor without fear, no more than without sense."[37] In chapter 11, Hobbes again underscores that, in this life, felicity does not lie in the "repose of a mind satisfied," making the rejection of some *finis ultimus* the focus of his discussion.[38]

Felicity, here treated in a formal manner—that is, beyond the presence or the absence of the object—is also assessed in a negative manner. Hobbes insists that it is not to be defined as perpetual success in obtaining what one desires. Rather, it is "a continual progress of desire, from one object to another, the attaining of the former being still but the way to the latter." From this continual progress of desire, Hobbes makes his famous inference—given as a "general inclination of all mankind"—to wit, "a perpetual and restless desire of power after power that ceases

51

only in death."[39] The transition from the precariousness of men's instant enjoyment to the assuring of a contented life is here specifically mediated by "the acquisition of more," that is, by the generalization to all appetites of the passions we have seen to be determined by inequality. Hobbes is clear on this point. He gives conquest, competition, honor, command, desire of praise, and ambition as paradigms of felicity. The cause of this, Hobbes explains, "is not always that a man hopes for a more intensive delight, than he has already attained to; or that he cannot be content with a moderate power: but because he cannot assure the power and the means to live well, which he hath present, without the acquisition of more."[40]

The role which the reference to death plays in this account of felicity deserves attention, for when Hobbes writes, "I put for a general inclination of all mankind, a perpetual and restless desire of power after power, that ceaseth only in death," the hope to meet with continual success is predicated of the end of life. In the immediate context of chapter 11, the reason for this transition from instant enjoyment to the striving for more is presented as man's foremost desire. Hobbes writes, "The object of man's desire is not to enjoy once only, and for one instant of time; but to assure for ever, the way of his future desire."[41] But this cannot mean that men desire the continuance of any enjoyment or the obtaining of what one desires, because, as we know, there is a continual mutation in the object of any man's desire, while obtaining the object of desire is not felicity. Nor can this mean that the logic of felicity could be explained by some *finis ultimus,* a notion rejected by Hobbes together with the "beatific vision" or the thinking of felicity in terms of some unintelligible afterlife.[42] This transition from the precariousness of enjoyment to felicity as striving for power is mediated by reference to death as the *terminus ad quem,* that is, the only expectation whose logical possibility is sure to coincide with a real possibility at some point in time.

However, death cannot relieve men from the insecurity of specific desires without putting an end to desire itself. "Nor can a man any more live, whose desires are at an end, than he, whose senses and imaginations are at a stand."[43] And it is on this basis that the generalization of felicity as power to all human beings becomes possible, even to those who would rather exhibit "desire of ease" (or sensual delight) or "desire of knowledge" (or arts of peace) rather than, let us say, "desire of riches" or "desire of office."[44] Even to them, passions determined by inequalities can be universalized because, in the face of death, all objects of desire become interchangeable, as well as the obtaining or not obtaining of those objects. Inequalities, in a word, become negligible. Whether one desires more dominion or more excellence in some art, more riches, or more ease, one cannot live without desiring more. One cannot live without structuring one's present desire within the absence of goods carried by the notion of the future. It is then impossible to live without structuring one's present desire by passions determined by inequalities.

The "acquisition of more" is thus more than a *conditio sine qua non* of felicity. It is the only available specification of the future, the only form of "future desire."[45] It is the only way not to be dead-alive on the way to death as the foremost equalizer. It is the only way that desire, as a restless (but not endless) pursuit can activate mutation in a manner that does not bar the road to felicity in this life. In other words, passions determined by inequalities are the only alternative for human desiring when present living is set up against the futility of a life terminated by inevitable death.[46] In Hobbes's system, far from proving the inanity of life, the reference to death as the *terminus ad quem* rather proves the futility of inequalities. It puts all objects of desire on a par, as well as the obtaining or the not obtaining of what one desires. Beyond the impossibility of any *summum bonum* and of any *finis ultimus,* death equalizes not by putting an end to inequalities in power, but by putting an end to desire itself, thus equalizing all forms of felicity.

OBLIGATION AS THRALLDOM

There is, in chapter 11, another passage referring to equality. Commenting on the saying "benefits oblige," Hobbes describes the receiving of benefits as hateful thralldom or mutual desire, according to whether it comes from an equal or from an inferior. He writes, "To have received from one, to whom we think ourselves equal, greater benefits than there is hope to requite, disposeth to counterfeit love; but really secret hatred; and puts a man into the estate of a desperate debtor, that in declining the sight of his creditor tacitly wishes him there, where he might never see him more."[47] This passage is curious because, although the obvious criterion would seem to be whether there is some hope of requital (on this reading, therefore, only unrequitable benefits are thralldom), the equality or the inequality of the partners is also at stake. Hobbes writes, "For benefits oblige, and obligation is thraldom; which is to one's equal, hateful."[48]

The end of the section confirms this reading: it is only the receiving of benefits from superiors or inferiors that will lead to definite conclusions. Hobbes writes, "To have received benefits from one, whom we acknowledge for superior, inclines to love," the reason for this being that the obligation does not produce a "new depression." Therefore, "cheerful acceptation, which men call *gratitude*" becomes possible. It is "such an honour done to the obliger, as is taken generally for retribution."[49] Similarly, to receive benefits from an inferior also inclines to love. One supposes the possibility of requital to be obvious in the situation.

It is only in the case of equals that "benefits oblige" disposes either to conceited love or to secret hatred—in both cases, a negative feature.[50] This is to suggest that, however defined, "benefits oblige" can hardly pertain to equals, at least not without creating a dilemma.[51] In other words, however much the hope of requital could stand as the criterion, the plausible feature of requitals as between equals is here dismissed.

Despite its oblique phrasing, Hobbes's comment on obligation as a possible thralldom between equals and between equals only is important. I surmise that it shapes his first statement about natural equality. When he writes in chapter 13, that "Nature has made men so equal . . . [that] the difference between man and man is not so considerable that one can thereupon claim to himself any benefit to which another may not pretend as well," there is no way to understand that, between equals, the hope of requital could obtain as a criterion for obligation. There is no way to expect that between equals benefits should oblige. As a matter of fact, in Hobbes's subsequent deductions, obligation will be thematicized with reference to superiors and inferiors, including the laws of gratitude toward superiors and love toward inferiors.[52]

NATURAL EQUALITY: THE DEDUCTION

Keeping the preceding discussion in mind, let us now briefly sketch the function of equality in Hobbes's famous analysis of the state of nature in chapter 13 of the *Leviathan*. The first statement about equality—the one quoted in the preceding paragraph beginning with the words, "Nature has made men so equal . . ."—refers to an "equality of ability," namely, the strength of the body ("the weakest has strength enough, by machination or confederacy, to kill the strongest") and to the faculties of mind, in which Hobbes finds yet a greater equality among men. From this "equality of ability" arises, says Hobbes, "equality of hope," and from equality of hope, "enmity if any two men desire the same thing which they cannot both enjoy."[53] From enmity derives the "endeavour to destroy or subdue one another." From this comes "diffidence," and from diffidence, the universal "augmentation of dominion" sought for the sake of man's conservation. Thus, if there is no common power to keep men in awe, competition, diffidence, and glory lead men to the war of every man against every man. From this state of war, it follows that "nothing could be unjust." It follows, Hobbes concludes in chapter 14, that "every man has a right to everything, even to one another's body." Before turning to natural equality as the right of all to all, it is important to analyze the logic of the deduction within the limits of chapter 13, because Hobbes is not merely giving a clear instantiation of negative equality as the main form of human equality—the war of every man against every man. He is doing so in such a manner that equality and inequality become interchangeable by reference to death as the foremost equalizer. This occurs in a striking feature of Hobbes's deduction—namely, that under the name of equality, he is assessing the consequences of the inequalities that he has already posited in the logic of human passions.

When Hobbes affirms "the equality of ability," whether of mind or of body, his assertion is comparative and it is systematically stated in a negative manner. Men are so equal in their faculties of body and mind that the difference between them is not so considerable as to allow anyone to claim a benefit to which another cannot pretend as well. The greater equality here ascribed to the faculty of the mind is not the assertion of the equality of reason.[54] Rather, it is the fact that, concerning reason, every man is contented with his share.[55] This contentment arises because of one's feeling of superiority toward others, especially the "vulgar."[56] Pride itself, a passion determined by inequality, becomes here the foremost proof of natural equality. Commenting on the fact that men, "howsoever they may acknowledge many others to be more witty or more learned, will hardly believe there be many so wise as themselves," Hobbes observes that "this proves rather that men are in that point equal, rather than unequal. For there is not ordinarily a greater sign of the equal distribution of anything than that every man is contented with his share." Notice here the inversion: there is no better sign of equal distribution than unequal distribution when people are contented with their share.

Furthermore, to rest contented with one's share, even within modest bounds, is precisely what the state of nature disallows.[57] The fear of death and its correlative search for security make it impossible to define human beings as equals even in the relative sense of each being contented with his or her own share. Hobbes writes, "Because there are some that pursue their acts of conquest further than their security requires, others that otherwise would be glad to be at ease within modest bounds enter the augmentation of dominion for they could not subsist by standing only on their defense."[58] The argument is not that all men have the actual desire of what in *De Cive* Hobbes called the "arrant wolf."[59] The argument is that the existence of the "fiercests" determines the rule by forcing even the "temperates" to search for dominion.[60] This is to say that egoism in the form of *homo homini lupus* is not the basis of Hobbes's deduction here. The basis of his deduction is that when confronted with the possibility of death—here, by sudden killing—passions determined by inequalities make the search for dominion the universal rule, forcing even the temperates to comply with it as the exclusive rule of the social, but not yet civil, game.

Inequality, in the sense of a general search for dominion, is made the exclusive rule of the social game, and is made such under the name of "natural equality," as Hobbes's summary of "Men by nature equal" indicates. What is asserted, however, is not the equality either of the body or of the mind, but rather the negligibility of observable degrees in the distribution of faculties when related to the body (strength) or to the mind (pride).[61] And this negligibility is asserted by referring to death as the foremost equalizer. In Hobbes's terms, "the weakest has strength enough to kill the strongest, either by secret machinations, or by confederacy with others, that are in the same danger with himself." The rationale for this, as stated in *De Cive*, is that "they who can do the greatest thing (namely to kill) can do equal things" and hence "*are* equal."[62] The same applies to the faculties of the mind—in *De Cive*, "the combat for wits" was stated as "the fiercest"—where the search for dominion determined pride as the rule of the game whose extension in anger, rage, and fury is predicated of death in the *Leviathan*.[63]

Within the limits of chapter 13, therefore, natural equality makes room for the rejection of "equality of ability."[64] Equality of hope is also rejected for things which are desired and could not be enjoyed in common.[65] Equality of worth is also impossible, because not only is the worth of a man his "price," but where there is no power, "every man looks that his companion should value him at the same rate as he sets upon himself."[66] What is being generalized, even to those who would rather be contented within modest bounds, is thus the ill condition of mere nature, understood here as the human condition without a power to overawe all men. In other words, under the name of natural equality, what is generalized throughout is the system of passions determined by inequality. The inequality of strength and mind and the inequality of power and riches are presented under the name of natural equality because of death as the foremost equalizer. All are condemned to death as the *terminus ad quem* and all exposed also to sudden death by killing—the only form of death to which voluntary powers can apply, hence its central role in the deduction. Negative equality, here dramatized as the state of war, thus plays the role of the foremost form of natural equality.

Within the limits of this chapter, a last remark must be made. The "natural right of every man to everything" is neither Hobbes's premise, nor even his assumption. In fact, this notion does not even occur in chapter 13 but, for the first time, in chapter 14. In chapter 13, the logic of the argument is to switch from partial, relative, and negative comparisons to the nightmare of total war. The logic of the argument is to predicate natural equality upon the assumption of negative equality—that is, on death as the ultimate standard by which to assess human equality. In the face of death, the various forms of inequality vanish and the difference between equality and inequality becomes so negligible that the terms become interchangeable. This is the reason why Hobbes's predication of inequalities in human relations has been misread as the vindication of natural equality. For under the name of natural equality, Hobbes was deducing a consistent universalization of inequality on the assumption that equality is impossible except as a negative concept.[67]

THE RIGHT OF ALL TO ALL

Let us now turn to the final step of Hobbes's argument—that is, the transition from natural equality as defined within the context of total war to natural equality as the right of all to all.[68] The logic of the argument will be to switch from the indiscernibility of equality and inequality in the nightmare of total war (chapter 13) to the right of all to all as the logical dread awaiting any step beyond negative equality (chapter 14). This is another way of saying that, in the specific context of the *Leviathan,* the natural right of every man to everything is neither Hobbes's premise, nor his assumption. It is the ultimate deduction from the state of nature understood as the state of war.[69]

As I just mentioned, natural equality as the right of all to everything does not even occur in the famous deduction of chapter 13. The closest statement to it was phrased negatively when Hobbes said that nature has made men so equal that the difference between them is not so considerable that any man can claim to himself any benefit to which another may not pretend as well.[70] The right of all to all first occurs in chapter 14 and there, explicitly, as a deduction. Indeed, Hobbes writes, "Because the condition of man, as hath been declared in the precedent chapter, is a condition of war of every one against every one . . . it followeth that in such a condition, every man has a right to every thing; even to another's body."[71]

This right occurs as the culminating point of Hobbes's argument against the ill condition in which man is placed by mere nature, or, to be clear, as a foil. And it is made a foil not as a consequence of men's so-called natural equality (remember that it is competition, diffidence, and vainglory that lead to the state of war) but the necessary premise for concluding with the total surrender of one's rights to the Leviathan.[72] This was the point of Hobbes's rejection of any *summum bonum.* There is no common rule of good and evil in a commonwealth, but "from the person that representeth it."[73] This was also the point of his insisting on felicity as power, paving the way to monopoly. "The greatest of human powers is that which is compounded of the powers of most men, in one person, natural or civil, that has the use of all their powers depending on his will."[74] This was, of course, the point of deriving war itself from nature, by generalizing only the negative features of the human condition: "Men have no pleasure, but on the contrary a great deal of grief, in keeping company, where there is no power able to over-awe them all."[75] Concerning this power—which may be described as the political version of negative equality to the extent that it is essentially defined by total surrender of one's rights—Hobbes's concern is not the equality of benefits and burdens arising from the government as could obtain among subjects.[76] Rather, his concern is the equality of benefits and burdens between the ruler and the subject—"the same and common to both"—which does not imply that power and honor be the same, for the latter "vanisheth in the presence of the sovereign."[77]

Thus, the right of all to all (otherwise called "natural equality") is the reference needed for the articles of peace (otherwise called "laws of nature") to rephrase retrospectively the negative features of the absence of right which were said to characterize the state of war. It does so by adding to the negligibility of inequalities between all human beings the logical impossibility of natural equality as a relation between any two individuals. Indeed, to the negative situation described in chapter 13—"if any two men desire the same thing which they cannot enjoy in common, they become enemies"—chapter 14 adds the proof that in any such situation natural equality could not logically obtain. This is the point of Hobbes's phrasing that "in such a state [universal war of all against all], every man has a right to every thing," its main logic being that, even in the state of nature, the effects of this right are "the same, almost, as if there had been no *Right* at all."[78] Bearing in mind the whole of Hobbes's deduction, the reasoning behind this assertion can be schematized as follows:

From the observations that one individual man does not always desire the same thing, that all individual men cannot agree in the desire of the same object, and that two individual men may sometimes want something which they cannot both enjoy, Hobbes moves to the stronger claim that it is logically impossible for all individual men to enjoy all individual things. From this he deduces that equality between any two individuals, here defined as each wanting and enjoying all, is also impossible. Notice that, in this reasoning, the notion that two individuals could share something is not at all the issue. Rather this is stipulatively precluded for the sake of his argument. What must be emphasized is that, once logically understood, natural equality—the right to all—is the culminating point of Hobbes's whole argument against mere nature. It makes natural equality something that we should fear. So much so that, from then on, natural equality will stand as the logical dread awaiting any further step beyond negative equality.

EQUALITY IN THE LAWS OF NATURE

Hobbes's final deduction confirms this reading, as may be shown from his further references to equality within the enunciation of "articles of peace," otherwise called "laws of nature." The "right of all to all"— Hobbes's deduction, rather than his premise—is, indeed, given also as a preamble to the derivation of articles of peace, including chapter 14 (on the two first laws of nature) and chapter 15 (on other laws). In total, there are nineteen. What must be emphasized is that, in Hobbes's further inferences about laws of nature, natural equality as the right of all to all remains throughout the foil.

The first law of nature—to seek peace and follow it, and, by all means we can, to defend ourselves—is indeed given as the logical consequence of the fact that natural equality is something that we should fear. The second law of nature makes the rejection of natural equality the specific referent of the surrender.[80] It intimates "that a man be willing, when other are so too, as far-forth, as for peace, and defence of himself he shall think it necessary, *to lay down this right to all things,* and be contented with so much liberty against other men, as he would allow other men against himself."[81] Again, when the two first laws are summarized in chapter 15 as the premises of the third law—"that men perform their covenants made"—this is given once more with the specific exclusion of the right of all men to all things.[82] A similar approach is taken in several other articles deriving laws of nature where the dread of war (henceforth indistinguishable from natural equality) is repeatedly the main argument.[83]

Besides these systematic references to the right of all to all as the dread awaiting natural equality, a second feature of Hobbes's further references to equality in his derivation of articles of peace deserves attention. Beyond the right of all to all, but still within the performance of the covenant, articles of peace must be understood under the express condition that the right of all to all is not merely rejected but systematically dispelled. Hence, for equality and within the covenant, a new form of negativity.

The most important of Hobbes's further references to equality, minus the state of war, appears in the enunciation of the ninth law of nature (to acknowledge every other man as his equal by nature) and in the eleventh law (if a man is trusted to judge between man and man, he must deal equally between them).[84] Notice that the ninth law—"to acknowledge other men as equal by nature," which is offered against Aristotle's statement that some are slaves by nature—is predicated of an interesting instantiation of interchangeability. Hobbes has concluded, indeed, that we must acknowledge other men as equals by nature whether "nature have made men equal" or whether "nature have made men unequal."[85]

In both cases, a new negative function for equality is asserted. Thus, as with law nine, to acknowledge every other man as equal is a law of nature "against pride,"[86] whereas as with law eleven, to judge between man and man in dealing equally with them is against the "acception of persons."[87] A similar approach is taken against the excess of pride (in the fourth law), against contumely (in the eighth law), against arrogance (in the tenth law), against one being his own judge (in the seventeenth law), and against partiality and bribes for arbitrators (in the eighteenth law).[88] In other words, once negative equality is admitted as the ultimate standard of human equality, the further content of human equality becomes vague, unless its specification is given in negative terms. In the present context, equality is stated against pride (that is, against too much pride, as may be inferred from the eighth law against contumely)[89] and against the acception of person (that is, against partiality, as the seventeenth and eighteenth laws will further make clear).[90] The reference to death is not irrelevant to these phrasings for, as Hobbes explains, revenge or controversies will otherwise be determined by war. Nor is total surrender to the Leviathan indifferent in the matter, for its basic equality—profits and disprofits arising from the government are the same for the ruler and the subjects[91]—implies that "as in the presence of the master, the servants are equal, and without any honour at all, so are the subjects in the presence of the sovereign."[92]

A more complex and yet similar approach is taken in Hobbes's five laws of nature dealing with the question of property. These include the twelfth law of nature ("equal use of things common"), itself predetermined by free gift (the fourth law, on gratitude), and accommodation (the fifth law, against holding the superfluous when others need the necessary) and further specified by lot (the thirteenth law), then by primogeniture and first seizing (the fourteenth law)—that is, by a series of laws predicated on economic inequalities. The whole discussion is a clear deduction that, in matters related to property, one should reject the Aristotelian distinction between commutative and distributive justice, as the latter is not a right.[93]

Indeed, according to Hobbes, once the third law (that men perform their covenants made) is recognized as the fountain of justice, the classic Aristotelian distinction must be rephrased, considering the idea that the worth of a man is his price.[89] Justice *commutative* then becomes the justice of the contractors and, if it includes the inequality of value of the things contracted for (or arithmetical proportion), it is in the following new sense that may be taken as the extension under the laws of nature of felicity as power. Hobbes explains, "The value of all things contracted for is measured by the appetite of the contractors: and therefore the just value, is that which they be contented to give." On the other hand, justice *distributive* here becomes the justice of an "arbitrator" and, if it includes "the distribution of equal benefit, to men of equal merit" (or "geometrical proportion"), it is in the following new sense which may be taken as the extension, under the laws of nature, of the dilemma of obligation as between equals. Hobbes explains that besides that which is by covenant, "merit is not due by justice but is rewarded by grace only."[95]

What is revealing here is that, in Hobbes's objections to the Aristotelian connection between equality and justice, the general pattern of argumentation from the passions determined by inequalities remains intact. This is specifically the case for the impossibility of equality of worth and equal sharing which, in the latter case, is further spelled out in five related laws. This is also the case of the "equal use of things in common," stated in the twelfth law, in which alternate possession, primogeniture, and first seizing are given as alternatives to the failure of equal use. In other words, what is operative is the impossibility of sharing things, which was already stated in the earlier steps of Hobbes's deduction.

Once put in this context, the phrasing of the twelfth law is revealing. It stipulates that "such things *as* cannot be divided, be enjoyed in common, *if* it can be; and *if* the quantity permit, *without* stint; *otherwise proportionably* to the number of them that have a right."[96] This hypothetico-deductive phrasing does not imply that equal sharing is a right. What it implies is that, given the logical impossibility of two individuals having the same thing if they cannot enjoy it in common (or what we have seen to be Hobbes's rendering of the right of all to all), the laws of nature must leave to grace, charity, alternate possession, lot, primogeniture, and first seizing this civil step beyond negative equality. Equal sharing here evokes the type of contingency stated in *De Cive*, that men come together in a positive manner "by Accident."[97] To share, even accidentally, is then related to the request to do it "without stint, a point which evokes Hobbes's former discussion of liberality against envy and of parsimony (a form of miserableness).[98] To enjoy "proportionably to the number of them that have right" evokes the "proportionals" defined in *De Cive* as "the same inequality in the number of them to whom it is distributed."[99] Hence, Hobbes's predetermination of "equal use of things common" on free gift and charity in laws four and five, and his further transference of equal use of things common to alternate possession (lot, primogeniture, and first seizing) in laws thirteen and fourteen.[100] Those laws are given as the alternative to the expected failure of equal sharings, leaving intact the logic of passions determined by inequality.

In Hobbes's entire deduction from the state of nature to the civil state, therefore, it is not just the case that, under the name of equality, what is generalized throughout is the system of passions determined by inequalities, because of their nullification in the face of death as the foremost equalizer. Nor is it only the case that by means of this negative equality taken as the standard of natural equality, equality and inequality become interchangeable. It is also the case that, beyond natural equality as the foil by which to determine the covenant, any further step toward equality must remain negative—unless one is willing to confront once again the dread of natural equality.

At this point, strikingly enough, the search for more equality than what the laws of nature negatively allow is bound to meet egoism, as Hobbes's penultimate "easy sum" explains. Beyond his "subtle deduction," he makes clear, the basic rule by which to examine all laws of nature is the negative duty: *Do not that to another, which thou wouldest not have done to thyself.* [101] His negative formulation of the foremost moral rule is not advanced as a check on inequalities. Rather, it is proposed as a check on egoism. Hobbes explains that one "has no more to do in learning the laws of nature, but when weighing the actions of other men with his own, they seem too heavy, to put them into the other part of the balance, and his own into their place, that his own passions, and self-love, may add nothing to the weight." Otherwise, one will come back to the state of war and mere nature—that is, to "private" appetites as the measure of good and evil.[102]

The ultimate interchangeability between equality and inequality is accomplished here by having equality, beyond negative equality, closed to the egoist's undifferentiated desire for more. In this search, negative equality gets its proper status as an assumption, as the underlying message behind equality as egoism, including the fact that now "all men are equal in their mutual disavowal of equality."[103] Thanks to death as the foremost equalizer, this message became so plausible that nobody bothered to check whether it was equality or inequality which Hobbes had universalized. The interchangeability between equality and inequality here finds its ultimate logic. It was necessary to show that beyond negative equality, one necessarily confronts egoism anew—that is, positive equality as a dread.

MACPHERSON'S LEGACY

C. B. Macpherson concluded *The Political Theory of Possessive Individualism* by citing equality, and especially this new Hobbesian "equality of insecurity" as the main difficulty awaiting us today. If the present analysis is correct, there is more to be said about equality within the liberal-democratic tradition than what Macpherson suggested. The relationships between equality and possessive individualism are not exhausted by the reduction of liberty to property in liberal-democratic theories. Nor are the relationships exhausted by the fact that, from Hobbes to Locke, all moral values were converted into market value with the universal (but not equal) subordination of all to the market. Possessive individualism did inform the liberal-democratic tradition even more fully than Macpherson showed, because there were specific assumptions about equality, distinct from the generalization of the property model, that contributed to the rejection of equality as an ideal.

I have focused here on one reason for this rebuttal, the idea that equality stands for egoism. However palatable Hobbes's description of men as equal egoists could have been as a mirror of possessive individualism, his argument was made plausible because negative equality was a commonly shared assumption. The reason why Hobbes could plausibly argue from the natural right of all to all (total equality or equality as egoism) to a total surrender to the Leviathan was that negative equality was taken both as a fact and as the paradigm for thinking about human relations with regard to equality. In Hobbes, we find a consistent but negative approach to equality stultifying egalitarianism by making equality and inequality interchangeable terms.

What the study suggests, therefore, is that in its possessive-individualist opposition of liberty to equality, the liberal tradition was not so much at variance with its professed ideal of equality as consistent with its negative assumptions about it. Beyond inconsistencies as a clue to shared assumptions, there is a peculiar form of consistency that also points to the role of presuppositions in moral and political theories. This includes assumptions that are obliquely stated and the consistency of which is difficult to ascertain because they are stated as negations.

Such is the case of negative equality which, taken as a fact about human nature and as an ultimate model for human relations, proceeds from the assertion of the human fatal destination to the blurring of the distinction between equality and inequality in the human condition. By negating the importance of this distinction, negative equality can thus make equality and inequality interchangeable. It can also dismiss the search for more equality as a mere variant of egoism. It can, in fact, deny that the moral issues of distributive justice could be at stake when attempting to transcend the actual relations of a possessive market society. The liberal understanding of equality is shaped by social assumptions that limit and distort equality so that this concept, like the liberal concept of liberty, stands in need of "repair."

NOTES

1. Evidence for this may be found in my *La thématique contemporaine de l'égalité. Répertoire, résumés, typologie* (Montreal: Presses de l'Université de Montréal, 1984), and in my study "Problèmes contemporains de l'égalité: Le motif de l'envie," *Cahiers du Départment de Philosophie,* no. 9102 (Université de Montréal, 1991), forthcoming in C. Porset, ed., *L'égalité,* Actes du colloque de Mulhouse. Ayn Rand, "The Age of Envy," *Objectivist* (formerly *The Objectivist Newsletter*) 10, no. 7 (July-August 1971). See also Ayn Rand, *The Virtue of Selfishness* (New York: New American Library, 1964). For a discussion of Rand, see in particular R. Nozick, "On the Randian Argument," *The Personalist* 52 (1971): 282-304; D. U. Douglas and R. Douglas, "Nozick on the Randian Argument," *Personalist* 59 (1978): 184-205; and P. Blair, "The Randian Argument Reconsidered: A Reply to Charles King," *Reason Papers* 10 (1985): 91-100.

2. C. B. Macpherson, *The Political Theory of Possessive Individualism. Hobbes to Locke* (Oxford: Oxford University Press, 1962). For Macpherson on Hobbes, see chapter 2 (on Hobbes) and chapter 7 (conclusion). For Macpherson's reading of Hobbes on equality, see in particular pp. 25, 74-78, 83-86, 88-90, 93, and 106.

3. On Hobbes and inequality, see the entry "Hobbes" in my *La thématique contemporaine de l'égalité.* For recent discussion, see also Gegg Franzwa, "The Paradox of Equality in the Worlds of Hobbes and Locke," *Southwestern Philosophical Review* 5 (1989): 33-37; Gayne Nerney, "The Hobbesian Argument for Human Equality," *Southern Journal of Philosophy* 24 (1986): 561-76; Larry S. Temkin, "Inequality," *Philosophy and Public Affairs* 15 (1986): 99-121; Timothy Sullivan, "The Negative Dialectic of Equality and Freedom," *Dialogos* 15 (1980): 83-95; Richard Schottky, "Epistémologie et philosophie politique chez Hobbes, Locke et Rousseau," *Archives de philosophie* 31 (1968): 657-63; Gary B. Herbert, *Thomas Hobbes: The Unity of Scientific and Moral Wisdom* (Vancouver, B.C.: University of British Columbia Press, 1989); Franck Tinland, "Hobbes, Spinoza, Rousseau et la formation de l'idée de démocratie comme mesure de la légitimité du pouvoir politique," *Revue philosophique de la France et de l'étranger* 175 (1985): 195-222; Jan H. Blits, "Hobbesian Fear," *Political Theory* 17 (1989): 417-31; Howard C. Cell and James I. MacAdam, eds., *Rousseau's Response to Hobbes* (New York: Lang, 1988); Maurizio Viroli, *Jean-Jacques Rousseau and the Well-Ordered Society* (Cambridge: Cambridge University Press, 1988); and Charles Yves Zarka, *La décision métaphysique de Hobbes* (Paris: Vrin, 1987).

4. See Macpherson, *Possessive Individualism,* 26-28. The "two-stage logical abstraction" refers to the state of nature in which "man's natural proclivities are first disentangled from their civil setting and then carried to their logical conclusion in the state of war." This makes room for the "transition from neutral power to power over men" (that is, from chapter 10 to 11 and then 13 of the *Leviathan*), where Macpherson finds the greatest inconsistency in Hobbes's system—namely, the view that although only some men are said to desire ever

more power (p. 41), all men in society will be concluded to have an innate striving for ever more power over others (pp. 34-35, 45-47). Hobbes was then adding a social assumption to his physiological postulates (34-35, 45-47), namely, the equal subordination of all to the market (p. 85).

5. All quotes are from book 1 of the *Leviathan, or the Matter, Forme and Power of a Commonwealth, Ecclesiastical and Civil,* edited by Michael Oakeshott (Oxford: Basil Blackwell, 1946). Quotes from *De Cive* will be taken from *De Cive,* the English version, entitled in the first edition *Philosophical rudiments Concerning Governments and Society,* edited by Howard Warrender (Oxford: Clarendon Press, [1983]1987). In the present analysis, the main difference between the *Leviathan* and *De Cive* is that, in the former, natural equality as the right of all to all is clearly articulated as a deduction from the state of war.

6. *Leviathan,* bk. 1, pt. 1, chap. 2, p. 32. As will appear, the "almost" clause stands for the one thing that all men will be said to desire (peace), given their fear of death and thus their aversion for the state of war. Notice the negative formulation of the transition from the individual to all men.

7. *Leviathan,* introduction, 6.

8. Ibid.

9. *Leviathan,* chap. 6, p. 32.

10. Ibid., p. 33.

11. Ibid., p. 39: "And because in deliberation, the appetites and aversions are raised by foresight of the good and evil consequences, and sequels of the action whereof we deliberate; the good or evil effect thereof dependeth on the foresight of a *long chain of consequences of which very seldom any man is able to see to the end.* But for so far as a man seeth, if the good in those consequences be greater than the evil, the whole chain is that which writers call *apparent* or *seeming good.* And contrarily, when the evil exceedeth the good, the whole is *apparent* or *seeming evil*" (emphasis added). Expectation and anticipation are crucial premises for the fear of death to play its role in the final step of the deduction. Consistent with the logic of expectation, the nature of war will not be defined as actual fighting but "the known disposition thereto" (*Leviathan,* chap. 13, pp. 82-83). The same thesis (to fear is not to be affrighted) is in *De Cive,* chap. 1, annotation to pt. 2, p. 45.

12. *Leviathan,* chap. 6, p. 32. The elimination of the object of desire also makes room for the notion of felicity as power, as I will show.

13. *Leviathan,* introduction, p. 6. This complexity includes the fact that some passions are born with men, that some proceed from experience, that passions are in continual mutation, that "simple" passions have diversified names, from opinion men have of the likelihood of attaining what they desire, from the object loved or hated, from the alteration of succession itself, and so on. (See *Leviathan,* chap. 6, pp. 32, 34.)

14. The explicit rejection occurs in chap. 11, p. 63.

15. This borrows from Michael Oakeshott: "There can be no final end, no

summum bonum for man's active powers. There is, however, a *summum malum*, and it is death; its opposite, being alive, is only a primary good." See his introduction to the *Leviathan*, p. 31.

16. This deduction belongs specifically to the field of ethics, to the extent that *science* (knowledge of consequences) which is also called *philosophy*, has a subcategory (under the heading of consequences from the qualities of *men in science*) dealing with "Consequences from the *passions* of men." See *Leviathan*, chap. 9, p. 55.

17. *Leviathan*, chap. 6, p. 34. Emphasis added. Magnanimity in the use of riches is *liberality*, pusillanimity in the same is *wretchedness, miserableness*, or *parsimony*, as it is liked or disliked (p. 35). It may be noticed that these two definitions capture the main features now ascribed to envy, but on Hobbes's notion of envy, more below.

18. Ibid., p. 36. See also *Leviathan*, chap. 8, p. 46: "The passion whose violence or continuance make madness is either great *vainglory* which is commonly called *pride* and *self-conceit* or great *dejection* of mind."

19. *Leviathan*, chap. 6, pp. 36-37. "*Grief*, for the discovery of some defect is SHAME" and "the *contempt* of good reputation is called IMPUDENCE." In chapter 8, Hobbes will show how dejection inclines to causeless fear, then to melancholy, then to madness (see *Leviathan*, chap. 8, p. 47).

20. *Leviathan*, chap. 6, p. 35.

21. This paves the way to the universalization of diffidence in the final step of the deduction, when only the aversive relation between two persons will be discussed—that is, only envy.

22. This was the point of Hobbes's argument in *De Cive*—which is not reproduced in the *Leviathan*—that men come together and delight in each other's company *by accident*. See *De Cive*, chap. 1, pt. 2, p. 42. Notice the negative phrasing of the alternative: men's meeting by "mutual poverty and glory" (p. 43).

23. The distinction between jealousy and envy is more systematic in the *Leviathan*. In *De Cive*, the impossibility of the generalization of love was stated thus: "If by nature one Man should Love another [that is] as Man, there could no reason be return'd why every Man should not equally Love every Man, as being equally Man, or why he should rather frequent those whose Society affords him Honour or Profit" (see *De Cive*, chap. 1, pt. 2, p. 42). There being no consent in the object of desire, all (individual) men cannot love all (individual) men. Hence, in the *Leviathan*, the restriction of love to two persons.

24. This is interesting given the tendency to use *jealousy* and *envy* as synonymous terms in the general argument against equality sketched in the first part of this paper. This is a powerful instantiation of Macpherson's thesis that possession of things (rather than, say, self-ownership) pervades the liberal tradition. For a counterexample, however, see my study on Thomas Paine, "Egalité et appropriation," in A. Burgio, dir., *Egalité/Inégalité* (Bologne: Quottro Venti, 1991), 117-38.

25. *Leviathan*, chap. 6, p. 37. Notice the negative formulation of indifference: "those things which we neither desire, nor hate, we are said to *contemn*; CONTEMPT being nothing else but an immobility or contumacy of the heart in resisting the action of certain things" (ibid., 32)—paving the way to the generalization to all human beings of the passions determined by inequalities.

26. The dual relation becomes central in the final step of the argument where "natural equality" is restricted to the clause "if *two men* desire the same thing" (*Leviathan*, chap. 13, p. 81), whereas in *De Cive*, the "strongest/Sword" situation was when "many men at the same time have an Appetite to the same thing which yet very often they can neither enjoy in common, nor yet divide it" (see *De Cive*, chap. 1, pt. 6, p. 46).

27. An interesting example of interchangeability between equality and inequality, mediated by envy, appeared in *De Cive*, where arguing against some who were discontented with the government because it was under one, Hobbes wrote: "but this exception against *one* is suggested by *envie*, while they see, one man in possession of what all desire: for the same cause they would judge it to be as unreasonable, if a *few* commanded, unless they themselves either were, or hoped to be of the number; for if it be an unreasonable thing that all men do not have an equall Right, surely an Aristocracy must be unreasonable also. But because we have shewed that the state of equality is the state of warre, and that *therefore* inequality was introduc'd by a general consent; this *inequality* whereby he, whom we have voluntarily given more to, enjoyes more, is no longer to be accompted an unreasonable thing" (*De Cive*, chap. 10, pt. 4, p. 132; emphasis added).

28. *Leviathan*, chap. 8, p. 47. "Pride subjecteth a man to anger, the excess whereof is the madness called RAGE and FURY. And thus it comes to pass that excessive desire of revenge, when it becomes habitual, hurteth the organs and becomes rage: that excessive love, with jealousy, becomes also rage: excessive opinion of a man's own self . . . becomes distraction and giddiness: the same, when joined with envy, rage; vehement opinion of the truth of any thing, contradicted by others, rage."

29. Then, the relation *between two individuals* desiring the same thing *cannot* obtain, because *all* (individual) men *obtaining all* (individual) things is a logical impossibility.

30. *Leviathan*, chap. 6, pp. 35-36. Remember that in *De Cive*, laughter was a crucial (experimental) proof of the nonnaturally sociable nature of man. See *De Cive*, chap. 1, pt. 5, p. 46. One reason this is not reasserted in the *Leviathan* is that, whereas *De Cive* presented the "combat of wits" as the "fiercest," the *Leviathan* will present knowledge (or sciences) as "small power" (*Leviathan*, chap. 10, p. 57).

31. Rather parallel to Hobbes's rejection (chap. 6, p. 36) of Aristotle's notion that some men are, by nature, slaves (see *Leviathan*, chap. 19, 100-110), the notion that paternal dominion obtains by generation will be also rejected (see *Leviathan*, chap. 20, pp. 130-31), in both cases by ascribing those inequalities to "consent."

32. "*Grief* for the calamity of another is PITY and ariseth from the imagination that the like calamity may befall himself; and therefore is called also COMPASSION, and in the phase of the present time a FELLOW-FEELING and therefore for calamity arising from great wickedness, the best men have the least pity; and for the same calamity, those hate pity, that think themselves least obnoxious to the same" (*Leviathan*, chap. 6, p. 37). Similarly, "*contempt* or little sense of the calamity of others is … CRUELTY; proceeding from security of their own fortune." "For that any man should take pleasure in other men's great harm, without other end of his own I do not conceive it possible."

33. *Leviathan*, chap. 8, p. 42. Emphasis added.

34. *Leviathan*, chap. 10, p. 56. Emphasis added. See Hobbes's long list—riches, reputation, success, affability, nobility, eloquence, and more are power (chapter 10 of the *Leviathan*, p. 56ff.)—power being generally defined instrumentally as man's "present means to obtain some future apparent good," the corresponding notion being "to honour" (or to value a man at a high rate); hence the corresponding list (to pray for aid, to obey, to give great gifts, to give way, to show sign of love, and others are "to honour").

35. "Luck" reappears as "lot" in the thirteenth law of nature, and then as a remedy to the failing of "equal use of things common" in the twelfth law, an eventuality which the logic of human passions makes highly previsible. (See *Leviathan*, chap. 15, p. 101).

36. *Leviathan*, chap. 6, p. 39.

37. The symmetry between desire and aversion does not imply the symmetry between hope and fear in desire.

38. *Leviathan*, chap. 11, p. 63.

39. Ibid., p. 64.

40. Ibid.

41. Ibid.

42. *Leviathan*, chap. 6, p. 39. Hence, religion—to which the whole of chapter 12 is dedicated—is but a way to "take hold" of men's fear and ignorance (*Leviathan*, chap. 12, p. 78), including fear of death, of poverty, and other calamity (p. 70). The anxiety of time to come is the natural cause of religion, an abduction to (legitimate) power (pp. 77) by "unpleasing priests" (p. 80).

43. *Leviathan*, chap. 11, p. 63.

44. Ibid., p. 64. As will appear, the reference to "ease and sensual pleasure" puts the "vulgar" and the "fiercest" in the same category. "Desire of knowledge" or science was described in chapter 10 as "small power because not eminent; and therefore, not acknowledged in any man; nor are at all, but in a few, and in them, but of a few things" (*Leviathan*, chap. 10, p. 57). Both cases are said to be "power" because they "dispose to obey a common power." To have power and to be disposed to obey a common power becomes undiscernible as required by the (final) surrender to the Leviathan.

45. See Michael Oakeshott, introduction, p. 31. Oakeshott insisted that Hobbes's

notion of felicity has a conditional and a negative feature (introduction, pp. 36-37).

46. The reference to death as a proof of the vanity of life implying devaluation of power, honor, and riches is another variant of negative equality. On this see my "L'égalité à l'aube des lumières: La double norme de Bossuet," forthcoming in H. Méchoulan, ed., *L'etat classique* (Paris: Vrin).

47. *Leviathan*, chap. 11, p. 65.

48. Ibid.

49. Ibid.

50. Significant here is Hobbes's phrasing in *De Cive* that "all free congress ariseth either from ... mutual poverty or from vain glory." On this, see Macpherson, *Possessive Individualism*, 27.

51. Similarly, no rule will later be stated concerning "profits and disprofits arising from government" among subjects, Hobbes's concern being rather "benefit equall to the Ruler and his subjects."

52. See the fourth law of nature (for benefits received of mere grace) and the fifth law (not to retain what is superfluous while to others necessary) in *Leviathan*, chap. 15, p. 99. Hobbes writes, "Ingratitude has to grace the same relation that injustice has to obligation by the covenant. As justice dependeth on antecedent covenant, so does GRATITUDE depend on antecedent grace." Notice the egoist/dissimulation evocation in the justification of this law: no one gives "but with the intention of good to himself," which intention, if frustrated, reconducts to the state of war (*Leviathan*, chap. 5, p. 99).

53. *Leviathan*, chap. 13, p. 81. Remember that it is a logical impossibility that all men desire the same thing, hence the reference here to "two" (individual) men wanting the same.

54. In chapter 8, Hobbes has systematized the inequality of reason, for example, by opposing "good wit" (natural) to "dullness" and "stupidity," the difference being caused "by the difference of men's passions" (see *Leviathan*, chap. 8, p. 43). As for "acquired wit" (by method and instruction), the causes of their differences are again the passions, principally the more or less of desire of power, of riches, of knowledge, and of honor, all which may be reduced to desire of power (see *Leviathan*, chap. 8, p. 46). The only passage of the *Leviathan* close to asserting the equality of reason occurs in chapter 5, p. 28: "To him that can avoid these things [the seven causes of absurdity], it is not easy to fall into any absurdity, unless it be by the length of the account; wherein he may perhaps forget what went before. For all men by nature reason alike, and well, when they have good principles. For who is so stupid, as both to mistake in geometry and also to persist in it when another detects his error to him?" (*Leviathan*, p. 28). Notice the hypothetico-deductive feature of this statement. Prudence is the sort of wit in which Hobbes finds "not so much difference of men as there is in their fancies" (*Leviathan*, chap. 8, p. 45).

55. On each content with his share of reason, see Descartes, *Discours de la*

méthode ("Le bon sens est la chose du monde la mieux partagée: car chacun pense en être si bien pourvu que ceux même qui sont les plus difficiles à contenter en toute autre chose n'ont point coutume d'en désirer plus qu'ils en ont") and Montaigne's *Essais* 2:17 ("On dit communément que le plus juste partage que Nature nous ait de ses grâce, c'est celui du sens, car il n'est aucun qui ne se contente de ce qu'elle lui en a distribué!"). For an analysis of Descartes's approach, see my article, "L'héritage cartésien: L'égalité épistémique," *Philosophiques* 15, no. 1 (1988): 77–94.

56. Notice Hobbes's negative formulation of common reason: "I can imagine no reason, but that which is common to all men, namely the want of curiosity to search natural causes and their placing felicity in the acquisition of gross pleasures of the senses, and the things that most immediately conduce thereto" (see *Leviathan*, chap. 8, p. 50). This is given against the existence of *demoniacs*, or men "possessed with spirits."

57. Although dissimulation can make room for the generalization to all human beings of the extreme degree of passions here determined by inequalities—"the most sober men when they walk alone . . . would be unwilling the vanity and extravagance of their thoughts at that time should be publicly seen . . . " (*Leviathan*, chap. 8, p. 48)—Hobbes is clear that this is not the manner in which his deduction is construed. Both in the *Leviathan* and in *De Cive*, he specifically denies that all men actually share the extreme degree of passions that will be henceforth generalized as "mere nature," even to the temperate (*De Cive*, preface, pp. 32–33) or to those who would be "glad to be contented with modest bonds" (*Leviathan*, chap. 13, p. 81).

58. *Leviathan*, chap. 13, p. 81.

59. This was the point of Hobbes's denial (in *De Cive*) that his egoist hypothesis implied *all* men to be wicked by nature. He explained that "though the wicked were fewer then the righteous, yet because we cannot *distinguish* them, there is a necessity of suspecting, heeding, anticipating, subjugating, self-defensing, ever incident to the most honest, and fairest condition'd" (see *De Cive*, preface, p. 33; emphasis added).

60. For the temperate, see *De Cive*, chap. 1, pt. 4, p. 46.

61. A similar approach is taken in Hobbes's statement on prudence: "In which [prudence] there is not so much difference in men; as there is in their fancies and judgment; because the experience of men equal in age, is not much unequal as to the quantity; but lies in the different occasions; every one having his private designs" (*Leviathan*, chap. 8, p. 45). Prudence is then experience "which equal time, equally bestows on all men in those things they equally apply themselves unto" (chap. 13, p. 80). Notice the negative turn (there is less difference in prudence than in reasoning and fancy) and the conditional form (if all men applied themselves equally to the same things with the same quantity of experience and time—a logical impossibility for men in "continual mutation").

62. Notice that Hobbes here justifies the term *natural equality* as one of the

two causes of mutual fear: "For if we look on men fullgrown, and consider how brittle the frame of our humane body is, (which perishing, all its strength, vigour, and wisdome itselfe perisheth with it) and how easie a matter it is, even for the weakest man to kill the strongest, there is no reason why any man trusting to his own strength should conceive himself made by nature above others: *but they who can do the greatest things (namely kill) can doe equal things.* All men *therefore* among themselves *are* by nature equal; the inequality we now discern hath its spring from the Civill Law" (*De Cive,* chap. 1, pt. 3, p. 45; emphasis added).

63. *De Cive,* chap. 1.

64. My reading here differs from Macpherson's assertions that Hobbes begins with "equal rational individuals" (*Possessive Individualism,* 106), postulating an "equality of ability" and an "equality of expectation," both taken as facts in setting up an "equality of right" (p. 74).

65. This reappears in the twelfth, thirteenth, and fourteenth law of nature (see *Leviathan,* chap. 14, pp. 101-2).

66. "The *value* or WORTH of a man, is as of all other things, his price; that is to say, so much as would be given for the use of his power: and therefore is not absolute; but a thing dependent on the need and judgment of another. . . . And as of other things, so in men, not the seller, but the buyer determines the price. For let a man, as most men do, rate themselves at the highest value they can; yet their true value is no more than it is esteemed by others" (*Leviathan,* chap. 10, p. 57). This will reappear in Hobbes's definition of justice (*Leviathan,* chap. 15, p. 98).

67. In this reading, *negative equality* is thus "the factual equality which men can see as overriding all their factual inequalities" that Hobbes needed for his view on equality to be consistent. On this, see Macpherson, *Possessive Individualism,* 83.

68. *Leviathan,* chap. 14, p. 85.

69. The *Leviathan* made natural equality a clear *deduction* from the state of war, whereas in *De Cive* civil equality and war were either *intertwined* or *separate.* In the preface it says the "state of men without civill society [which state we may properly call the state of nature] is nothing else but a meere warre of all against all; and in that warre all men have equall right unto all things." In chapter 1, "the rights which all men have to all things, that is the rights of Warre," relate to the two causes of "mutuall fear": the natural equality of men and their mutual will of hurting, causes not "equally to be condemned." See *De Cive,* preface, p. 34, and chapter 1, pt. 3, pp. 45-46.

70. *Leviathan,* chap. 13, p. 80. The sense in which this deduction is predicated on inequality was clearer in *De Cive* when Hobbes explained, "To have all, and do all is lawfull for all" is to say that "Profit is the measure of *Right*" (*De Cive,* chap. 1, annotation to pt. 10, p. 48).

71. *Leviathan,* chap. 14, p. 85. Emphasis added.

72. This was the point of Macpherson's concluding remark on the paradox of Hobbes's individualism "which starts with equal rational individuals and

demonstrates that they must submit themselves wholly to a power outside themselves," this power from outside being at variance with the physiological model of self-moving mechanisms. On this, see Macpherson, *Possessive Individualism*, 77-78 and 106. This was also the point of Macpherson's argument that in Hobbes the sovereign power must override traditional property rights. See C. B. Macpherson, "Hobbes's Political Economy," *Philosophical Forum* 14 (1983): 211-34.

73. *Leviathan*, chap. 6, pp. 32-33.

74. *Leviathan*, chap. 10, p. 56.

75. *Leviathan*, chap. 13, p. 81.

76. This was the point of Rousseau's criticism in his *Discours sur l'origine et les fondements de l'inégalité parmi les hommes* (1754): "C'est ici le dernier terme de l'inégalité et le point extrême qui ferme le Cercle et touche au point d'où nous sommes partis: C'est ici que tous les particuliers redeviennent égaux parce qu'ils ne sont rien" (see J.-J. Rousseau, *Oeuvres complètes*, bk. 3 (Paris: Gallimard, La Pléiade), 191. Notice, however, Rousseau's own formulation of the fundamental clause of social contract as "l'aliénation totale de chaque associée avec tous ses droits à toute la communauté" (*Le Contrat social*, 360).

77. To object to this is to reason from envy. "While they see, one man in possession of what all desire: for the same cause they would judge it to be as unreasonable, if a *few* commanded, unless they themselves either were, or hoped to be of the number" (*De Cive*, chap. 10, pt. 4, p. 132; emphasis added).

78. *De Cive*, chap. 1, pt. 11, p. 49. The "almost" clause stood for the thesis that, in the state of nature, right was decided by the "strongest" and the "sword" (*De Cive*, chap. 1, pt. 6, p. 46) or that profit was the measure of right (*De Cive*, chap. 1, pt. 10, p. 48).

79. As stated in *De Cive*, chap. 1, pt. 11, p. 49: " ... although any man might say of every thing, *This is mine*, yet could he not enjoy it, by reason of his Neighbour, who having equall *Right*, and equall power, would pretend the same thing for his."

80. The right of all to all being a logical impossibility, the clause according to which "a man be willing when others are so too" is a negative transposition of the logical necessity of surrender to the Leviathan.

81. *Leviathan*, chap. 14, p. 85; emphasis added. Notice the negative phrasing of liberty as "against" other men.

82. *Leviathan*, chap. 15, p. 93.

83. See laws numbered four, five, eleven, seventeen, eighteen, and, to a lesser degree, six (dread of hostility) and eight (dread of hatred or contempt).

84. *Leviathan*, chap. 15, p. 101.

85. "If nature therefore have made men equal, that equality is to be acknowledged: or if nature have made men unequal; yet because men that think themselves equal, will not enter into condition of peace, but upon equal terms, such equality must be admitted" (*Leviathan*, chap. 5, pp. 100-101). As the context indicates, the clause "yet because men that think themselves equal" refers to the

illusory victory of the wise or the strong concerning command in the civil government. The negative assumption behind this interchangeability is clearer in *De Cive*. Hobbes wrote: "Whether therefore men be equall by nature, the equality is to be acknowledged, or whether unequall, because they are like to contest for dominion, its necessary *for the obtaining of Peace, that they be esteemed as equall*" (*De Cive*, chap. 3, pt. 13, p. 68).

86. But not against "honour" (see the fourth law on gratitude). *Leviathan*, chap. 15, pp. 99-103.

87. Clearly related here to the state of war. See ibid., p. 101. This appears as Hobbes's amendment to Aristotelian equity as a moral norm by which to judge the generality of the laws, restricting it to the juridical rule against the acception of persons.

88. Ibid., pp. 99-103.

89. The eighth law ("no man by deed, word, countenance, or gesture, declared hatred or contempt of another") complements the seventh law about revenge ("the retribution of evil for evil must look at the good to follow from revenge rather than at the greatness of evil past") as the rule of choice between hazard (fight) and revenge. Hobbes explained that because all signs of contumely provoke fight, "insomuch as most men choose rather to hazard their life than not to revenge," no man should declare them. See ibid., p. 100.

90. Ibid., p. 102. The thirteenth law (lot), as an alternative to the failure of "equal use of things common" is a further derivation of equity against the acception of persons. Besides lot, "other means of equal distribution cannot be imagined" (see ibid., p. 101).

91. *De Cive*, chap. 10, pt. 4, p. 132.

92. *Leviathan*, chap. 18, pp. 119-20. Hobbes argues here against the view that sovereign kings, *singulis majores/universis minores*, bear less power than their subjects all together. The next sentence is a good example of interchangeability: "And though they shine some more, some less, when they are out of his sight; yet in his presence they shine no more than the stars in the presence of the sun." A similar approach occurs in Hobbes's section on "Equal taxes," to be referred not to the equality of riches but to the equality of debt which everyone owes to the commonwealth for his defense. This negative equality (or being in debt) proceeds from the fact that "the benefit that every one receiveth thereby is *the enjoyment of life*, which is equally dear to poor and rich." See *Leviathan*, bk. 2, chap. 30, p. 226; emphasis added.

93. *Leviathan*, chap. 15, p. 98. Emphasis added. The distinction pertains to the "justice of actions," not to be confused with the "justice of men" or the "justice of manners." See *Leviathan*, chap. 15, pp. 97-98. Hobbes was objecting then to the Aristotelian connection between equality and justice, as the corresponding passage in *De Cive* makes clear (see *De Cive*, chap. 3, pt. 6, pp. 64-65).

94. *Leviathan*, chap. 10, p. 57.

95. *Leviathan*, chap. 15, p. 99. As Macpherson insisted on Hobbes's view of

commutative and distributive justice: "Hobbes's scorn for these concepts is unconcealed" (*Possessive Individualism*, p. 63).

96. *Leviathan,* chap. 15, pp. 101-2.

97. *De Cive,* chap. 1, pt. 2, p. 42. The argument against universal love ("if by nature one man should love another there could be no reason why every man should not equally love every man") could be restated against equal sharing: if by nature one man should help another, there could be no reason every man should not equally help every man.

98. *Leviathan,* chap. 10, p. 56. "Riches without liberality is not power because in this case they defend not but expose men to envy, as a prey." See also chap. 6, p. 35: "Miserableness: pusillanimity in the use of riches, wretchedness, miserableness, or parsimony, as it is liked or disliked."

99. *De Cive,* chap. 3, pt. 14, pp. 68-69. See also chap. 3, pt. 6, p. 65.

100. *Leviathan,* chap. 15, pp. 100-101. Later in the *Leviathan* Hobbes will refer charity—toward those who, by accident inevitable, are unable to maintain themselves by their labor—to the "laws of commonwealth," that is, objecting to the "hasard of such uncertain [private] charity" on the grounds that "uncharitableness" must not characterize the sovereign. On this, see *Leviathan,* bk. 2, chap. 30, p. 227.

101. *Leviathan,* chap. 15, p. 103. Hobbes explains his "easy sum" by the fact that men are, for the most part, too busy in getting food, and for the rest, too negligent to take notice of his deduction.

102. *Leviathan,* chap. 16, p. 104.

103. The quote is from Charles Yves Zarka, *La décision métaphysique de Hobbes* (Paris: Vrin, 1987), 305.

Chapter 4
The Individualist/Holist Debate and
Bentham's Claim to Sociological
and Psychological Realism

Nancy L. Rosenblum

No piece of the conceptual apparatus of political theory gets greater use than the dichotomy of individualism and holism. It is put to work across the board, from studies in methodology and metaethics to concrete studies of rights and citizenship, so that the basic terms of this dichotomy are familiar.

Individualism is associated with what C. B. Macpherson, in one influential formulation, called "the Hobbes-to-Bentham concept of man," and of course with Kantian autonomy. The unifying idea here is that the voice of ethics, indeed of norms and values in general, speaks with authority directly to individual consciousness, and that individuals are the explanatory starting point for understanding social actions and structures. Ordinarily, the political corollary of ontological individualism is either a legalistic society of persons bearing rights or, in hostile terms, a marketplace of "Benthamite utility maximizers unrelated to others except as potential buyers and sellers of commodities."[1]

In holism, by contrast, authoritative values arise from communal purposes with which individual actions and ends are identified. Holism has Idealist, Romantic, and Marxist versions, as well as traditionalist and conventionalist ones. Typically, in holist politics, community good takes priority over personal freedom. Following Hegel, holists often cast individualism in historical terms as a falling off from some original or possible unity: "The people is not the organic body of a common and rich life" but is reduced to "an atomistic, life-impoverished multitude."[2]

Charles Taylor has cautioned against overly simplistic versions of this conceptual dichotomy. Individualism/holism has both an ontological and a political face, and ontological issues and advocacy issues are separable. While ontology may be part of the essential background of the political view a person advocates, taking a position on one does not commit that person to some corresponding position on the other. To illustrate, Taylor points to atomist individualists such as Nozick and holist collectivists such as Marx, but also to atomists who advocate a communitarian politics and holists who are good liberals—Humboldt, for example.[3] One interpretation of Bentham's utilitarianism—which sees in it both a radical individualist ontology and a teleological moral theory concerned not with persons but with a state of affairs that aims at maximizing a condition of social welfare—should make the usefulness of the warning clear. Nowhere in *political* theory is the overlap between individualists and holists more dramatic and unexpected, I think, than in the case of Bentham and Hegel. For both philosophers, the defining institution of the modern state is a public culture of legalism. Both also emphasize citizenship marked by legal standing over participation, administration by a universal class over democracy, and rights in context over natural rights. Macpherson, as I will show, falls into the common error and writes as if liberal politics in support of capitalist property flows automatically from individualist assumptions.[4]

Because ontology does not determine politics, there is an overlap in the political preferences of individualists and holists. Because individualist ontology is compatible with a variety of theories of motivation and of self-development, there is an overlap with holists along any scale that has abstract and atomistic at one end, and contextualist, socially constituted, and intimately connected at the other. In this essay, I focus on the holist claim that individualists are committed to an unrealistic perception of the separateness and independence of the individuals.[5] On this view, individualism conceives of persons as rigidly bounded and impermeable to one another—a charge made vivid in the phrase *atomistic individual-*

ism. In detaching desires and purposes from constitutive social contexts, the charge continues, individualists are unable to account for a range of moral and political experiences that have connection or identification with others at their heart. As a result, individualism is incapable of comprehending the attachments and internalized social norms that make even the most individualist of political societies—procedural liberalism—viable, and it is left to holists to explain that contractual relations rest on underlying trust and shared values, national defense on patriotic identification, and so on.

I pursue the business of complication by using Bentham's individualism to assess competing claims to sociological and psychological realism. Bentham embodies individualism's arid utilitarian extreme. Macpherson, for one, took Bentham as a model of the family of errors that seemed to him to follow necessarily from individualist ontology. By showing that even Bentham's work challenges the individualism/holism dichotomy, I hope to indicate how much in the way of useful psychology and social history is lost by this simplification.

In attributing atomistic assumptions to individualism, holists tend to lump together a set of claims that are distinct and independent of one another, and, in assessing Bentham's individualism, I identify and take them up in turn. I start by considering one standard holist charge: because Bentham's individualism is based on a "reductivist" sensationalist psychology, it gives priority to impulses that are arbitrary and contingent (and therefore without essential moral or motivational significance), and entails a view of persons as isolated by their separate sensational experiences. I go on to show that Bentham was committed to an account of the social origin of desires, and that, with his focus on "sinister interests" and "security of expectations," he was not only a contextualist, but conceived of identity as a social construction. I also suggest that Bentham's notion of "expectation" is a more fruitful approach to socially constructed aspects of the self than those employed by contemporary theorists who dismiss his psychology out of hand. In this connection, I show that expectations about property were not at the heart of Bentham's social psychology, and why Macpherson's reading of the relation between Bentham's ontology and politics is misleading and obscures what is genuinely characteristic in his discussions of labor, reward, and inequality. Finally, I analyze the most important and defensible aspect of the individualist/holist dichotomy: the contrast between calculating and expressive selves.

NANCY L. ROSENBLUM

REDUCTIVIST PSYCHOLOGY, FALSE
UNIVERSALISM AND RADICAL SEPARATISM

The familiar first sentence of *An Introduction to the Principles of Morals and Legislation* announces a manifestly universalist, sensationalist psychology. The classic criticism of this position and others like it is Hegel's: "Empiricism lacks . . . all criteria for drawing the boundary between the accidental and the necessary; i.e., for determining what in the chaos of the state of nature or in the abstraction of man must remain and what must be discarded."[6] Does Bentham's sensationalist psychology give central place to motives that are arbitrary and contingent, so that utilitarianism is the incoherent adjustment of society to satisfy random desires? The "scientific" claim that Bentham made for his psychology has less to do with weighing and comparing pleasures than with the fact—amenable, he thought, to the test of personal experience—that avoiding pain is a more powerful imperative than increasing pleasure. Bentham may have been notoriously indifferent between pleasures but not between pleasure and pain, meaning physical pain and the awful emotional and physiological suffering of fear. His psychology is not the system of a dry calculator, but of a sensibility horrified by pain, for whom the distinction between essential and inessential feelings was clear (I, 34).

Bentham's loathing focused on the suffering of the weak at the hands of the powerful. So long as some men have power, the rest are vulnerable. Political officials especially inflict suffering at will, and often unexpectedly, in order to achieve advantages for themselves. No one has catalogued all his references to the vulnerable, but their range has something to satisfy both eighteenth- and twentieth-century sensibilities. Women subject to domestic tyranny are on his list, as are persecuted homosexuals, privates in the army, employees, and "potential legatees," to name a few. But Bentham's work is first of all about the victims of deliberate political cruelty. Recall that the calculating apparatus appears in the *Introduction* in a discussion of punishment. The subject was officially inflicted pain, legal torture, and Beccaria was its inspiration. The whole point of introducing categories like intensity, duration, propinquity, and so on, was to help legislators think about keeping punishment to a humane minimum. Bentham was certain that the worst crimes are regularly perpetrated by those with the most power. They act from antipathy and incline to severity.[7] Bentham goes back and forth, sometimes using slavery as the paradigm of defenselessness against arbitrariness, and sometimes using the willful torment of animals to describe the condition of slaves. The point is that where power is unlimited, it will be difficult to check even flagrant abuses, and that vulnerability is bound to entail cruelty, which is always appalling. "The blackness of the skin is no reason why a human being should be abandoned without redress to the caprice of a tormentor. It may come one day to be recognized, that the number of the legs, the villosity of the skin, or the termination of the os sacrum are reasons equally insufficient for abandoning a sensitive being to the same fate." His *Constitutional Code* was to have had a section on cruelty to animals.[8]

Bentham was determinedly reductivist in giving priority to minimizing pain over higher purposes, which is why he abhorred moral fanaticism. He had no patience with those willing to inflict suffering for the sake of some ideal, however altruistic or inspired. Well-meaning sympathies and noble moral antipathies are perfectly capable of producing errant violence, and Bentham reserved his most intense revulsion for the human type who sees the present as "but a point" and is prepared to sacrifice existing generations "for the sake of the species" (I, 360). When causes are not evaluated with a view to their consequences in actual suffering, they are simply excuses for cruelty.

For Bentham, then, pain was an ineliminable part of social life, and political theory begins with mistrust of authority. Democracy was one element (and not the most important) in the armory of protection along with publicity and the revelation of abuses of authority, official crimes. But mainly he looked to codes of law. Bentham's obsessive codification was aimed at reining in extravagant and often brutal governments. Of course, because pain is "that instrument to which the law itself owes all its powers," it was perfectly clear that some degree of pain is necessary and inevitable." However, it should be kept to a minimum, employed only to prevent worse evil, and leveled in ways that are regular and expected. This is what his utilitarianism is all about. Bentham's psychology undermines the view of utilitarianism as a teleological theory aimed at maximizing aggregate happiness regardless of its effect on individuals. Instead, it supports a view of utilitarianism as a moral theory in which the equality of persons—certainly with respect to their interest in avoiding physical pain and fear—operates as both an ontological assumption and a limitation on justifiable social choices.

Arguably, Bentham's reductivist preoccupation with pain is bedrock psychological realism, and the political cautions drawn from it are the very definition of mature political realism, and should be apparent to anyone with a sense of history and of common human suffering. In "Two Concepts of Liberty," Isaiah Berlin repeated more than once Bentham's dictum that every law with its attendant sanction is an infraction of liberty and causes some person pain. He also cited Bentham when he wanted to express horror at those who torment the living under the pretense of promoting the happiness of the unborn.[10] Even for liberal theorists who judge minimizing pain and fear an inadequate basis for a theory of government dedicated to the most extensive personal liberty, it is an irreducible starting point.[11]

Holists would not be satisfied with evidence that Bentham's psychology discriminates between arbitrary and essential desires, however. The problem of atomism remains regardless of what motivations are sovereign, and, on the holist view, Bentham's individualism posits the irreparable separateness of persons. What can the separateness of persons mean? The idea is not used as it is in rights theory, in which separateness of persons is shorthand for a moral, not an ontological, proposition about the inviolability of individual rights or interests. Instead, it signifies the absence of (or inability to explain) significant connections to others. Because attachment and identification are essential aspects of social and moral experience, atomistic individualism is either impossible or pathological. Clearly, Bentham thinks that pain and pleasure, including the admitted pleasures of community, are experienced by the self alone and motivate men and women personally and individually. However, unless they subscribe to some notion of group mind, holists rarely challenge this thought. The question is whether Bentham casts individuals as unrealistically isolated, trapped in their separate sensational experiences, with no basis for mutual insight or moral connection.

In the *Introduction,* Bentham's justification of the principle of utility proceeds by a process of elimination. The principles of *aestheticism* and *asceticism* are incapable of providing a criterion for agreement when moral consensus does not already exist. If the object is justifying moral sentiments to the community—still more so if the object is a public rationale for legislation—this failure is disqualifying (I, 9n).[12] Utility can serve as a public criterion and universalist ethic because it puts every question upon "an issue of fact" about the reasonably predictable consequences of a law or action for actual suffering (II, 495). Plainly, casting utilitarianism in general terms is tenable because the sovereignty of pain is supposed to be a real, felt experience. Everyone would evade pain and fear at the hands of men in power if only they could. They would say so if given the opportunity, and would recognize misery in others if only they looked. Bentham could assume this much as universal: "What all men are disposed to suffer by, all men are disposed to hate" (I, 10). He could adopt the point of view of victims and say with assurance that it is certain that the condition of slavery is painful to slaves since "no man who is free wishes to become a slave, and there is no slave who does not wish to become free" (TL, 202; I, 344). And he was confident of sufficient identification with the suffering of others to make the pain of "alarm" a principal consideration for utilitarian legislators. He assumed, in short, mutual understanding and universal assent to the imperative of minimizing the arbitrary infliction of suffering.

The thought that sympathetic identification with pain and fear is possible, and that it is both a source of norms and an impetus to action, was commonplace among Enlightenment thinkers. Its part in utilitarian theory was taken for granted by Bentham's contemporaries, and examined by Elie Halevy in *The Growth of Philosophic Radicalism*. Sympathy was as widely accepted as the idea of the natural identity of interests. Bentham speaks of sympathy often, and he thought that, to a benevolent mind, misery can never be an object of indifference. "The less an injured party is capable of defending himself, the stronger ought to be the natural sentiment of compassion. The law of honour, coming to the support of this instinct of pity, makes it an imperious duty to be tender with the feeble, and to spare those who cannot resist. The first index of a dangerous character is *oppression of the weak*" (TL, 258). Bentham did not rely on either sympathy or the natural harmony of interests when it came to political prescriptions. Instead he looked to institutionalized rewards and punishments to effect an artificial identification of interests. The principle of utility was a more reliable public rationale than consulting one's own feelings, because people's sympathies and antipathies are variable in content and capricious in their reach. Still, there is something perverse (and willfully ahistorical) about the eclipse of sympathy for physical pain and fear as an element of Bentham's psychology.

In the absence of sustained argument by holists, there is no reason to reject the thought that some experiences of pain are universal rather than historically or culturally specific, available to the understanding of anyone who cares to look, as Bentham thought, and an occasion for identification with others. Nor is there reason to think that, because sympathy is potentially universal in content and scope, it is necessarily diffuse in practice, so that it forms a weaker connection—less concrete, less emotionally compelling, or less instructive as a guide to action—than identification with the particular values of a particular group or community, which is often the starting point of holist ontology. At this point, the rigid dichotomy of individualist separateness and holist connection, of arbitrary individual desires and ones deeply rooted in communal values, becomes messy. It disintegrates into a competition over whose insight into essential human goods (or bads) and what sort of identification (with which others?) is more substantial and efficacious.

ABSTRACT INDIVIDUALISM, CONTEXTUALISM, OR A SOCIALLY CONSTITUTED SELF?

According to another family of holist claims, individualist ontology is abstract and atomistic because it refers to pleasures, pains, beliefs, and values as if they were given, or simply "there," detached from social contexts, with neither a psychological nor a political history. Individualism also sees the self as disconnected from its own beliefs and desires, which are neither deep nor gripping. In short, individualism lacks a concept of identity. This piece of the conventional mold in which individualism is cast needs breaking down as well.

Abstract and atomistic are peculiar charges to level against a philosopher who enjoys a secure place in the company of eighteenth-century ideologists, and whose whole subject was the connection between ideas and social order, and how ideas operate as a means of exercising power. The Enlightenment project was to attack what Helvetius first called "interested error" and Bentham called "the elaborately organised, and anxiously cherished and guarded products of sinister interest and artifice" (Fragment, 508). His *Fragment on Government, Book of Fallacies,* and *Official Aptitude Maximized, Expense Minimized* are standard works of this type. They are representative of what is referred to today as "the politics of interpretation" and designed to bring the political conditions of "discourse" (Bentham used the term) to light. The conventional Whig notion of "sinister influence" referred exclusively to bribery and patronage by the crown, which could be remedied by a restored constitutional balance of power. However, Bentham's "sinister interests" goes much further. In the spirit of the continental Enlightenment, he has a broader, less conspiratorial notion of ideology. His subject was how organized social groups secure authority and exercise power by monopolizing knowledge, influencing emotions and beliefs, and ultimately producing a state of habitual dependence on others. Bentham applied this perfectly typical eighteenth-century social analysis to churchmen,[13] aristocracy[14] and "expert cultures"—above all, to the legal profession, whose corner on technical knowledge of the law, exploitation of legal fictions, and systematic practice of obfuscation were lifelong objects of Bentham's outrage and efforts at reform.

This suggests that, even if Macpherson were correct in characterizing Bentham as a possessive individualist and apologist for capitalist inequality, he goes about things indirectly. Bentham's chief concern in the bulk of his writings is uncovering the way in which knowledge and language create and support authority. It would seem to follow that if Bentham's psychology has a characteristic weakness, it is less that he saw happiness purely in terms of material acquisition—for he did not—than that he was naïve about the efficacy of unveiling ideas as disguises for interests. This was a limitation he shared with other Enlightenment thinkers who placed their faith in education, and with contemporary deconstructivists and proponents of "discourse analysis" who have little more to say than these early ideologists about the mechanism by which exposure accomplishes a change of belief. In fact, unlike Helvetius, Bentham did not imagine that a benign social order would follow automatically from liberation from tutelage or that "enlightenment" was the equivalent of a useable standard for concrete reform. He did not imagine that error could be easily overcome, either. As evidence, there is his self-censorship of writings originally intended for his penal code in which he argued against the criminalization of sexual nonconformity. Bentham knew that neither refutations of the standard arguments for outlawing homosexuality nor utilitarian arguments showing that legalization of homosexuality might reduce excess population growth would have much effect in dissolving this powerful prejudice, rein-forced as it was by religious authority.

Bentham was a far less vulgar ideologist than the phrase *sinister interests* suggests. He had a sophisticated view of the relation between interest and belief. For one thing, he was no facile voluntarist. We read in *The Book of Fallacies* that the influence of interest may be a secret even to a man himself (I, 372-73). There is also his wonderfully Freudian observation that "fig-leaves cover our unseemly parts," so that if we were to look into our own minds we would be repelled, and exposure would be cause for mortification (I, 218-19; II, 478). That is why "not infrequently, as between two persons living together in a state of intimacy, either or each may possess a more correct and complete view of the motives by which the mind of the other, than those by which his own mind is governed."[15] Self-deception plays a part in sustaining ideology, too, and Bentham conceded that even the legal fraternity was not entirely cynical. Nor did he think it possible to choose beliefs simply because it is in our interest to do so. We read, again in *Fallacies,* that by themselves rewards and punishments cannot produce belief (I, 65). His massive work on judicial evidence recommends methods for generating and collecting information, but also considers the motivations that people have to resist becoming informed. Bentham was no epistemologist, however. Whereas Helvetius had written about attention and Hartley about the association of ideas, Bentham was not interested in the cognitive processes involved in the formation of beliefs in individuals. Wondering about the origin of something as familiar yet complex as a "habit of obedience," for example, Bentham was happy to wave the problem aside. "The enigma . . . may be satisfactorily solved upon the principle of association, of the nature and force of which a very satisfactory account may be seen in Dr. Priestley's edition of Hartley on Man" (I, 57). This lapse is not unique to Bentham, of course. Holist ontology does not come complete with epistemological accounts of belief formation either, or with cognitive or emotional accounts of how the self, "thick" with shared meanings and values, comes to learn them—still less with a developmental theory of how the self comes to be identified with some group or larger whole.

In short, Bentham's analysis of pleasures and pains, interests and ideas, and purposes and actions is straightforwardly contextualist; they are not only occasioned by social experiences but draw their meaning and value from concrete social contexts. For example, the pleasures associated with honor are bound up with a peculiar social order and set of practices with which individuals are identified, and about which Bentham wrote a great deal. He did not attend to idiosyncratic feelings or assign importance to individual preferences available only to possessors. Instead he assumed (as he had to if psychology were to serve as the material for a rationale for legislation) that it was possible to make public sense of an action in a specific context. Nothing in his psychology precludes the powerful, formative effects of socialization. The improbable alternatives to some notion of socialization are a person ceaselessly buffeted by ephemeral sensations and aroused by present situations, or radical existential self-creation—and Bentham subscribed to neither. Thus, he criticized churchmen as corrupt for exploiting people's religious beliefs, but, at the same time, recognized them as "but the children of the system—bred under the system," so that "had the existing individuals never had existence, under that system others exactly like them, differing in nothing but name, would have occupied their places."[16] To imagine that desires and beliefs were either natural or self-generated is simply a delusion.

By itself, however, a contextualist account of pleasures and pains or beliefs and purposes does not satisfy the distinct but related holist concern that these should run deep and have a powerful hold on individuals. Does Bentham propose a self socially constituted in some stronger sense than contextualism alone suggests—a self genuinely identified with its beliefs and feelings? The best approach to Bentham's thoughts on social attachment and identity is by way of his well-known assertions about the ends of law, where "expectation" emerges as the key to his social psychology and as an important point of convergence with holism.

EXPECTATIONS AND THE
SOCIALLY CONSTRUCTED SELF

We know that in Bentham's theory of legislation fear and insecurity are reasons for government, and the object of utilitarian legislation can be refined from instituting "positive good" to securing expectations. Care of security is the law's entire work, Bentham wrote (I, 307). "The goodness of the laws depends upon their conformity to general expectation" (TL, 148; V, 266; III, 388-89). The principle of nondisappointment is the legislator's chief and all-directing guide.[17] It is, therefore, imperative to distinguish radically contingent or purely personal pleasures and pains from politically relevant expectations. The general thrust of security of expectation as an object of legislation is clear enough. Expectation is the alternative to dumb habit and blind routine on one side, and to everything spontaneous and purely visionary on the other. Securing expectations is the alternative to both rigid custom and revolutionary fanaticism.

Bentham had nothing against conventions per se, but he did oppose traditionalism and any principled rejection of new or changing expectations. The idea was that legislation must take into account more than just existing rights at law and interests protected by a dominant ideology. Bentham's radicalism consists in acknowledging expectations not previously afforded legal recognition. He literally defines property as the established expectation of enjoyment from a thing (I, 19, 308), announcing his distance both from any thought of a natural right of property and from direct utilitarian calculations of the best distribution of rights or goods, unmediated by special concern for existing expectations. This definition of property in terms of expectation requires that property rights reflect shifts in the sorts of things that are generally thought to be appropriable (and those that are not—the paradigm case for him was political office), forms of property relations, ways of transferring and disposing of property, and so on. Indeed, this definition implies that when a formal right of ownership is unaccompanied by actual expectations of enjoyment, it could be violated in the interest of other ends of legislation, including equality. In the *Civil Code,* Bentham proposes what the legislator ought to do about existing distributions:

> There is nothing more different than the state of property in America, in England, in Hungary, and in Russia. Generally, in the first of these countries, the cultivator is a proprietor; in the second, a tenant; in the third, attached to the glebe; in the fourth, a slave. However, the supreme principle of security commands the preservation of all these distributions, though their nature is so different, and though they do not produce the same sum of happiness. (*Civil Code* I, chap. 11)

This passage sets property in the context of security and defends existing distributions. Contrary to Macpherson's reading, it does not single out one form of property over others. Plainly, it does not make a case for capitalism as the universally best arrangement.[18] Bentham's ostensible purpose here is to give priority to existing expectations over effecting a system of natural justice or, more interestingly, a system that maximizes production. But we cannot conclude from this that Bentham always gives security of property priority over ever other good—including, say, subsistence—much less that he commends material expectations over all others. There is nothing to suggest that Bentham shared Hegel's philosophy of property as the institutional embodiment of the right of personality.

Security of expectations stands opposed not only to traditionalism but also to utopian revolutionism with its contempt for established practices. Bentham has himself been charged with utopianism in proposing a rash of codes for adoption by everyone from Catherine the Great to governments in Spain and Portugal and the new democracy in Greece. In sober moments, however, he knew that "the influence of time and place in legislation" is everything—that no place was a "clean paper," that a kind of expectation exists everywhere. Only in the eyes of an "English capitalist" is Mexico a land of "utter darkness" (II, 569). He knew that "the constitution of a state is one thing, the conduct of the government and of the people under the constitution, another" (II, 568). Bentham was not Montesquieu. But utilitarianism is a theory of rights in context, and Bentham's justification of rights is governed by the end of securing existing expectations.

Of interest here is that the priority of security of expectations among the several ends of legislation stemmed from its status in Bentham's ontology. Bentham believed that sensations unite men and women with animals in a single moral field, but the fact that people are not limited to the present time is what distinguishes them from "brutes." "It is by means of this we are enabled to form a general plan of conduct; it is by means of this, that the successive moments which compose the duration of life are not like insulated and independent points, but become parts of a continuous whole. Expectation is a chain which unites our present and our future existence, and passes beyond ourselves to the generations which follow us. The sensibility of the individual is prolonged through all the links of this chain" (I, 308). With expectations, Bentham takes up the themes of contemporary political theorists for whom certain desires and purposes are "constitutive." In fact, expectation may be a more resonant and flexible concept than those employed by political theorists today. Bentham defined expectations as gripping in a way that most desires are not. The satisfactions associated with them are regularly anticipated, and their disappointment is a particularly acute pain and a cause of real disorientation. Expectations are always conscious, of course, and involve self-reflection. They are ingredients of purposes and plans, as passing desires are not. As Bentham conceives it, expectations also entail social consciousness. An expectation is forward-looking, incorporates prediction, and signals recognition that fulfillment depends on the actions and purposes of others personally and on the working of social institutions. Expectations are elements of identity, then, but it is not the case that specific expectations are either fixed or wholly defining. Bentham made these considerations explicit and applied them to politics in practice in his writings on public office, from polemical pieces like *Official Aptitude*

Maximized to the synthetic *Constitutional Code.* These writings amount to an elaborate case study of shifting expectations about the business of government and the nature of public service, and they are important here because they illustrate how, in the course of political development, expectations become elements of an individual's social identity. "Bentham on Bureaucracy" is a favorite subject among scholars of late eighteenth- and nineteenth-century political and intellectual history, but historians typically overlook the framework of social psychology in which he sets his institutional prescriptions and ideas about political development, while philosophers typically ignore the subject altogether.[19] The gist of Bentham's story is the transformation of office from a form of property secured by custom and law to a largely hereditary class (and from which they anticipated benefits in the form of remuneration and honor) to the idea of a responsible professional public administration akin to Hegel's universal class. Bentham documented this transformation by examining changes in the institutional practices of executive officers, judges, officials of the British India Company, and so on, and by analyzing speeches on the subject. Edmund Burke's parliamentary speeches on office and reward were a sign that the traditional class of public men was on the defensive, and evidence of the turbulent state of contemporary thinking about class, honor, and public service. Bentham called Burke hypocritical, saying that he was anxious to guard against the "depravity" of the lower orders who desperately desired wealth, but condoned the present system of "predatory exactions" by men of noble birth (V, 268). But hypocrisy was a minor matter compared to the larger historical issue of changes in expectations. Office had become increasingly divorced from its earlier associations with virtuous self-sacrifice and contempt for money, Bentham observed, and it was increasingly exploited by an identifiable fraternity as a business for private financial gain. He criticized this system, calling it a "solid peace ... between pride and cupidity." The response to corruption was not, however, a reassertion of the ideology of aristocratic honor, but an emerging conception of public administration as a form of professional service and responsibility.

The problem Bentham faced was how to promote this modern notion of office-holding within the constraints of his own "disappointment prevention principle," which required him to attend to the residual expectations of traditional office-holders. His detailed answer combined proposals for compensating former officials with proposals for managing bureaucracy by means of a rational system of rewards and punishment that would join interest and duty and enforce objective standards of aptitude, efficiency, and answerability. The important unifying theme was the new ethos of professional service and responsibility, its institutionalization, and the social groups or "carrier classes" most likely to make it their own—or to internalize it.

This large body of work on the origin and institutionalization of expectations of public service is a more just measure of Bentham's understanding of the social construction of the self than *Panopticon*. For one thing, works like *Official Aptitude* indicate, as *Panopticon* does not, his sensitivity to a range of intermediate conditions—institutional and group identity, for example—that are the actual settings for self-development. The problem is to identify constitutive contexts, which fall somewhere between the dramatic alternatives of complete individual privacy, license, and irresponsibility, on the one side, and the total surveillance of a carceral environment, on the other. Bentham's writings on the organization of officialdom also suggest that while moral identity is at stake in forming responsible public officials and reforming criminals, Bentham's idea of character formation and of the type and severity of public norms that figure among the defining elements of the self was modest. His preferred institutions mainly teach habits of rule-making, rule-following, and responsibility. While a legalistic public culture involves considerable internalization and self-control, it does not pretend to encompass the sum of a person's values—even moral ones—or interests, or to exhaust personality as a whole. Even in his writing on penal communities, Bentham worried about accommodating the domestic ceremonies of Jews in institutions designed for Protestants, and proposed a separate workhouse for Jews with their own rabbis, cooks, and butchers (IV, 24).

In contrast to Bentham's discussion of the origin and function of expectations, contemporary holist assertions about the constituted self appear confusedly double-edged. For some theorists of the constituted self, norms, interests, and even sexual identity are brittle constructs amenable to virtually unlimited manipulation and rapid change. As Foucault argues, the constituted self is both wholly determined and decentered, no self at all. The constitutive disciplines of the modern state organize behavior in such a way that people have only the illusion of intention and responsibility. At the opposite extreme from Foucault are communitarians who typically use *constituted* to refer to a kind of self that is as far as possible from deliberately managed, fractured, and contingent. For them, the constituted self is meant to evoke deep, formative connections to a social whole from which a self emerges with an unshakable moral and social identity. The danger here is portraying too deep a connection, so that what comes to mind is less a strong identity than a primitive, regressive merging with an authoritative whole. This is why communitarian theorists often take a step back and advise that the self is only "partly constituted" by its connections. With "expectation," Bentham indicates a sensible, elastic middle ground between a socially constructed but brittle, "selfless" self, on the one side, and a self fully and inescapably constituted by some set of original attachments, on the other. "Expectation" also invites greater specificity about both the formative context and the actual elements of identity than today's all-or-nothing references to the self and its presumptive constitutive "whole."

Even so, Bentham's treatment of the subject is not entirely satisfactory. No sociologist, he offers few general propositions about the kinds of social orders that generate stable expectations and those subject to radical discontinuity that may produce marginalization, anomie, and severe psychological decentering. The exception was slavery. Bentham insisted that the circumstances of slavery—insecurity without compensation and without remedy—inhibit the formation of expectation, so that "there is no tomorrow for the greater number of slaves" (I, 345). Certainly, Bentham's position must be supplemented with writings from cognitive or psychoanalytic theory on the developmental dynamics of self-formation and identification. The same can be said of most holist theories, however; again, we rarely find holist ontology accompanied by propositions about the origin or preservation of constitutive "wholes," about which ones generate strong selves, or about the psychodynamics of identification.

MACPHERSON ON PROPERTY, INEQUALITY AND POSSESSIVE INDIVIDUALISM

The question remains whether property as a form of expectation has a special place in Bentham's theory of the self or in his politics. Macpherson not only argues that the security of property was an absolute for Bentham and that his political theory "was really concerned only with the rationale of the capitalist market society," but also that material ownership and the political imperative of securing private property follow directly from Bentham's individualist ontology.[20] In making his case, Macpherson moves back and forth between two different readings of possessive individualism.

On one reading, the universal necessity for protecting private property rights over other ends follows from Bentham's sensationalist psychology, according to which no one will labor unless he or she is rewarded with (presumably private) ownership. The thought that labor is painful and is best exacted or impelled by the incentive of some reward is a familiar, plausible axiom, which Bentham adopts.[21] But the axiom is unspecific as to kinds of labor and reward, and Bentham applied it across a very wide range of activities, not all of them economic. He spoke of his own work in these terms: only those "oppressed by their insignificance" are moved to perform the "ardent and persevering" labor of thought (II, 249). His writings on public officialdom—his attack on sinecures, for example—employed a rhetorical reversal of the axiom to read "no benefit without burden." Bentham liked to describe labor both of the brain and of the hand as a species of "drudgery." His thought was to make every form of service, including public service, appear banal. His purpose in dwelling on labor was to demystify the business of authorities, to unintimidate the uninitiated. He was also keen to argue that, for every type of labor, there is a necessary and appropriate reward. Bentham was preoccupied with securing services at minimum cost, but there is nothing peculiarly capitalist about economy per se. In fact, he was enthusiastic to multiply kinds of rewards besides property or profit, especially when it came to public service, and he would add to the armory of rewards the distinctly modern, nonaristocratic honor of professional reputation.

Still, it may be that, at least when it comes to ensuring economic production, Bentham thought the unlimited accumulation of property was the only efficacious reward, and he was prepared to secure it against the other ends of legislation, including equality. In the passage Macpherson cites more than once in support of this reading, Bentham writes that "without law there is no security; and, consequently, no abundance, and not even a certainty of subsistence" (TL, 109). Macpherson concludes from this that Bentham not only defends existing distributions generally, but explicitly sets security of property in opposition to equality. Macpherson argues that Bentham was driven by his psychology of labor and reward to a hysterical fear about productivity, and was blind to the fact that systems of property can be overturned and more equal distributions effected without bringing civilization to an end.

Bentham did fear ideological egalitarianism. He said so plainly and often, and he did set property in opposition to the demand for equality in the abstract. His writings on the subject are of a piece—they are either reactions against the French "Declaration of the Rights of Man and Citizen," or they echo the arguments developed in the 1790s for *Anarchical Fallacies,* in which Bentham judged that in actual practice the promised rights to property and equality always conflict. Between them, he would secure property first, as the principle of nondisappointment demands. But on Bentham's own terms, this would follow only if material equality were not a real expectation that must be weighed against established expectations of ownership. This is what he said, insisting repeatedly that equality is an empty, rhetorical phrase. All of the consequentialist reasons he gives for protecting existing property rights against claims to equality flow from this. The demand for material equality is inspired by envy. It knows no determinable limits—certainly none capable of fixed expression in law. It invites "continual, fresh divisions of the earth," incessant invasions to correct the inequalities that inevitably recur. That egalitarianism may vastly increase the policing role of government is a danger taken for granted today, and not assumed to imply a defense of capitalism. In short, in the context of the revolutionary rhetoric of equality, which Bentham thought inherently incapable of being fulfilled but entirely capable of wreaking destruction, he wrote that the pursuit of equality requires endless divisions, leaving nothing to divide: "devant eux des cités, derrier eux des deserts" (I, 312).

This is not the unmitigated defense of existing property rights nor the rejection of every redistribution that Macpherson makes it out to be, however. Things are different, Bentham says, if property is invaded for the sake of subsistence or in order to lessen identifiable inequalities, where the actual suffering of indigents can be set against the disappointed expectations of property owners. Also, formal property rights unaccompanied by expectations can be overturned in an effort to diminish inequality, making sense of his proposal for a severe tax on inheritances in "Supply Without Burden."[22] A good summary of Bentham's position is this: "When security and equality are in opposition, there should be no hesitation; equality should give way.... The establishment of equality is a chimera: *the only thing which can be done is to diminish inequality*" (I, 311; emphasis added).[23]

Macpherson is on stronger ground with his second interpretation, which has it that Bentham assigns priority to securing property over policies of redistribution because, under present conditions, it is the necessary incentive to the accumulation of capital, and because present circumstances in England make private capital accumulation the best way to increase the material well-being of the whole society.[24] Here, productivity and a distribution of benefits that makes everyone better off than any presently conceivable alternative arrangement are the justifications for private ownership and a market system. This is a contextual, empirical claim, not a universal one, and Macpherson does not indicate where, in Bentham's writings, and in view of what conditions he asserts the independent premise that private ownership is necessary for production and hence satisfaction.[25] It is not the peculiar mark of defenders of capitalism (Marx shared the view, too), nor does it flow logically or necessarily from individualist ontology.[26]

Taken together, the passages Macpherson cites to support the claim that Bentham was imbued with the "capitalist ethos" compose themselves, on closer inspection, into a different picture that is dominated, as I have already argued, by the general theme of securing expectations. Bentham wanted to shift away from the traditional focus on natural rights and historical rights at common law, which fail to capture the full range of expectations. On his view, legal relationships should mirror nonlegal ones, and Bentham looked for some overarching concept besides property rights to capture the array of social relations and the expectations to which they give rise and that it is the business of law to secure. The term he settled on as sufficiently flexible and comprehensive was *services.* Bentham cast social relations as a system of mutual services. Law secures expectations by ensuring the regular performance of an array of services, which include economic production (TL, 197, 187; I, 470; OLG, 57-58, 60). From this perspective, Bentham's model of society is not the exchange of goods in the market, but the responsible performance of services—public services chief among them—and his model social role is neither that of entrepreneur nor consumer, but of responsible professional.

In this picture, authority and dependence are inescapable parts of social life, and property is not the only structure of inequality, nor is it even inherently the most painful. The advantage of thinking in terms of services is precisely that it looks beyond property claims and public enforcement of contracts, broadening the range of expectations afforded by political and legal recognition. It also infuses both public and private authority with an ethos of responsibility for performance, acting as property rights alone do not, as a reminder of the consequences of actions for others. With the idea of service, Bentham also applies to expectations standards of publicity and justiciability, thus providing dependents in public and private life with both a justification and minimal practical means of holding others accountable. This is Bentham's broad, frontal attack on the vulnerabilities created by an array of inequalities. With his attention fixed on what Bentham has to say about property, Macpherson misses Bentham's more inclusive objective of casting social relations in terms of expectations, services, and accountability. As a result, Macpherson had no part in formulating an alternative interpretation that links Bentham to industrial capitalism via his interest in "scientific management." This line of thought has the advantage of taking seriously his obvious preoccupation with the division of labor and hierarchy, record keeping, efficiency, communications, and accountability. However, as a way of making Bentham out to be an apologist for capitalism, this focus has its own problems. Bentham's attention to rewards had as much to do with ensuring individual performance and responsibility as efficiency. In any event, economy meant minimizing costs, not maximizing profits. He aimed at a general theory of management that would apply to the operations of government rather than industrial production. In fact, he seemed to think that, as political development proceeds, and with it the capacity of government to provide responsible management, the public agenda could be greatly extended.[27]

CALCULATING VERSUS EXPRESSIVE SELVES

The most important claim Macpherson makes about Bentham's individualism is that he takes the essence of human nature to be maximizing utility and fails to admit the difference between maximalization of wealth and maximalization of utility.[28] There is little to support this view, and, in at least one instance, Macpherson admits that Bentham saw utility in terms of a wide range of valued things, not wealth alone. Citing chapters 5 and 10 of the *Introduction*, Macpherson surveys the field. "Man's utilities included the pleasures of curiosity, of amity, of reputation, of power, of sympathy, of ease, of skill, of piety, of benevolence, and so on."[29] But whether the individual is said to live to maximize pleasure, or material goods, or utility generally without limit, Bentham stands out as the exemplary theorist of the arrantly calculating self. The self as instrumental, calculating, and maximizing are all elements of the holist picture of individualism, etched on the imagination of romantics in particular. It remains to show that at the heart of this final family of holist claims is the charge that individualism disavows the psychological and sociological significance of expressivism.

In fact, instrumental, calculating, and maximizing are conceptually distinct and do not apply equally well to any version of individualism. Instrumentalism is as old as human action, and characterizing the self as "instrumentalist" appears to tell us very little, unless we realize that holists use the term to refer to a systematic preoccupation with means, rather than with purposes or ends—and not so much with appropriate, fitting, or aesthetically pleasing means as with efficient ones. While it is possible to imagine blinkered, unreflective adjustments of means to achieve ends economically in practice, it is hard to imagine a purely instrumental self. Moreover, Bentham's individualist psychology is associated with utilitarianism, which is all about consequences. Indeed, by collapsing ends into one chief end—minimizing pain—Bentham only points up its significance. There is nothing automatic or coldly efficiency-minded about "instrumental reasoning" to find ways to protect the vulnerable from arbitrary suffering.

The idea of a calculating self reflects a stronger and more specific antipathy toward individualism than does instrumentalism alone. Macpherson sometimes asserts that, for Bentham, utilities are the only human ends, and that all utilities are quantifiable, although it seems that Bentham never used the phrase *felicific calculus*, which was invented by his translator Etienne Dumont. A more restrained version of this charge has it that utility, as a valuational device, gives special place to ends that are quantifiable and that can be expressed in economic terms. For holists, calculation is abhorrent by itself as an inferior form of reasoning hostile to imagination and spontaneity. Beyond that, it is abhorrent because its ends are ignoble. The calculating self has no use for nonquantifiable, hence nonmarket, goods like beauty or community—which is why romantic sensibilities are particularly repulsed by it. Of course, many individualists have judged economic rationality to be limited—if not loathsome, too—for a variety of other reasons, including the thought that, by themselves, market calculations are indifferent to exploitation and inequality.

"Maximizing" gives calculation an even sharper edge by suggesting that all relevant human goods are not only reducible to economic terms, but can be pursued endlessly, without limit. The self is infinitely desirous and characteristically engaged in a senseless, obsessive, and insatiable quest for satisfaction. The implication of Macpherson's discussion is that the maximizer is necessarily an accumulator or appropriator—hence the connection to possessive individualism. But this conflation is not obviously true; *infinite desirer* is not synonymous with *infinite consumer*, and neither translates necessarily into *infinite appropriator* of a specific form of property. The link that Macpherson wants to forge between maximizing and capitalism requires the additional independent premise that private ownership is the necessary condition for satisfaction. I have already argued that this is a contingent claim about political economy, not one that flows logically from individualism.

It emerges that, even for Macpherson, the key objection to individualism is philosophical. He identifies it with the maximizing self, not acquisitiveness per se. This becomes clear when Macpherson extends his criticism of individualism from Bentham to J. S. Mill. Macpherson argues that Mill had to "fight his way out of the Benthamite position" of maximizing wealth, and redefined human nature in terms of developing and enjoying human powers. But Mill did not succeed in breaking away from the errors of individualism because he replaced maximizing happiness with maximizing powers. It is hard to know what "maximizing powers" can mean, hard to imagine a hunger for self-development analogous to the bundles of appetites that impel men and women to limitless consumption or accumulation, and hard to assimilate perfectionism to maximization. It is certainly difficult to recognize Mill's account of self-development, which invokes Humboldt's "beautiful individuality" and romantic notions of "the expression of one's own nature," in Macpherson's description. What exactly is Macpherson's criticism of Mill? He might have restricted his criticism to Mill's politics, accepting Mill's modified individualism while insisting that equality of individual rights to make the most of oneself requires access to resources that is possible only in a nonmarket, socialist state. But Macpherson goes further and claims that like Bentham, Mill misconceived the human essence.

This is not the place to investigate whether Macpherson had a fully developed ontology and whether it was faithfully Marxist and had creative labor at its heart, or what he envisioned uninhibited, unexploited realization in a democratic community to be, or how successfully his democratic theory flows from his concept of human nature. It is enough to say that democracy is not just instrumental, the best condition for realizing natural wants and creative human powers. Democracy—which Macpherson sees prefigured in certain non-Western concepts of the general will and in communism—is constituted of true self-formation. Reunification with a democratic whole is an essential and independent good. Rational individual purposes are expressions of the general will of a democratic community. With this, Macpherson joins in the holist claim that expressivism is the defining characteristic of the self, and that expressions of true human values and purposes reflect membership in some constitutive whole. Of the several aspects of the individualist/holist dichotomy I have surveyed, the juxtaposition of calculating to expressive selves is probably the most widespread among political theorists today and is insisted on with the greatest intensity.

The contrast between instrumental rationality and expressivism makes sense if we assume that men and women are turned perpetually outward in response to external stimuli, so that pleasures, purposes, and the like are contingent and simply "there." On this view, the self lacks depth and identity. But if we assume that the self is identified with its desires and purposes, as Bentham does with his focus on the social psychology of expectations, then even narrow calculations to ensure that expectations are not disappointed can reasonably be thought of as self-expressive. If we assume, further, that individual purposes are constituted by social attachments, as Bentham also appears to do, then instrumental rationality is perfectly compatible with the expression of collective values and converges with some modest holist accounts.

Several versions of expressivity have no place at all in Bentham's individualism, however, and for these cases, the contrast between expressivism and instrumentalism holds up well. Bentham does not see beliefs and feelings emerging from some deep inner nature. As I have shown, he had a sociological, not a romantic, account of the origin of beliefs and feelings. Bentham gives every evidence of disavowing the possibility of selves being genuinely seized by natural feeling, intuition, direct vision, or internal light. Certainly, these distinctively romantic aspects of the self, in contrast to socially constructed expectations, do not come into play in his social psychology for legislators. Although once again, nothing in his antiromantic picture of the self denies depth, as I have suggested, Bentham was perfectly aware of unconscious desires and motives, and of their consequences for self-deception.

Nor—and here holist antipathy to Bentham's individualism is most compelling and seems to hold for Macpherson—does Bentham imagine desire and purposes as expressive of Hegel's geist, or reason in history. Like Hegel, Bentham defined the modern state as a public culture of legalism, which imposes its distinctive discipline on members. But he does not share the Hegelian thought that "as the state comes to its 'truth' as the expression of universal reason in the form of law, it brings the individual with it toward his ultimate vocation."[30]

Even so, the conventional picture of Bentham as the premier target of the expressivist reaction against utilitarian calculation could use a bit of touching up. The "sovereignty of pleasure and pain" and Bentham's account of men and women moved by "alarm"—which imagination alone can produce—cast in doubt the arid, mechanistic, life-impoverished individualism often attributed to him. More importantly, romantic individuality is simply unthinkable without his insistence on the uniqueness of individuals. Certain forms of romantic expressivism would have been impossible without Bentham's devastating attack on asceticism and his emancipation of will and desire. Intellectual history is full of cases of unintended and paradoxical influence—for example, the way in which Hume's skepticism fueled the German antirationalists' turn to faith and revelation in the mid-eighteenth century.[31] But there is a direct, well-charted path from utilitarianism to romanticism via William Godwin, whose *Political Justice* fired the imagination of Shelley. *Prometheus Unbound* is utilitarianism romanticized, a poetic account of the world of the greatest happiness. Godwin's anarchism enjoyed an affinity with some forms of romanticism that Bentham's legislation plainly did not, but arguably Bentham's liberation of desires has had even more far-reaching (if more diffuse) consequences for romantic individualism. From some perspectives, Bentham's own work appears as an extravagant "fantasy of reason." His ideal of legislators weaving a "fabric of felicity" out of a vast multiplicity of desires brings visionaries like Fourier to mind. Bentham commanded public respect for a potentially fantastic array of fears and expectations, and thus for a potentially fantastic company of social relations and uncensored schemes for increasing happiness.

But Bentham is saved from crossing the boundary of sociological and psychological realism by his sober recognition that the "fabric of felicity" is held together by severe, unromantic laws and punishments, and that within it authority and dependence are inevitable. He also argued that an individual's sense of belonging in the modern state ought to come from a sober recognition of his or her legal standing and claim to public consideration in making and enforcing laws. One's sense of membership is a matter of stern understanding, not of love or mysterious attunement. Belonging has nothing to do with lovely sentiments of attachments, on the one hand, or the grim, inescapable structural correspondence between the self and its constitutive whole, on the other.

At this point, the divergence between individualist and holist politics enters. For holists, expressivity is the standard for judging the meaning and value of an action or practice. The fact that beliefs or interests are spontaneous reflections of underlying shared values is their merit, and expressions of community ought to be authoritative. In this view, nothing is more dangerous or debilitating than moral views and purposes that detach individuals from communities and shared ethical frameworks. For Bentham, by contrast, the fact that expectations and actions are expressive of shared values is an important descriptive element but not a normative one. Prescriptively, Bentham wants the "latent" shared values of social groups brought to light in order to be assessed. As the term *special interests* suggests, the social foundations of individual beliefs or desires is rarely benign. The political import of his social psychology is that reflections of social meanings and values in individuals' expectations and fears are amenable to understanding and reform.

NOTES

Roman numerals refer to the volume number of *Works of Jeremy Bentham*, edited by John Bowring, 11 vols. (1832–43; reprint, New York: Russell and Russell, 1962). Other standard volumes cited include *The Theory of Legislation*, edited by C. K. Ogden (New York: Harcourt, Brace, 1931), cited as TL, and *Of Laws in General*, edited by H. L. A. Hart (London: Athlone Press, 1970), cited as OLG.

1. C. B. Macpherson, *Democratic Theory: Essays in Retrieval* (Oxford: Oxford University Press, 1973), 11. For alternative characterizations of individualism and liberalism, see George Kateb, "Democratic Individualism," in Nancy L. Rosenblum, ed. *Liberalism and the Moral Life* (Cambridge: Harvard University

NANCY L. ROSENBLUM

Press, 1989), and Nancy L. Rosenblum, *Another Liberalism* (Cambridge: Harvard University Press, 1988).

2. Cited in Steven Smith, *Hegel's Critique of Liberalism* (Chicago: University of Chicago Press, 1989), 84.

3. Charles Taylor, "Cross Purposes: The Liberal-Communitarian Debate," in *Liberalism and the Moral Life*, ed. N. L. Rosenblum, 159-82. On Humboldt, see Rosenblum, *Another Liberalism*.

4. For Macpherson, "the assumption . . . that Man is the proprietor of his own person" is not simply a way of posing the ethical assumption that we owe nothing to society, but a political error that flows directly from ontology.

5. I leave aside a host of questions surrounding methodological individualism and its alleged triviality or falsity, which are surveyed in Steven Lukes, *Individualism* (Oxford: Basil Blackwell, 1973) and in Richard Miller, "Methodological Individualism and Social Explanation," *Philosophy of Science* 45 (1978): 387-414. Bentham seems to fall into Miller's category of moderate individualism, which says that social phenomena must have a "rock bottom" explanation in terms of psychological characteristics of participants but does not limit these characteristics to participants' reasons for acting as they do (p. 412).

6. Hegel, *Natural Law* (Philadelphia: University of Pennsylvania Press, 1975), 64.

7. Bentham considers gentler punishments for homosexuality (which ought not to be punishable at all, in his view) than the current one. "If population were the only object, the mischief that a rich bachelor did by giving himself up to improlific venery might be amply repaired by obliging him to give a marriage portion to two or three couples who wish for nothing but a subsistence in order to engage in marriage." "Pæderasty," unpublished ms., quoted in Lea Campos Boralevi, *Bentham and the Oppressed* (New York: Walter de Gruyter, 1984), 47.

8. Bentham is one of the rare, nontheological sources for this position. Foucault's attack on humanitarianism as the elimination of physical torture—his implicit approval of cruelty—is the more interesting and usually neglected juxtaposition with Bentham.

9. Ms. cited by Ross Harrison, *Bentham* (London: Routledge and Kegan Paul, 1985), 135.

10. Isaiah Berlin, "Two Concepts of Liberty," in *Four Essays on Liberty* (Oxford: Oxford University Press, 1969) 171n.

11. Judith Shklar, "The Liberalism of Fear," in *Liberalism and the Moral Life*, ed. Rosenblum, 32. It is adequate for Richard Rorty, *Contingency, Irony, and Solidarity* (Cambridge: Cambridge University Press, 1989), 65, 192.

12. "Look the world over, we shall find that differences in point of taste and opinion are grounds of animosity as frequent and as violent as any opposition in point of interest . . ." Cited in Boralevi, *Bentham and the Oppressed*, 56.

13. The intensity of Bentham's feelings here, relative to those of his continental counterparts, emerged only when C. K. Ogden published excerpts from

writings on religion that had been omitted by Bowring from the collected works.

14. The people's "conceptions, their judgments, their suffrages, their language, have till this time been placed almost completely under the guidance, and almost, as it were, at the disposal" of the aristocracy. IX, 44.

15. Ms. cited by Ross Harrison, *Bentham*, 205.

16. Church of Englandism, ms., pp. 52-53, cited in L. J. Hume, *Bentham and Bureaucracy* (Cambridge: Cambridge University Press, 1981), 189.

17. For a more complete discussion, see Nancy L. Rosenblum, *Bentham's Theory of the Modern State* (Cambridge: Harvard University Press, 1978).

18. Macpherson, *The Life and Times of Liberal Democracy* (Oxford: Oxford University Press, 1977), 31.

19. The intellectual history of Bentham's thought on this subject is the focus of L. J. Hume, *Bentham and Bureaucracy.*

20. Macpherson, *Life and Times,* 33.

21. Most theorists would (and do) agree. Rousseau thought that foresight, labor, and abundance were one, but he saw them all as terrible and unnatural and resulting in nothing but misery. An exception, of course, is the exotic, psychologically sophisticated Charles Fourier.

22. Even so, Bentham drew a distinction between destitution or lack of subsistence (which must be corrected by government action) and poverty (which is always relative to abundance). See Rosenblum, *Bentham,* 49ff. Much of what Bentham wrote on a range of economic topics and on subjects like abortion must be considered in the context of his gradual adoption of Malthus's view of overpopulation and his (often secretive) rejection of Malthus's prescriptions. Macpherson does not attend to this historical debate and thereby misses one key to Bentham's humanitarianism and its redistributive implications.

23. The most important example Macpherson could have cited of the priority of property over equality has nothing to do with redistribution per se, but with the emancipation of slaves. Bentham proposed only gradual abolition-ism, with slaves purchasing their own freedom or limitations being set on the right of inheriting slaves.

24. Macpherson, *Democratic Theory,* 7-8, 26, 130.

25. Ibid., 18, 20, 30. Macpherson sometimes argues that a justification of private property follows inexorably from this ontology of a desirous self, but he also argues in the opposite direction from political conclusion to ontology, insisting that capitalist incentives and power relations depend upon unlimited accumulation, so that a defense of capitalism requires a self defined as infinitely desirous.

26. If it is not the case that a society with prosperous agriculture, manufac-ture, and commerce tends to progress toward equality, Bentham's principles suggest a justification for positive state action to achieve that end. Most Bentham scholars conclude that his thoughts on economy were qualified, and that his theory is open on the matter of free market versus government regulation,

NANCY L. ROSENBLUM

ownership, and control, and that it is pretty much an empirical judgment in each case whether and how trade-offs can be made.

27. L. J. Hume suggests, but does not demonstrate definitively, that Bentham was inspired to think about management by what he knew about industrial enterprise. Hume argues convincingly that Bentham worked out a theory of stages in the development of institutional forms of economic activity—the first suitable to purely individual enterprise, and the more advanced stages in which government management had progressed enough to allow government to increase its functions, taking over from private enterprise. See Hume, *Bentham and Bureaucracy*, 138.

28. Macpherson, *Life and Times,* 34.

29. Ibid., 26, 58.

30. Charles Taylor, *Hegel and Modern Society* (Cambridge: Cambridge University Press, 1979), 51.

31. Isaiah Berlin, "Hume and German Antirationalism," *Against the Current* (New York: Viking, 1955), 173-74.

Chapter 5
Stretching the Limits of the Democratic Imagination

John Keane

MAXIMIZING DEMOCRACY

During the past three decades, the work of C. B. Macpherson has been blown about by almost every wind of criticism. It has been dismissed as old-fashioned, as neglectful of the "perennial problems" of political philosophy, as an "unhistorical" distortion of past realities or, simply, as trapped on the wrong (or losing) side of the class struggle.[1] These criticisms are unconvincing. They should be doubted, for they miss the fundamental and lasting importance of C. B. Macpherson's project—his bold, lifelong attempt to revive the postwar democratic imagination.

For the good part of Macpherson's distinguished career, the subject of democracy excited little passion among political philosophers. It was widely assumed that the theoretical foundations of contemporary Western democracies were self-evident and therefore uncontentious, and that the study of democracy was largely an empirical enterprise. Macpherson refused to accept this settled assumption. He supposed, correctly, that the meaning of democracy is not timeless, and that the principles of democracy have been interpreted in diverse ways as their custodianship has changed hands. Guided by this insight that the struggle to control the definition or meaning of democracy is an intrinsic feature of modern societies, Macpherson challenged the belief that democracy is simply a method of choosing and authorizing governments, whose leaders are meritorious and whose citizens are passive and self-restrained subjects. He battled against the view that citizens in liberal democracies should "neither raise nor decide issues ... the issues that shape their fate are normally raised and decided for them" (Schumpeter). He denied that democracy is a market-like process in which the leaders of political parties act as entrepreneurs, offering competing parcels of political goods to voters, who as consumers choose which party's promised parcels they will buy at election time.

From the time of his essays of the early 1940s, Macpherson proposed a radical alternative to this vertical conception of democracy.[2] He envisaged a postliberal and participatory democracy, by which he meant a social order which guarantees that all its members are equally free to actualize their human capacities. To defend a more participatory democracy in this sense is to work for the principle of the equal self-expression of individuals. It is to anticipate their emancipation from the outdated and contingent rules and regulations of long-established institutions. Democracy is an equitable and humane society which facilitates all individuals' maximum self-development. In a fully democratic society, to use words Macpherson loved, "individuals would understand themselves as exerters and enjoyers of their own uniquely human capacities."

THE METHODS OF DEMOCRATIC RENEWAL

There is a striking hiatus between this vision of democracy and the forms of "vertical" democracy celebrated by most democratic theorists during the period of the postwar settlement. This hiatus was reinforced by several methodological premises within Macpherson's writings. Among the most important were his attempt to inject utopian themes into the discourse about democracy; his efforts to retrieve, question, and to develop liberal and democratic traditions of the early modern period; and his generous use of conceptual models, which aim to clarify and to highlight the most important elements of the complex reality addressed by his theory. These methodological premises require further examination, since they help to clarify the strengths and weaknesses of Macpherson's project of maximizing democracy.

To begin with, Macpherson is best understood as a utopian in the philosophical sense. His call for participatory democracy was always intoxicated with the standard utopian technique of presenting exaggerated arguments which serve as positive standards against which the existing world and its justifications can be measured and judged as inadequate. Macpherson sensed, correctly, that today's reality is often yesterday's utopia and that tomorrow's reality is often today's utopia. In this respect, his utopia was a deliberate provocation of the status quo. Democracy was, for him, not a system of power to be preserved, but a condition to be sought after. Under less than favorable conditions, his theory asked for more democracy—for a "revolution in democratic consciousness."[3] Consonant with this utopian mode of thinking, Macpherson never provided a detailed picture of how to move from the present into the future. To criticize Macpherson, say, for disregarding the empirical subjects who would be capable of instituting a more democratic society is therefore beside the point, for this is only to describe his mode of thinking.[4] Macpherson's approach is better judged by its productivity—that is, by its capacity, first, to question the apparently natural and fixed boundaries of the present by drawing our attention to neglected problems; and second, by its ability to anticipate or open the way for democratic developments which cannot yet be institutionalized. In short, the success of Macpherson's defense of democracy must be judged by the extent to which it functioned as a "fertile utopia" (Ernst Bloch).

A second methodological premise of Macpherson's theory of democracy is its turn toward the Anglo-American liberal/democratic traditions of the past. Macpherson's quiet conviction that this past speaks to us with a directness that wipes out the centuries impressed everyone who knew him. That is not to say that he was an archivist of old political ideas, or that he thought that we should live as though we were dead. Macpherson rather supposed that democratic traditions are as easy to lose as they are difficult to regain, and he therefore rebuked his contemporaries for their theoretical amnesia, for their embrace of a model of democracy founded on a condescending attitude toward the past. He perceived, correctly, that the past cannot be left to conservatives, and that contemporary democratic theory must develop eyes in the back of its head. It must nourish itself upon attempts to "rescue" the past by demonstrating its positive or negative meanings for those living in the present. According to Macpherson, the task of enquiring after what we have become, or what we may become, obliges us to enquire after what we once conceived ourselves to be.

Those who wish for the maximization of democracy must zealously prevent things of great importance to democracy from passing into oblivion. The viability of democratic theory must therefore be judged, not by its forgetfulness of the past and embrace of "the new," but at least in part by its capacity to retrieve, extend, and to imaginatively transform the subversive themes of old bodies of political thinking. Democrats need to cultivate a remembrance of things past, for under contemporary conditions memory is a subversive weapon. The present survival and future growth of democracy require the extension of the vote to the most disenfranchised of all constituencies—our silenced ancestors. Democracy among the living requires democracy among the dead.

While Macpherson never assumed that the political principles of the past are sufficient for a changed and more complex late twentieth-century world, he did insist—to borrow an opening metaphor of *The Political Theory of Possessive Individualism*—that these founding principles can be built upon. The foundations of democracy may have cracked and tilted, but they can—if they are not to be demolished entirely—be repaired, preserved, and renewed.[5]

No doubt, Macpherson's retrieval of the liberal and democratic past was highly selective. This was quite in accordance with the deliberately excessive or utopian character of his concern to maximize democracy. Criticisms of the "unhistorical" character of Macpherson's interpretations of the history of modern political thought are therefore mistaken.[6] The alleged weakness of Macpherson—this misrecognition of an actual historical past—was in fact one of his key strengths. He never attempted to faithfully "record" the past (as spectator theories of historical interpretation wrongly assume to be possible). His account of the past was deliberately selective. It was framed by analytic models (of different forms of society, or of different historical phases of the development of liberal/democratic theory) which served to isolate and emphasize certain (but not other) aspects of a past which, from Macpherson's point of view, are of great relevance to the task of democratizing the present.

It is true that he was sometimes tempted to say that these models reflect an underlying reality, and that they therefore correspond to actual thinkers and their actual contexts.[7] Despite these occasional claims to having "clearly identified" the deeper objective significance of thinkers and societies of the past—claims which are refuted by recent developments in the theory of textual interpretation[8]—Macpherson's defense of democracy always relied upon models which highlighted the important point that the definition of the past cannot ultimately be separated from the evaluation of its normative significance. These models addressed certain questions to their objects of analysis, setting them apart and treating them as worthy of recognition and analysis. Such questions served as something like one-sided vantage points from which the past could be classified, analyzed, understood, explained, and evaluated. In this precise sense, Macpherson's interpretation of the liberal/democratic tradition was consistently subjective. It was a species of ideal-typical analysis (in Max Weber's sense) that emphasized that certain aspects of modern reality are of crucial significance for the future of those who are living within the present.

THE PROPERTY QUESTION

Relying upon these three methodological premises, Macpherson explored the contemporary significance of the modern liberal/democratic tradition originating with Hobbes. His interpretation of this tradition both praised its central achievement—its positing of the free rational individual as the criterion of the good society—and criticized its basic assumptions as self-contradictory and, therefore, as practically unrealizable as such. Macpherson's affirmative criticism of the liberal/democratic tradition most often took the form of exposing strict inconsistencies within its theoretical structures. He worked within the terms of this tradition in order to transgress them. In other words, he demonstrated that certain crucial elements of the liberal tradition cannot be reconciled with democracy, and that, therefore, the vision of a liberal democratic society is self-paralyzing and impossible in practice.

Of fundamental importance to Macpherson's affirmative critique of liberalism was the question of property. In his view, nothing has given liberal/democratic theory more trouble than its conception of property rights. The argument, in brief, is that the fundamental problem of liberal/democratic theory consists in its difficulty of reconciling the liberal property right—the right of capitalist acts among consenting adults —with another right which is the grounding ethical principle of both liberal humanism and democracy: the equal effective right of all individuals to use and to develop their capacities. The self-paralysis of liberal/democratic theory is traced to its various attempts to shelter these two contradictory sets of rights. For when the de facto liberal property powers are written into law and protected by the state as a natural individual right to the exclusive use and disposal of the resources provided by nature and of portions of the capital created by past labor on this nature; and when this political and legal guarantee of property rights is combined with liberal assumptions about infinite desire and a corresponding system of market incentives and rights of free contract, then liberal doctrine necessarily justifies a concentration of ownership of property and, hence, a system of power relations among individuals and classes which negates the ethical goal of autonomous individual development.

Macpherson's critique of liberalism echoed the words of Shakespeare's *Merchant of Venice,* which Marx himself quoted in *Das Kapital:* "You take my life / when you do take the means whereby I live." Within a possessive market society, in which there is a market in labor as well as in products, the liberal belief that unlimited desire is natural or rational encourages the establishment of the right of unlimited appropriation, which in turn leads to the concentration of ownership of the material means of labor. This concentration of property disadvantages the propertyless, who lose free access to the means of turning their capacity to labor into productive labor. Because they rarely have access to the means of independent production, and because they cannot demand in wages an amount equal to what would be the product of their labor on property of their own, the propertyless are disempowered. By employing the labor of others, those who monopolize property can effect a continual net transfer of powers (or some of the product of those powers) of the propertyless. According to Macpherson, an insoluble contradiction therefore lies at the heart of liberal/democratic theory. If, as this theory insists, an individual right to saleable property is a fact of human nature, it ought not to be denied or hindered. However, unless this right to private property is denied or hindered, it leads in practice to an effective denial of the possibility of equal individual human fulfillment. This difficulty—the contradiction between the rights of property and the entitlements of individuality—was inherent in liberal theory and possessive market society from the beginning. Under contemporary capitalist conditions, or so Macpherson argues, it continues to be so.

Macpherson pointed to the undemocratic effects of this contradiction through at least three different, if overlapping, lines of argument. In his classic and best-known text, *The Political Theory of Possessive Individualism,* this difficulty was traced to a unifying assumption—"possessive individualism" within liberal discourse of seventeenth-century England. Articulating the organizing principles of the emergent market society, liberalism assumed that individuals are essentially the proprietors of their own persons or capacities, owing nothing to society for them. Yet this same assumption was also incompatible with the great achievement of seventeenth-century liberalism: its insistence that what makes an individual human is freedom from dependence upon the will of others. The individuality defended by seventeenth-century liberalism was, at the same time, a fundamental denial of individuality. The freedom of individuals to enter voluntarily, if self-interestedly, into relations with other individuals was premised on their exercise of exclusive control over their bodies, capacities, and properties. In Macpherson's view, it is precisely this exclusive control by some individuals that denies other individuals access to property and power, forcing them to alienate their capacity to labor and, with that, to relinquish their full powers of individual autonomy. The individuality of some—property owners—is therefore possible only insofar as they consume the individuality of others—laborers—within the institutional framework of a possessive market society. In sum, the market capitalism justified by seventeenth-century liberalism generated class differences in the effective rights and powers of individuals, yet required for its justification assumptions about equal natural rights and powers.

Elsewhere, the undemocratic implications of this contradiction are spelled out by analyzing the incompatibility between two concepts of the human essence. According to Macpherson, these two concepts of human nature—humanity as infinitely desirous consumers of utilities, and humanity as active developers of their unique potential—have coexisted less than peacefully for more than a century within the liberal/democratic tradition.[9] They emerged at different historical moments, and in response to changes in the constellation of power in modern societies.

The first postulate—individuals as insatiable consumers and appropriators, as infinite antagonists of scarcity—was an invention of the emerging capitalist market society of seventeenth-century England. It was expressed most forcefully in the utilitarianism of Bentham and James Mill. This postulate was not only compatible with the activity required of individuals under capitalist conditions. It also functioned to justify the right of unrestricted individual appropriation, which was so necessary as an incentive to continuous effort in this new type of society. But from the time of the nineteenth century, Macpherson claimed, this liberal postulate was challenged increasingly by the democratic thesis that individuals are capable of freely exerting their manifold capacities. J. S. Mill's critique of utilitarianism is exemplary of the manner in which the democratic postulate soon became an integral part of the theory of liberal democracy and its emphasis on the need for respect for individuals as human beings.

The ideal of maximizing human powers was supposed to counterbalance the older assumption that individuals are maximizers of their utilities. According to Macpherson, the attempt democratically to amend and to transform liberalism has been wholly unsuccessful, and it must remain so, because it supposes the possibility of reconciling what cannot, in fact, be reconciled. Under market capitalism conditions, life cannot be lived fully by individuals who are considered as equals so long as they devote themselves to the acquisition of utilities and, consequently, to denying effectively the equal right of individuals to make the best of themselves.

Finally, in his book *Property,* Macpherson analyzed this central difficulty with specific reference to the property question.[10] The individual right to private property—which liberal theory has inferred from the nature of the species—was seen to be overly narrow and in need of broadening, exactly because it contradicts the liberal assertion that all individuals are naturally free and equal. Guided by the precept that property is not a thing in itself, and that it is always subject to transformations of form and meaning, Macpherson argued for a new property paradigm. The argument drew upon, and considerably amended, Isaiah Berlin's famous distinction between negative and positive liberty.[11] Property, although it must always be an individual right, need not be confined to a negative right to exclude others from the use, benefit, or disposal of the fruits of labor and/or of the means of life. To suppose that property is a natural right to prohibit others from what one commands or produces—property as exclusively *meum* and *tuum*—is to be seduced by liberalism. It is to assume, falsely, that the denial of the humanity of others—who are without property in land or capital, and must therefore alienate their labor—is somehow natural.

Yet property, Macpherson continued, may equally be considered as an individual right not to be excluded by others from the use, benefit, or disposal of the means of life and the fruits of labor. When property is understood in this positive sense, the problem of liberal/democratic theory is no longer one of infringing, narrowing, or putting absolute limits on the individual property right. It is rather a problem of *supplementing* the individual right to exclude others—a right that would persist, say, in the form of consumables, such as toothbrushes (one of Macpherson's favorite examples), which can be enjoyed only as exclusive property—with common property, the individual positive right not to be excluded by others. Property in land, capital, labor, and the consumable means of life is a right required by all to enable them to express their human essence. The right not to be excluded by others to the means of life is a necessary condition of the right of all to full human development. Through this reasoning, Macpherson envisaged not the abolition of the right of property, but rather the generalization of property ownership into a form of "autogestion" which ensures, for all members of society, the ability to dispose of the social forces of production and to enjoy the fruits of productive activity. Macpherson always regarded this positive right to property as not only preferable, but as actually required by the liberal/democratic ethic of individuals as creative actors. Democratic control over the uses to which the amassed capital of society is put would not destroy, but in fact emancipate, the liberal/democratic vision from its self-destructive, half-democratic premises.

POSTLIBERAL DEMOCRACY

Although Macpherson's vision of postliberal democracy as the maximization of human powers is only briefly sketched here, its chief strengths should be apparent. It powerfully called into question the postwar class compromise secured by the Keynesian welfare state. It demonstrated the implausibility of the free market case against the welfare state. Macpherson's vision challenged the consensus that democracy equals the rule of political elites. It drew attention to the vital importance of thinking historically about democracy, and, by emphasizing the ways in which the distribution of social and political power is conditioned by property relations, it pointed to a muddle within liberal/democratic theory. In each respect, Macpherson's vision proved to be a fertile utopia. Yet it is also possible to discern several serious weaknesses within his defense of a postliberal democracy. Although these difficulties within Macpherson's otherwise fruitful approach are not immediately obvious, they are of profound importance to anyone concerned with the future of democracy. These difficulties include the failure of Macpherson's democratic humanism to come to terms with ethical pluralism, his attraction to the

113

JOHN KEANE

myth of collective harmony and the abolition of the state, and his excessive trust in modern scientific-technical progress. These problems are analyzed further in this chapter. In each case Macpherson's arguments are employed in order to demonstrate their internal limits—that is, what they have excluded or concealed from discussion.

ETHICAL PLURALISM

To begin with, questions must be raised about Macpherson's argument that democracy is equivalent to the humanization of the world. His humanism supposes that democracy is not merely a set of procedures, but a normatively structured way of life. It also supposes that qualitative distinctions between good and bad are possible—that being human is a defensible good.

As I have shown, Macpherson attempted to stimulate the democratic imagination by celebrating the principle of "the free development of human capacities."[12] This principle rests on the surprising assumption that competing or contradictory validity claims are not of the essence of being human. It is as if democratic humanism is a privileged form of life that is incontrovertible and hence insulated against political controversy.

Consider Macpherson's discussion of the possibilities of maximizing democracy.[13] Here individuals' human attributes were taken to include the capacities for rational understanding; moral judgment and action; aesthetic creation or contemplation; and emotional activities of friendship, love, and, sometimes, religious experience. A cascade of questions concerning the criteria of validity of these human attributes is prompted by this list:

- Are there not diverse forms of rationality and, if so, are they all equally human?
- Are there not different types of moral judgments and action and different forms of aesthetic creation and contemplation?
- Which particular religious experiences should be counted as essentially human?

Even if convincing and binding responses could be given to such questions, could we assume that these different human attributes are compatible with each other—Presbyterianism with Marxism-Leninism,

114

gay and lesbian politics with Islam, and feminism with trade unionism? In short, as Max Weber asked: Are these gods sometimes not at war with each other and, if that is the case, which of them should we serve?

Macpherson would have rejected this line of questioning as an example of rational-calculating thinking, as the type of market reasoning that converts and downgrades all human values and forms of life into self-interested, greedy behavior. From this perspective, the very possibility of democratic emancipation depends upon warding off market irrationalism by forming the correct conception of the very essence of morality: that is, being human. Only with that could democracy be secured against the antidemocratic assumption that any belief, including those avowedly hostile to humanity, is as good as any other.

This conclusion is unwarranted. Philosophical questions about the diversity and potential incommensurability of normatively structured forms of life are among the most pressing frontier problems of contemporary democratic theory. Paradoxically, Macpherson's efforts to justify the vision of a democratic society which maximizes the "uniquely human capacities" of individuals brings this problem of ethical diversity and conflict into sharper focus. His assumption that democracy—the free exercise of subjects' humanity—is obviously preferable to heteronomy reveals that this preference is far from obvious, and that the justification (and possible redefinition) of democracy therefore requires further and more careful philosophical consideration.[14]

The need to reconsider the political implications of ethical pluralism is, of course, peculiar to modern societies, as de Tocqueville and others first suggested. Under modern conditions, the search for objective ethical truth—for rules which determine, once and for all, how rational agreement can be secured among forms of life that evidently are in conflict—has been both singularly unsuccessful and (as in the extreme cases of Stalinism and Nazism) politically destructive. Modern societies severely weaken the power of norms referring to cultural tradition or to a natural order of things. Consequently, they begin self-consciously to summon up their normative identities from within themselves. Modernization processes terminate the natural determination of ethics. In destroying the old reference points of ultimate certainty, modern social actors begin to sense that they are not in possession of any ultimates based on knowledge, conviction, or faith, and that they are continually and forever obliged to define for themselves how and why they wish to live. It becomes evident to these actors that theirs is a society marked by ethical indeterminacy. They sense that the so-called ultimate ends do not correspond to an immutable and "real" origin or essence, and that these normative goals are therefore always subject to debate, conflict, and resistance—and, hence, to temporal and spatial variation. Actors within modern societies discover, even if intuitively, that the processes of creating, developing, and implementing norms can be analyzed only through a theory of ethical pluralism that understands that norms come to appear as ultimate or grounded only insofar as they are conventionally differentiated from, and come to predominate over, *other* and *different* norms. Ethical standards, from this perspective, are seen not as positive and fixed entities in themselves, but as the product of a system of practically established, contingent, and therefore highly precarious differences and similarities among individuals, groups, movements, and institutions of various kinds.

The more that modern societies liquidate the assumption that ethical standards have an essential or ultimate basis, the more a theory of ethical pluralism is required to make sense of the political processes of contestation and alliance through which normative standards are established., transformed, or undone. Emphasizing the radical indeterminacy and possible incommensurability of these standards, a theory of ethical pluralism suggests, contrary to Macpherson, how a theory of democracy can do without a standpoint of humanism, which is itself defined as "essential" and closed to further questioning.

As I have argued against Lyotard and Habermas, there is an intimate relationship between ethical pluralism and democracy.[15] The theory of ethical pluralism, itself not a metatheory based on First Principles, rejects all forms of power and politics which are hell-bent on stifling this indeterminacy and pluralism by demanding the general adoption of particular forms of life that have been clothed in the familiar repertoire of metaphors, such as that every woman needs a man just as the herd needs the shepherd, the ship's crew a captain, and the proletariat the Party; that the end justifies the means; that doctors know best; that capitalism is the best and most efficient form of economy; and so on.

This connection can be clarified by asking after the presuppositions of ethical pluralism—that is, by reflecting counterfactually upon the theoretical and sociopolitical conditions necessary for its institutionalism as such.[16] Consider the following line of reasoning.

The pluralist thesis that ethical values may be incommensurable, and that they are intelligible and interpretable only in terms of their difference from, or similarity with, other values and their criteria of adequacy implies an opposition to all claims and institutional contexts which thwart or deny this pluralist thesis. That is to say, a self-consistent pluralism is compelled to devote itself to the theoretical and political project of questioning and disarticulating all absolutist or ideological truth claims. That means, for example, that ethical pluralism cannot rest content with prepolitical assertions about the need for supporting our culture conversationally, through the telling of stories.[17] It also means that it cannot cling naïvely to the melancholic, complacent, or cynical views often associated with various forms of ethical relativism: that every belief about every matter is as good as every other.

Pluralism implies the need for institutional arrangements that guarantee that advocates of similar or different forms of life can openly and continuously articulate their respective norms. At the least, it implies a civil society comprising a plurality of interdependent, self-organizing social institutions. This further implies the need for political mechanisms of conflict resolution and compromise that limit and reduce the serious antagonisms that frequently issue from struggle among incompatible forms of social life. The pluralist insistence upon the diversity and incompatibility of the structure, styles of reasoning, and substantive content of life-forms also supposes—and this point is fundamental—the need for democratic procedures which guarantee openness within and between state institutions and civil society and, therefore, ensure that individuals and groups can fairly defend their particular norms in relation to other, possibly incompatible, norms.

This line of argument, which is so near and yet so far from Macpherson's democratic humanism, suggests that democracy is an implied condition of the ethical pluralism initiated by processes of modernization. To embrace ethical pluralism is to anticipate, and to support the establishment of, a civil society and publicly accountable state institutions, within which individuals and groups can openly express their agreement with (or their opposition to) others' ideals. In this sense, democracy can no longer be understood, as Macpherson sought to understand it, as a substantive norm, or as a type of heteronomous principle which can be foisted upon social and political actors. Democracy is better understood in terms of procedures which have normative implications. Democracy comprises a system of procedural rules that specify who is authorized to make collective decisions and by which institutional means such decisions are to be made. In contrast to all forms of heteronomous government, democracy comprises procedures for reaching collective decisions by means of the fullest possible and qualitatively best participation of interested parties and their representatives. Understood in this way, democracy cannot be interpreted as merely one procedural condition among others, as if groups struggling to defend or to realize their ideals could decide legitimately to play by democratic rules for a time, only later to abandon them. Their rejection of democracy would evidently contradict the particular and contingent character of their ideals. Their proclaimed universalism would cover up the wholly conventional social and political processes of conflict and solidarity through which all particular ethical ideals are established, maintained, and transformed.

From this pluralist perspective, finally, democracy can no longer be viewed as a synonym for the withering away of social division and political conflict, as Macpherson's theory of the nonopposition of essentially human capacities encouraged us to do. The foundations of fully democratic societies are permanently unstable. The well-known adage that democracy is a tedious process derives from this fact. Democratic procedures are rarely taken for granted, and decisions taken by means of these procedures are rarely accepted fully, as if power struggles and controversies about means and ends, techniques and ethics, could be resolved once and for all. Consequently, under democratic conditions reliance on the faculty of judgment is indispensable. A democratic society cannot flatter itself on its capacity to know and to subsume everything under hard and fast general rules. Its members understand the need to be sensitive to particulars and to avoid moralizing categorical imperatives. They also know that they cannot rely upon universally applicable rules and methods, and consequently they appreciate their own ignorance, which is to say—compare the Socratic attitude—that they know that they cannot know everything. To defend democracy in this sense is, therefore, to recognize the power of indeterminacy, controversy, and uncertainty. It is to be prepared for conflict, for the appearance of the unexpected, and for the constant probability of novelty.

THE ABOLITION OF THE STATE?

Macpherson's tendency to suppress the problems of uncertainty, diversity, and conflict is related to, and strengthened by, his fascination with the nineteenth-century goal of abolishing state institutions. I have observed already that Macpherson attempted to criticize liberal justifications of market-capitalist society and its class divisions by, at the same time, retrieving, reconstructing, and affirming the liberal notion of individual self-development.[18] What is curious about this affirmative critique is that it takes little or no account of the specifically political and legal dimensions of the liberal/democratic tradition—including its theories of social contract and arguments about self-determined political obligation and consent; its theories of a free press, minority rights, majority rule, and formal and universal law; and its important emphasis on the division between the state and civil society.

Macpherson's silence about such issues is reminiscent of the young Marx's counterdeclaration of civil and political rights in *Zur Judenfrage*, and is especially evident in *The Political Theory of Possessive Individualism*. It is true that this work contains rare passages where Macpherson acknowledged that the classical liberal concepts of justice, obligation, rights, and freedom are not fully reducible to the liberal defense of market exchanges between proprietors conceived as possessive individuals.[19] This caveat usually remained unheeded. The state, or political society, was normally conceived by Macpherson as a mechanism for maximizing the security of the property-owning classes. For example, the differences between Hobbes's defense of a self-perpetuating sovereign state and Locke's defense of a more limited constitutional state were explained by referring to the growth of class cohesion within the emergent market society. In each case, political and legal procedures were viewed as mere engines for guaranteeing property, understood as saleable absolute rights to things. Macpherson also claimed that the English Levellers (consistent with their petit-bourgeois class position) identified freedom with property—an interpretation that underestimated the extent to which their broad concept of "propriety," which was common in seventeenth-century political discourse in England, covered not only rights to life and estate, but also to liberty from state tyranny.

The reductionism of Macpherson's account of liberalism was further evident in his conflation of the important differences between classical liberalism and utilitarianism, the latter being understood as only a restatement of the individualist principles worked out during the seventeenth century.[20] The thesis that "Bentham built on Hobbes" is repeated in *The Life and Times of Liberal Democracy*, in which the analysis of liberal democracy commences with utilitarianism, as if, say, the explicit rejection of the natural rights and social contract doctrines by Bentham and James Mill were of little consequence for democratic theory.

By concentrating on the market at the expense of the specifically political and legal concerns of classical liberalism—seeing them as appendages or functional requirements of a civil society dominated by commodity production and exchange—Macpherson's understanding of modern civil societies and states was overly narrow. It downgraded the important distinction between civil society and the state because it tended to reduce the state to a political organ of the property-owning classes, especially the bourgeoisie. On that basis, it further conflated the complex patterns of group organization, stratification, and the conflicts and movements of civil society to the logic and contradictions of a mode of production—the market-capitalist economy. The importance for democratic theory of other institutions of civil society—households, prisons, voluntary associations, hospitals, scientific and literary clubs, and churches—was thereby devalued. Macpherson's inability to come to terms theoretically with feminist concerns in *The Life and Times of Liberal Democracy* was symptomatic of this difficulty. He supposed, unconvincingly, that the fate of households and other institutions of modern civil society is tied to the overwhelming power of the market.

Macpherson also underestimated the extent to which liberal justifications of the market were not identical with early liberal arguments for and against the power of the modern constitutional state.[21] Liberal discourse from the time of the English Civil War until the abortive revolutions of 1848 did not merely seek to make the world safe for a capitalist system that permitted no other criterion of individuals' worth than that of market freedom, as Macpherson and his teacher Harold Laski supposed.[22] Early liberal political philosophy was also preoccupied with two fundamental problems: apportioning and controlling the exercise of political power, and reconciling the freedom of different individuals, groups, and classes with political order and coercion. Typically, the state was seen as a product of reason, as an institution which collectively restrains private interests and passions, and thereby secures a controlled and ordered liberty in the face of possible exercises of pure strength and/or disorder and chaos. Political reason is *raison d'État*. It served to justify an entirely new apparatus of anonymous power—the modern bureaucratic state—in which the monopoly of the weapons of violence is reinforced by means of collecting taxes, conducting foreign policy, articulating and administering law, and policing its subjects. The function of the state is to provide a secure foundation upon which patriarchal family life, as well as domestic and international trade and commerce, could flourish.

Most early modern liberal thinkers understood that the market economy emerged under the shadow of the modern bureaucratic state. They also saw that the unconditional recognition of its sovereign power could—and frequently did—result in the deprivation of the powers of its male, property-owning subjects. Consequently, while early liberal thinkers sought to justify the centralizing state as necessary, they attempted at the same time to justify limits upon its potentially coercive powers. Although blind to certain forms of power (such as markets, patriarchal households, and disciplinary institutions), these liberal thinkers displayed—certainly when compared with our times—a very deep sensitivity to questions concerning power, legitimacy, and obligation.[23] In other words, the history of liberal political thought from the midseventeenth until the midnineteenth centuries is the history of attempts to justify might *and* right, political power *and* the rule of law, and the duties of subjects *and* the entitlements of citizens.

Macpherson's imaginative defense of democracy can perhaps be excused on these finer points of interpretation. But his truncated understanding of modern civil societies and the political and legal dimensions of liberalism produced a deep ambiguity within his writings about the appropriate role of political institutions in democratic societies. In fact, his discussion of democracy vacillated between two extreme and diametrically opposed (but symbiotically connected) possibilities: a deep trust in state power and a belief in the fiction of the withering away of the state.

Consider Macpherson's statism, his insistence upon the duties owed by subjects to sovereign state power. There are several examples, of which one is his comments on the former state socialist regimes.[24] In the context of a discussion of whether the state apparatuses of these regimes could be described as democratic—if, by democracy, we mean a publicly accountable system of political, legal, and military institutions—Macpherson answered in the negative. Yet, Macpherson continued, if these societies are understood as transitional regimes, as in motion toward democracy in the sense of "a kind of society," a form of society without class divisions and orientated to the free development of human capacities, then they can indeed be described as democratic. The most striking instance of Macpherson's unintended statism is to be found in the concluding pages of *The Political Theory of Possessive Individualism.*[25] There he argued that a theory of political obligation that does not rely upon naturalistic, divine, or external standards of legitimacy can be valid only if it can point to a fundamental equality among all individuals, a shared equality that, in turn, can serve as the basis of their self-obligation to political power. In his view, liberal/democratic theory can no longer rely on the assumption that everyone is subject to the determining laws of a competitive market, the inevitability of which has been challenged increasingly during the past century by the enfranchisement and militancy of the industrialist working class.

Is a new concept of fundamental equality at all conceivable? Macpherson answered affirmatively by pointing to a new development: the possibility of global nuclear war which, in his view, has created "a new equality of security among individuals, not merely within one nation but everywhere."[26] Hobbes's depiction of the state of nature—in which life is solitary, poor, nasty, brutish, and short—is now a more frightening and actual possibility than Hobbes could ever have imagined. This global insecurity makes possible a new rational political obligation to a wider political authority.

Macpherson was correct, of course, about the unparalleled catastrophe implicit within a world bristling with nuclear arms. But by appealing to global insecurity as the condition of political obligation and obedience, his arguments lost contact with the democratic principles of self-assumed obligation and the restriction of state power. Fear is never the basis of democratic solidarity. It is its antithesis. Fear of losing power corrupts those who exercise it, just as it corrupts those who are subject to power. Fear also has a nasty habit of displacing itself onto overbearing personalities, parties, and institutions. As Hobbes himself acknowledged, the act of voluntary contract outlined in the *Leviathan* is highly involuntary, because it takes place under the threat of death. Moreover, as an act of mutual consent, it is the first and final contract because it is synonymous with the institution of a new political entity—a sovereign power—that can be resisted legitimately only under exceptional circumstances. It is a type of political authority before which, as Hobbes said, all subjects are little more than small stars in the presence of an overpowering sun.

Elsewhere, Macpherson's statism was jettisoned in favor of the opposite, but equally implausible, vision of the abolition of the state. From the time of his survey of political radicalism in Alberta, he was tempted by the chiliastic belief in a transparent, self-regulating social order, a democratic society marked only by rational harmony and near-perfect freedom and equality among creatively interacting individuals.[27] This belief followed directly from Macpherson's tendency to reduce all political problems to issues of property, and also by his reliance on what he described as the staggering postulate, which I have criticized above, of the nonopposition of essentially human capacities.[28] Macpherson always emphasized that democratic theory must recognize that human rights and freedoms are not mutually destructive. If freed from scarcity, individuals could live together harmoniously. Whatever tensions remained would be creative and noncontradictory tensions. They would form part of a process in which an individual's essentially human capacities could be exercised without hindering the use and development of other individual's human capacities. Fully humanized individuals could transform themselves self-consciously by codetermining their relations with other individuals and their material environment, without conflict and untroubled by second thoughts and unforeseen consequences. Individuals in motion would be reconciled with each other and with themselves.

In relying upon this postulate, Macpherson allied himself with the tradition of expressivist thinking which is traceable to eighteenth-century romanticism, to Humboldt and Schiller, *Sturm und Drang*, Herder, the young Marx, and J. S. Mill. Expressivism sustained itself upon a deinstitutionalized notion of freedom, and in this respect it can be seen as an attempted rebellion against the uniquely modern institutional division between state institutions and civil society. Individuals are seen to develop and externalize their subjectivity in peaceful cooperation with others. Individuals are the process of harmonious self-creation.

Macpherson's reliance upon this model of expressivism and its belief in collective harmony is problematic. His theory of democracy yearned for a perfectly substantive democracy, unhindered by procedural matters. It supposed that on the democratic Isles of Humanity there will be no foxes who trick cows, and that lions will be moved to lie down with lambs. In this democratic paradise, individuals would, at all times, be "for themselves." Their identity would be fused together organically. By expressing their humanity freely, individuals would at the same time express the humanity of the whole collectivity. The individual and the political community would become a fully realized unity.

Contemporary democratic theory must reject this mode of expressivism as an unrealizable daydream that, paradoxically, looks considerably less radical than the old liberal formulations it sought to replace. To suppose the possibility of collective harmony is to ignore the obvious reasons why state institutions cannot wither away. It is also to whet expectations about the need for collective harmony, thereby encouraging (often unintentionally) the growth of authoritarian measures designed to eradicate disagreement and to enforce collective harmony. To envisage collective harmony is also to ignore the perennial need for mechanisms—such as the separation of state and social powers—that prevent the concentration and abuse of power. Finally, the supposition of collective harmony discourages consideration of the following kinds of questions about the institutional preconditions of democracy:

1. Assuming, with Macpherson, the absence of large-scale systems of privately owned property, what would be the appropriate role and scope of state, cooperative, and individual forms of property?
2. Would there be a role for market mechanisms—a question ruled out *a priori* by Macpherson's identification of "the market" with capitalism and possessive individualism—and, if so, how could their negative effects be controlled without instituting new forms of bureaucratic administration?
3. Would producers be free to choose their forms of work activity and to retrain themselves?
4. Would a citizen's basic income be provided unconditionally to all adult citizens?

Macpherson's postulate of the nonopposition of essentially human capacities rules out these important types of questions for democrats. It rests on the misleading assumption that the transition to democracy could take the form of a leap into the realm of freedom untroubled by problems of complexity and controversies over procedural rules. It presupposes, unrealistically, that democratic humanity would become generic humanity, cheerfully and harmoniously united in a world of pure self-government.

TECHNOLOGY AND SCARCITY

Macpherson's counterargument against this type of criticism is that actual or projected technological developments within mature capitalist societies require, and make possible, a postscarcity form of democracy in which, at long last, it would be feasible to discard the market concept of humanity as a mere aggregate of acquisitive, contentious individuals driven by "numberless wants" (Hume). According to Macpherson, scarcity was for millennia the universal human condition. He denied the insight, developed in recent anthropology, that societies of plenty existed prior to modernity.[29] According to Macpherson, there has always been scarcity, and until the rise of modern capitalism it had been generally assumed to be a permanent and irreversible phenomenon. However, three centuries ago, with the advent of market capitalism, the phenomenon of scarcity underwent a profound transformation of meaning. Liberal societies invented a new view of scarcity, supposing that the permanent condition of humanity is a condition of scarcity in relation to *unlimited desires*, both innate and acquired. Certainly, before the emergence of liberal market society, nobody assumed that unlimited desire was the natural and proper attribute of the human being. It is not to be found in the writings of Aristotle or Aquinas, Macpherson pointed out. The view that satisfactions are permanently scarce, because they are relative to infinite desire, appears only during seventeenth-century capitalist society. This decisive change is expressed in the writings of Hobbes and Locke. At the beginning of the nineteenth century, it is carried to its logical conclusion by James Mill, for whom the "grand covering law of human nature" was the insatiable desire of all individuals for power to render the persons and properties of others subservient to their pleasures. Paradoxically, then, the concept of scarcity came to predominate only as capitalist society set about overcoming it. Scarcity was manufactured by the very process of organizing to abolish it.

In the present period, Macpherson claimed, King Scarcity can be deposed. He directly contested Keynes's view that we must remain trapped in the dark tunnel of economic necessity for at least another century, relying in the meantime upon economic growth to bring us into the daylight of abundance and freedom at the end of this tunnel.[30] The extraordinary development of the contemporary productive forces— what Macpherson called "the technological revolution"—is a positive (if self-contradictory) process because it contains the potential to undermine the rationale for unlimited freedom of acquisition. Macpherson, no doubt, recognized that the technological multiplication of productivity forms part of a corporate strategy of producing new quantities of desires, and that this threatens the democratic potential of the technological revolution.[31] But the rejection of market morality and its false assumption that individuals are infinite consumers and appropriators nowadays becomes logically as well as technically possible. Unwittingly, the technological revolution—the discovery and application of new means of communication and energy production are just two examples—aids the goal of a revolution in democratic consciousness.

This brief summary of Macpherson's observations on scarcity should suffice to indicate that they fell squarely within the tradition of those progressives who trust in the development of the modern forces of production, and who criticize the capitalist mode of production only for its failed potential to abolish material scarcity and to facilitate the dismantling of all relationships of arbitrary rule and blind obedience. This position underpinned the old communist belief in capitalistic production as a potential basis for socialism—Fordism without Ford, in Trotsky's version—and today informs proposals, championed by some industrialists, technocrats, and state planners, to adopt nuclear power democratically and for peaceful ends. The most forceful version of this thesis is the classical Marxian thesis concerning the fettering of the forces of production by capitalist relations of production. Macpherson's formulations closely resemble this thesis. According to both Marx and Macpherson, it is not modern science, machinery, or technical methods which overwork and enslave their producers. Pauperization or (as Macpherson would have said) dehumanization is, rather, the consequence of the mode of social and political relations of power within which the nonliving forces of production are embedded. From this standpoint, the potential of the mature forces of production serves as a critical measure of the immaturity of the existing class-dominated relations of production. In capitalist society, the scientific-technical forces of production—the accumulated products of social labor—represent a historical triumph of the producing species over outer nature. The existing stock of science, machinery, and techniques of producing contains the potential to reduce radically the unfreedom of the working day and to increase the democratically associated producers' wealth and freedom. Released from compulsory labor, and no longer preoccupied with labor as a necessary means of acquiring commodities, individuals could think and act as enjoyers and developers of their human capacities.

Macpherson's claim about the political innocence of the capitalist forces of production—his assumption that actors could democratically take over and dispose freely of the productive forces they inherit—is questionable in several respects. Macpherson insisted that nonownership of property—the lack of free access to "materials to work on or work with"—is the chief external impediment to democratic individuation. Yet he never considered the ways in which the *restriction* of nonowners' powers was an organizing principle of the Fordist phase of industrial production during which he wrote. The bureaucratic structuring of scientific research and development, and public and private sector attempts to subject the labor process to the principles of Taylorism, illustrate how, despite workers' pressure from below, the material forces of production are often the medium and outcome of the managerial will to control and to manipulate employees, who are regarded as just another badly designed machine in need of constant repair or replacement. The extent to which this process of subordination could be undone by the present growth of flexible specialization and the disintegration of the old technological paradigm based on the assembly line system and continuous flow industries, remains unclear.[32]

Unfortunately, Macpherson's account of science, technology, and the labor process is of little help in clarifying this trend. Its trust in the productive forces—in what Macpherson called "the technological advances made by capitalism"—is too deep.[33] It simply assumes that democracy and technology can advance hand in hand. Moreover, that unexplained assumption suggests why Macpherson's argument fails to consider the anguishing possibility that the democratization of certain types of socially necessary work might be unwise if the overall political goal is to maximize individuals' freedom from the exigencies of production and consumption. It is true that the production of, say, telephones, buses, bicycles, or computers could be democratized, that is, subjected to decisions of the members or representatives of producer and consumer groups equipped with the latest means of circulating information. However, the reliance on democratic procedures in the production process might sometimes be inefficient and time-consuming. In order to shorten radically the quantity of time given over to socially necessary work—a condition of democracy in Macpherson's sense—these forms of production might be better organized within large-scale, centrally administered institutions. In that case, technology and democracy would come into conflict. The scope of democratic participation would need to be limited in certain spheres in order to maximize democratic participation elsewhere.[34]

These difficulties in Macpherson's theory of democracy and technology are compounded by his argument that scarcity can be fully overcome. When reading Macpherson, one is struck by his frequent allusions to the adage which Marx appropriated from St. Simon: in democratic society, the maxim "from each according to his abilities, to each according to his needs" will finally prevail. The belief that all individuals could receive according to their own particular and general needs led Macpherson to anticipate a society of plenitude, a fairy-tale world of luxury and abundance in which each member of society will have open access to the legendary magic table that caters to each of their culinary wishes. After exerting their uniquely human capacities, individuals would need only to say, "Table, set thyself" in order to be served a sumptuous and satisfying meal.

Macpherson's belief in the possibility of material abundance corresponds to the early modern idea of uninterrupted progress in the mastery and domination of outer nature. Today, this idea is obsolete for several reasons. For a start, Macpherson's formulations eclipse the problem of defining distributive justice and the institutional conditions necessary for its ongoing realization. The problem of who gets what, when, and how appears to wither away in Macpherson's democratic society. Material scarcity and satisfaction are presented as determinate states of being. Liberated from scarcity and basking in a sunny world of material plenitude, individuals could thus develop their human capacities freely, that is, without external hindrance. Macpherson's secret affinity with Marx resurfaces in this formulation. Given material abundance, it is argued, each and every individual would be able to satisfy his or her material needs without disagreements, disputes, or hand-to-hand struggles. This vision is dangerous and impossible, because—to repeat an earlier point—it is shaped by the unworkable myth of a future democratic society marked by the immediate reconciliation of all with each and of each with him- or herself. Undoubtedly, Macpherson refused to think of human needs as naturally given. Needs have an inescapable historical character.[35] They are always defined and contested by social actors within a given temporal and spatial framework. But if needs are subject to fluctuation through time and space, and if the vision of free individuals living contentedly in harmony is thereby mythical, then questions about distributive justice can never be suppressed. Whatever the state of the productive forces, there will always be controversies about how, when, and where to divide the divisible. The likelihood of such controversies also implies the need for institutional procedures—within and between state institutions and civil society—for democratically expressing and equitably resolving them.

Macpherson's embrace of the idea of infinite progress in the mastery of nature is suspect for another reason. He supposed that the submission of nature to human domination is a condition of the democratization of humanity. The highest ethic of democracy might be summarized thus: Treat individuals as human beings, that is, as self-moving ends in themselves—and nature as a thing, as the raw material or means of human self-realization. Today serious doubts about the anthropocentrism of this ethic are emerging.[36] There is evidence that nature's enforced submission to human powers of technological control is stimulating nature's revenge on humanity. Anxiety about the effects of environmental waste and degradation on human life in the next century is growing.

There are justified fears that certain key resources will be depleted, that toxic wastes will affect our health, and that climatic changes may occur. Consequently, the early modern problem of scarcity tends to be superseded by growing concern about the global problem of waste.

Arguments for a sustainable economy are a plausible (if tentative) response to this new priority.[37] Industrialized societies are said to be ecologically unsustainable because they debase their natural environments to the point of jeopardizing future patterns or standards of living. Sustainability is a threshold concept with normative implications. It warns that we are acting recklessly, as if there were no tomorrow *(après nous, le déluge).* It therefore points to the need for a type of postindustrial economy in which current consumption of biospheric resources would not reduce the opportunity of future generations to enjoy the same level of consumption. A sustainable economy would be based on intergenerational equality in the consumption of biospheric resources. It would institutionalize the principle that we inherit the world from our ancestors and borrow it from our offspring, thereby requiring us to produce and to consume environmental resources in less reckless ways, so that an equivalent level of environmental consumption would be available to those not yet born.

Although the principle of sustainability appears to take us far from Macpherson's defense of democracy, it draws us in fact to the heart of democratic politics. Macpherson's anthropocentrism naturally shielded his analysis against this important connection, which therefore needs to be spelled out in more detail. It is often claimed that sustainability requires a slow-down or outright cessation of growth, and that the consequent shift toward a steady-state or no-growth economy would result in harmony in the overall relationship between the biosphere and the processes of investment, technological change, production, and consumption. In practice, things cannot be so simple. The reduction of aggregate growth cannot underwrite automatically the production and consumption patterns of future generations. This is because the sustainable rate for materials extracted from and wastes discharged into the environment varies greatly from one case to another. In practice, sustainable rates must therefore be established for each particular resource. Here the difficulty is that the complexity of the biosphere and our ignorance of it ensure that the rates so established can take only the form of approximate and uncertain estimates. Such uncertainty is compounded by the fact that many rates of sustainability are dependent on each other and—most importantly—by the fact that sustainability is

129

concerned with future effects, which are, by definition, not yet knowable.

For these various reasons, estimates of environmental impact and acceptable limits of waste will always remain controversial. Sustainability cannot serve as an incontrovertible principle or Archimedean point upon which to base a postindustrial politics. Sustainability certainly cannot be guaranteed automatically by such institutional mechanisms as centralized state planning, social ownership, scientific expertise, the market, or (as some Green activists claim) small-scale organization and natural living. Both the scale and complexity of present-day environmental problems and the difficult task of shifting to sustainable patterns of growth confront us with massive risks.[38] The production, distribution, and definition of environmental risks are now for the first time becoming problematic on a global scale. Contrary to Macpherson, it is not only the threat of nuclear war which has rendered us all equal. Smog, water pollution, and radiation are equally leveling in their effects. Risks are neither geographically nor sociologically limited. They crisscross national boundaries and boomerang on rich and poor, the powerful and less powerful alike. They tend to devalue the economic and aesthetic value of property, as the death of entire forests shows. Many of the new environmental risks—from poisonous additives in foodstuffs to nuclear and chemical contaminants—are also invisible, in the sense that they elude human perception and, in certain cases, are detectible only in the offspring of those who are currently affected. The growing quantity of these environmental risks suggests that we are in the midst of a massive, long-term experiment with ourselves and our biospheric environment, and that our productive powers are as awesome as the obligation to exercise them prudently.

Pressured by these environmental risks, democratic procedures today have a renewed and wholly novel pertinence. In the past, democracy was justified in various ways. There was the utilitarian claim that democratic mechanisms guarantee that the best interpreters of interests—the interested parties themselves—can sift through various options and decide for themselves. Others (including Macpherson) insisted that democracy is justified by its ability to maximize freedom in the sense of individual or group autonomy. Still others viewed democracy as superior because it is the strongest antidote to the abuse of power. Each of these conventional arguments is flawed, and new justifications of democracy are badly needed. The risk-based argument sketched here promises one such justification. It cuts across the grain of the conventional argument that the most important feature of democratic procedures is that they enable the approval of decisions of interest to the whole collectivity, or at least to a majority of citizens.Instead, it suggests that democratic procedures also enable the public disapproval and revision of established agreements, and that for this reason they are uniquely suited to societies grappling with environmental risks. Democratic procedures are superior to all other types of decision making, not because they guarantee both a consensus and good decisions, but because they enable citizens who are affected by certain decisions to reconsider their judgments about the quality and consequences of these decisions. Democratic procedures increase the level of flexibility and reversibility of decision making. They encourage incremental learning and trial-and-error modification (or "muddling through") and that is why they are best suited to the task of publicly monitoring, controlling, and sometimes shutting down complex and tightly coupled high-risk projects and organizations, the failure of which (as in Bhopal, Three Mile Island, and Chernobyl) can have catastrophic ecological and social consequences.

Only democratic procedures can openly and fairly select certain types of dangers for public attention, carefully monitor them, and bring to heel those responsible for managing risky projects, thereby minimizing the possibility of error and reducing the chances of the big mistake. Democratic procedures are, for this reason, an essential corrective to the wishful belief in the therapeutic powers of unbridled technical expertise. Unchecked technocratic power, with its belief in the omnipotence and beneficence of scientific-technical progress, has been partly responsible for the rising incidence and severity of environmental problems. Current attempts by professional experts to monopolize the process of defining and reducing risks are therefore as implausible as the claim to infallibility of a pope who has recently converted to Protestantism. The belief in technocratic solutions is also dangerous, insofar as it can bolster the temptation to deal with environmental risks through *dirigiste* policies or by resorting to states of emergency. Democracy is an unrivalled remedy for technocratic delusions. It is an indispensable means of rendering accountable those politicians and entrepreneurs who turn a blind eye to the environmental damage and "normal accidents" (Perrow) that plague high-risk projects; and it renders accountable those professional experts who seek to define acceptable levels of risk by means of technical analyses of probability—or simply by falling back on the childish solipsism that whatever isn't believed couldn't possibly be harmful.

131

JOHN KEANE

Unfortunately, Macpherson never pursued this unusual type of defense of democratic politics. Preferring to view democracy substantively, he clung to the neo-romantic notion that the peaceful emancipation of self-determining individuals is ethically and practically desirable. He therefore did not see that a great advance of democracy is that it is a type of decision-making procedure which enables its participants to monitor their own decisions. Democracy is a self-reflexive means of controlling the exercise of power. It is an indispensable weapon in the fight to question, restrict, and to dissolve arbitrary power, and for this reason a bad democracy is always better than a good dictatorship. That lesson is the unintended fruit of C. B. Macpherson's lifelong attempt to keep alive the democratic imagination. For provoking that insight, we should forever be grateful to him.

NOTES

1. The critical literature on Macpherson is vast. The most influential types of criticisms summarized here are to be found in I. Berlin, "Hobbes, Locke, and Professor Macpherson," *Political Quarterly* 35 (1964): 444-68; J. G. A. Pocock, "The Myth of John Locke and the Obsession with Liberalism," in J. G. A. Pocock and Richard Ashcraft, eds., *John Locke* (Los Angeles: University of California Press, 1980); J. Dunn, "Democracy Unretrieved, or the Political Theory of Professor Macpherson," *British Journal of Political Science* 4 (1974): 489-99; S. Lukes, "The Real and Ideal Worlds of Democracy," in A. Kontos, *Powers, Possessions and Freedom: Essays in Honour of C. B. Macpherson* (Toronto: University of Toronto Press, 1979); Andrew Levine, "The Political Theory of Social Democracy," *Canadian Journal of Philosophy* 6, no. 2 (June 1976): 191-93; and Ellen Meiksins Wood, "C. B. Macpherson: Liberalism and the Task of Socialist Political Theory," in *The Socialist Register* (London: Merlin Press, 1978), 215-40.

2. The most important of these essays are "The Meaning of Economic Democracy," *University of Toronto Quarterly* 9 (1942): 403-20; "The History of Political Ideas," *Canadian Journal of Economics and Political Science* 7, no. 4 (November 1941): 576-77; and "The Position of Political Science," *Culture* 3 (1942): 457.

3. *Democratic Theory: Essays in Retrieval* (Oxford: Oxford University Press, 1973), 184 (hereafter cited as *DT*).

4. Victor Svacek, "The Elusive Marxism of C. B. Macpherson," *Canadian Journal of Political Science* 9 (1976): 395-422.

5. *The Political Theory of Possessive Individualism: Hobbes to Locke* (Oxford: Oxford University Press, 1962), 2 (hereafter cited as *PTPI*).

6. See my "More Theses on the Philosophy of History," in *Meaning and*

Context: Quentin Skinner and His Critics, ed. James Tully (Cambridge: Polity Press, 1988), 204-17.

7. *The Life and Times of Liberal Democracy* (Oxford: Oxford University Press, 1977), 2-9 (hereafter cited as *LTLD*); cf. *PTPJ,* 4-8, 46-49.

8. See "More Theses on the Philosophy of History," cited in n. 6.

9. *DT,* 24-38.

10. C. B. Macpherson, ed., *Property: Mainstream and Critical Positions* (Toronto and Buffalo: University of Toronto Press, 1978), chaps. 1, 12.

11. Isaiah Berlin, *Four Essays on Liberty* (Oxford: Oxford University Press, 1969). Macpherson's critique of Berlin and his attempt to develop the distinction between "counterextractive" and "developmental" liberties are to be found in *DT,* 95-119.

12. *The Real World of Democracy* (Oxford: Oxford University Press, 1966), 58 (hereafter cited as *RWD*).

13. *DT,* essay 1.

14. This problem is evident within most recent contributions to democratic theory, in which the desirability of democracy is simply taken for granted. See, for example, Robert A. Dahl, *Dilemmas of Pluralist Democracy: Autonomy versus Control* (New Haven and London: Yale University Press, 1982), 2, 7.

15. "The Modern Democratic Revolution: Reflections on Jean-François Lyotard's *La condition postmoderne,*" *Chicago Review* 35, no. 4 (1987): 4-19; *Democracy and Civil Society* (London and New York: Verso, 1988), essay 7; and John Keane, "Democracy and the Media—Without Foundations," *Political Studies* 40 (1992): 116-29.

16. Cf. my "Democracy and the Theory of Ideology," in John Keane, ed., *Power/Ideology,* a special issue of the *Canadian Journal of Political and Social Theory* 7, nos. 1-2 (Hiver/Printemps 1983): 5-17.

17. This view is evident in Richard Rorty's *Philosophy and the Mirror of Nature* (Oxford: Basil Blackwell, 1980). Aside from its failure to deal with the type of counterfactual reasoning sketched here, the conversational model fails to acknowledge the need to mobilize against eschatological or totalitarian political solutions and methods, to which (as Claude Lefort has pointed out in *L'Invention démocratique* [Paris: Fayard, 1982]) modern societies are prone constantly because of their self-revolutionizing, quasi-democratic organizing principles.

18. This strategy is well summarized in "The Economic Penetration of Political Theory: Some Hypotheses," *Journal of the History of Ideas* 39 (1978): 101; and in "Humanist Democracy and Elusive Marxism," *Canadian Journal of Political Science* 9, no. 3 (September 1976): 423: ". . . what I have been trying to do all along (and am still trying to do) . . . is to work out a revision of liberal-democratic theory, a revision which clearly owes a good deal to Marx, in the hope of making that theory more democratic while rescuing that valuable part of the liberal tradition which is submerged when liberalism is identified with capitalist market relations."

19. For example, *PTPI,* 3.

20. Ibid.

21. In relation to modern contract theory and the theme of civil society and the state, I first argued this point in *Public Life and Late Capitalism* (Cambridge and New York: Cambridge University Press, 1984), essay 7. The general objection raised in this paragraph is summarized well by Norberto Bobbio, *Politica e cultura* (Torino: Il Mulino, 1955), 278: "It is simple to reject liberalism when it is identified with a theory or practice of freedom, understood as the power of the bourgeoisie. It is much more difficult, however, to reject liberalism when it is considered as the theory and practice of limiting the power of the state ... because freedom, understood as the power to do something, interests those fortunate enough to possess it, whereas freedom as the absence of restraint interests all humanity."

22. See Harold Laski, *The Rise of European Liberalism* (London: Penguin, 1962). A similar argument is developed in Anthony Arblaster, *The Rise and Decline of Western Liberalism* (Oxford: Basil Blackwell, 1984).

23. See my "Power, Legitimacy, and the Fate of Liberal Contract Theory," *Praxis International* 2, no. 3 (October 1982): 294-96.

24. *RWD,* chap. 2; cf. *DT,* 35-36, where the "different notion of democracy" defended by state socialist regimes is viewed as part of "the increasingly democratic temper of the world as a whole."

25. *PTPI,* 271-77.

26. Ibid., 276. Macpherson's concern with the nuclear weapons buildup is also in evidence in "Reluctant Duelists? Nuclear Arms for Canada: A Strong Case Examined," *Our Generation against Nuclear War* 2 (1962): 7-14; "Positive Neutralism for Canada?" *Commentator* 7 (1963): 9-11; and "Beyond the Nuclear Arms Issue," *Canadian Dimension,* Dec.-Jan. 1963/64, 14-16.

27. *Democracy in Alberta: Social Credit and the Party System* (Toronto: University of Toronto Press, 1953), 245: " ... the more homogeneous a society is, the less likely is the government to be regarded as a natural enemy. At the theoretical extreme of a society without class division, and with popular franchise, the people would regard the state's purposes as their own. ... Only in such a society is it possible to think of a general will sustaining a democracy without alternate parties."

28. *DT,* 54-55, 74.

29. Marshall Sahlins, *Stone Age Economics* (Chicago: University of Chicago Press, 1972); and Pierre Clastres, *Society Against the State* (Oxford: Basil Blackwell, 1977).

30. J. M. Keynes, *Essays in Persuasion* (London, 1932), 369-72; cf. *RWD,* 63ff.

31. *DT,* 25, 36-38.

32. See, for example, Alain Lipietz, *La croisée des chemins. Une alternative pour le XXIᵉ siècle* (Paris: Gallimard, 1989); David Wolfe, *Politics in the Information Age* (forthcoming); Christopher Freeman, "Keynes or Kondratiev? How can

we get back to full employment?" in P. Marstrand, ed., *New Technology and the Future of Work and Skills* (London: Frances Pinter); Michael Piore and Charles Sabel, *The Second Industrial Divide* (New York: Princeton University Press, 1985); and John Keane and John Owens, *After Full Employment* (London: Hutchinson, 1986).

33. *RWD*, 80.

34. See John Keane and John Owens, *After Full Employment*, cited n. 32.

35. "Needs and Wants: An Ontological or Historical Problem?" in Ross Fitzgerald, ed., *Human Needs and Politics* (Sydney: University of Sydney Press, 1977), 26-35; "Second and Third Thoughts on Needs and Wants," *Canadian Journal of Political and Social Theory* 3 (1979): 46-49.

36. Several aspects of the problematic relationship between democracy and the environment are discussed in my *Public Life and Late Capitalism,* essay 6, and *The Media and Democracy* (Oxford and Boston: Basil Blackwell, 1991), 164-93.

37. See R. K. Turner, ed. *Sustainable Environmental Management: Principles and Practice* (London: Routledge, 1988); and "The World Commission on Environment and Development," in *Our Common Future* (Oxford: Oxford University Press, 1987).

38. Ulrich Beck, *Risikogesellschaft—Auf den Weg in eine andere Moderne* (Frankfurt am Main: Suhrkamp, 1986), and *Gegengifte—Die organisierte Unverantwortlichkeit* (Frankfurt am Main: Suhrkamp, 1989).

39. See my "Democracy and the Decline of the Left," in Norberto Bobbio, *Dictatorship and Democracy* (Cambridge: Polity Press, 1989); the critique of foundationalist arguments for democracy in *Democracy and Civil Society,* 213-45; *The Media and Democracy;* and in "What's Left of What's Left?" *Times Literary Supplement* no. 4,603 (21 June 1991): 7-8.

Chapter 6
Freedom and Feminism

Virginia Held

There are many ways in which feminists share the perceptions and concerns of C. B. Macpherson. There are other ways in which his vision of a free, just, and democratic society leaves out much of what feminists have recently shown will be needed for women to be full participants and equal members of such a society. But the issues for feminists, in assessing Macpherson's legacy, are not only ones of omission; those issues could be handled by adding to his proposals some further appropriate ones. There are some ways in which recent feminist theory raises questions about certain of Macpherson's basic assumptions and categories at levels as fundamental as Macpherson's own doubts about the liberal tradition of possessive individualism.

In this chapter, I present some feminist concerns about the adequacy of Macpherson's criticisms of liberal democracy and his proposals for social change. In doing so, I emphasize how deep can be any feminist's appreciation of what Macpherson has contributed to furthering goals that we share with him. His analyses have been and can still be of enormous value to the feminist project, and, if I focus on our differences, it is only to contribute to further progress, not to decrease esteem for

137

Macpherson's legacy. His work has been for me, and I hope for many other feminists, of lasting importance.

Another preliminary clarification of intent that I wish to make is that, of course, I cannot present *the* feminist position on the issues that I shall discuss. At the moment feminism is a flourishing source of theory and practice. It is producing many different—and not always compatible —theories and suggesting a number of alternative approaches to social change. As Alison Jaggar points out, all feminists share the goal of over-coming the oppression of women, but we often disagree about the major cause of that oppression and about what should be done to end it.[1] These disagreements are part of a lively and healthy dialogue, one which is a remarkably cooperative exploration, not the internecine strife often hoped for by feminism's opponents. But they make clear that no feminist can speak for all. There is a growing awareness that we cannot talk about "women's experience" without qualifying our claims with respect to race, class, ethnic identity, sexual orientation, location in the global framework, etc. We are becoming more careful to make such qualifications and to listen to and to hear women who are not included in our own perspectives.

I suggest, then, what *some* feminists may think and feel about Macpherson's work, and I focus especially on his discussion of freedom.

FREEDOM AND SELF-DEVELOPMENT

For Macpherson, any adequate theory of democracy for our times must be a theory of society, not of merely political procedures. He argued for democracy as committed to maximizing the developmental powers of human beings—that is, their powers to fully develop their human capacities. He well understood that, for such democracy to exist, people would have to have access to what they need for human development. The principle that ought to guide democratic institutions, Macpherson asserted, is that "everyone ought to be able to make the most of himself, or make the best of himself."[2] On this conception, developing one's capacities includes the capacity for materially productive labor, but it includes much more. It sees a human being as "essentially a doer, a creator, an exerter of energy, an actor."[3] Macpherson also does not lose sight of the ways in which human beings are not necessarily the insatiably possessive individuals of classical liberal theory.

Feminists can admire and share Macpherson's emphasis on the

possibilities of increasing the developmental power of people, because this kind of power is not the zero-sum power-over-others of standard liberal theory, but a kind of power such that more for one person is compatible with more for any other. Macpherson acknowledges that this may be an optimistic view of human beings, but he sees their contentiousness as historically conditioned rather than essential. It is an optimism many feminists share.[4]

Macpherson's understanding of what it means to live as a free person has enabled him to argue eloquently that a person cannot be free without the means to live and work and act. Feminist views of liberation appreciate these understandings. The experience of women makes clear, for many who might otherwise fail to see it, how unsatisfactory is a conception of freedom that does not include access to the means to be free. Clearly, freedom from interference with our possession of property and our exercise of our rights cannot provide the liberation women seek if we have no property and are unable to acquire the means to live and to act and to feed our children.

Liberation is unmistakably connected with freedom. Thus, we can argue from one to the other in ways in which a concern with welfare or well-being may not allow. Liberation also requires that the means to be free be understood as an aspect of *freedom,* not only of welfare, or of separate preconditions for the enjoyment of freedom.[5] If freedom is separated from the means for its exercise, and if freedom is thought to have priority over other considerations, as it is in many theories and judgments, then the claims of those lacking the resources to live and to act freely will always have to yield to the claims of those already in possession of such resources, which are claims to freedom from interference with their enjoyment of the rights to property. The argument that the rights of those with property to freedom from interference must not be infringed for the sake of the welfare of those without property has been the bulwark—lately in libertarian guise—upholding the advantages of the advantaged. Women's experience of unfreedom can make a powerful contribution to arguments exposing the realities of who gains and who loses from such questionable construals of freedom. In this aspect, women's experience also upholds Macpherson's insistence that for a society to be one worthy of the name "free," it must assure its citizens access to the means to live and to labor.

I have disagreed with Macpherson's acceptance at the more strictly definitional level of freedom as negative only, as freedom from interference, freedom from external impediments.[6] Because he includes within the category of impediments the lack of resources needed to live and to act, he, of course, avoids the conclusion that a libertarian reaches with this analysis, and he argues forcefully for overcoming the "lacks" that prevent so many in capitalist society from being free and full participants in democratic life. However, it seems unduly awkward to me to construe such lacks as "impediments." I have found Gerald Mac-Callum's analysis to be persuasive, and I accept the view that freedom is a triadic relation in which we are free *from* x *to do* y.[7] We should be as concerned with the capacities and enablements that make us free *to do* what we choose as with the interferences that restrain us. Although he fits his concerns into the language of interferences, Macpherson agrees, and in one sense it matters less how we describe interferences and capacities than what they amount to in terms of social theory. In another sense, however, the definitional issues are important.

Macpherson calls attention to the ways in which a person can be incapacitated. In his discussion of how power is to be measured in terms of absence of impediments, he considers what are to count as impediments, and specifies three types of them:

1. Lack of adequate means of life, which includes the "material prerequisites for his taking part in the life of the community, whatever the level of its culture may be."[8]
2. Lack of access to the means of labor.
3. Lack of protection against invasion by others.

Because the third type of impediment can be removed by guaranteeing the civil liberties of traditional liberal theory, it is with the first two that Macpherson is primarily concerned. He answers such objections as that which notes that if the development of human capacities is infinitely great, the task of removing obstacles to this development would be insuperable. He argues that the material prerequisites of such development are not infinitely great, and are in fact within the capacity of democratic industrialized society to provide, in his view. As for the means of labor, the continuous transfer of powers from the non-owners of capital to owners that occurs in capitalist market societies can be ended, so that gains in productivity and in leisure can be used to enable all members to develop their capacities.

With such criticisms as these of existing arrangements that make it unduly difficult for women to acquire what they need to live and to develop, many feminists largely agree. Where a feminist might depart from Macpherson's view is in assessing the major requirements for what would be considered the absence of impediments or presence of empowerment. Macpherson sees the problems of existing systems that fail to offer the kind of democracy he advocates as problems caused by the ways in which such systems allow unjustified and unnecessary interferences with individuals' development. As we have seen, he writes of some having been stunted by "external impediments," and of the type of society he advocates as offering conditions in which such impediments would be removed. The images he uses are always of inner capacities in place, although their development may be thwarted by external conditions. He well recognizes that lack of access to the means to feed and shelter oneself will constitute such an external impediment. But he does not call attention to a range of problems that must be addressed if women are to be able to develop our capacities. To construe the lacks on which he does focus as "impediments" may further complicate the task of conceptualizing the components of freedom and democracy for women.

WOMEN AND EMPOWERMENT

Consider the discussion in a recent book by Sandra Bartky of a kind of disability that, at least under social conditions so far and in a given society, women are more apt to suffer than men: shame. Bartky considers the shame of embodiment attendant on women's sense of being a spectacle, of being continually on display, but she is concerned in this paper with a less specific type of shame. "This shame," she writes, "is manifest in a pervasive sense of personal inadequacy that, like the shame of embodiment, is profoundly disempowering; both reveal the 'generalized condition of dishonor'[9] which is woman's lot in sexist society."[10] She further characterizes this shame as "the distressed apprehension of the self as inadequate or diminished."[11]

In contrast with guilt that one may feel for one's actions, shame is felt for shortcomings rather than wrongdoings, and, for some, shame may be felt routinely rather than from a particular diminishment on a particular occasion. Shame, in Bartky's analysis, is a type of psychic distress occasioned by the "apprehension of oneself as a lesser creature."[12]

Bartky examines the "affective taste, the emotional coloration" of the traits which textbooks in the psychology of women report to be characteristic of women: lower self-esteem, less overall confidence, poorer self-concepts, as measured by women's beliefs and dispositions. She cites a variety of empirical observations confirming that women experience such disempowering feelings as shame more than men. Her discussion offers grounds for believing that "women typically are more shame-prone than men, that shame is not so much a particular feeling or emotion (though it involves specific feelings and emotions) as a pervasive affective attunement to the social environment, that women's shame is more than merely an effect of subordination but, within the larger universe of patriarchal social relations, a profound mode of disclosure both of self and situation."[13]

Bartky probes with care and insight the ways in which this affective attunement is disempowering. She writes, "The heightened self-consciousness that comes with emotions of self-assessment may become, in the shame of the oppressed, a stagnant self-obsession. Or shame may generate a rage whose expression is unconstructive, even self-destructive. In all these ways, shame is profoundly disempowering. The need for secrecy and concealment that figures so largely in the shame experience is disempowering as well, for it isolates the oppressed from one another and in this way works against the emergence of a sense of solidarity."[14]

What are the implications of such observations and reflections? Certainly such obstacles as a college climate in which instructors use sexist humor, or a dismissive tone of voice toward women, must be removed.[15] Certainly, the well-documented tendencies of men to interrupt women more than women interrupt men must also be made visible and corrected. These are not external impediments noticed by Macpherson, but they can be added, perhaps, to his list. However, it seems inadequate to think here primarily in terms of the removal of external impediments, especially of the type on which Macpherson focuses. Although removing such obstacles as the inability to find employment is certainly essential, it will be nowhere near enough to enable women to achieve such inner empowerment as provided by a sense of self-worth. The self-development of women involves changing the effective tastes and the emotional coloration with which we experience the world, not merely the outer obstacles in that experience. Doing so will require not that women learn to interrupt men as often as men interrupt women, or that women become as aggressive, assertive, or overconfident as male norms prescribe for men, but that women and men develop mutually respectful and shared practices of conversation and behavior, as well as mutually considerate and caring emotional relations.

Consider, next, a different kind of transfer of power than the one Macpherson examines. Macpherson enlightens us on how the transfer of power from non-owners of capital to owners conflicts with the principles of democracy. But consider the transfer of power in what Ann Ferguson and Nancy Folbre call "sex-affective production." In exploring the ways in which Marxist views of production and reproduction must be reconceptualized from a feminist point of view, Ferguson and Folbre focus their attention on the production of all that is required for childbearing, child rearing, and "the fulfillment of human needs for affection, nurturance, and sexual expression."[16] They discuss the ways in which women have been oppressed by a division of labor that demands that most of the requirements and responsibilities of sex-affective production are met by women. Women are socialized into a gender identity such that their sense of identity "keeps them willing to give more than they receive from men in nurturance and sexual satisfaction."[17] The division of labor that provides that the burdens of sex-affective production fall more heavily on women than on men is not a neutral division that assigns separate-but-equal roles. It is a division based on inequality and is upheld by social relations of domination that oppress women.

If we use Macpherson's category of extractive power,[18] we might say that men have employed extractive power to exploit women. We might also say that women have had to enter into unequal relations with men in which we have routinely given more affection to men than we have received, and in which we have devoted far more time and energy—to say nothing of far more of the caring concern that can drain the giver— to the mutual project of having and raising children. But again, it seems inadequate to think largely in terms of the removal of external impediments, especially of the kind focused upon by Macpherson. Of course, without the means to live, women will be unable to achieve any measure of self-development. But the means are as fundamentally necessary for the development of our children as for the development of women, and they are necessary in ways that contribute to, rather than disrupt, the relationships between all of us. To overcome the imbalance in "sex-affective production" between men and women, an almost complete reconstitution of relations between women and men will have to occur.

Access to the means of labor in the sense in which Macpherson has called for it is an important component, but only a component. As has often been noted, even when women work at paid jobs outside the home as long and as hard as do men, women routinely do a far larger share of the housework and child-care. Not only do women have less actual leisure, but concerns about whether a child is ill or in danger, or whether outside child-care arrangements are adequate, are more frequently present in women's minds, and more disempowering. These new relationships between women and men will also be inadequate if they merely cause women to be as concerned as men with their own unique (and essentially individualistic) self-development. The relations must be ones of mutual caring and concern, as well as of respect and noninterference.

In some of his later essays, Macpherson does consider the exploitation which women have suffered, and the difficulties women and various other groups will have in achieving full participation in Western liberal democracies.[19] Their primary difficulty, as he sees it, is that they cannot withhold services vital to the functioning of the economy. In discussing theorists of the seventeenth through nineteenth centuries, he explains why he thinks women were not a class: although women were exploited by a male-dominated society, this was, he holds, the result of legal arrangements akin to feudal ones rather than the results of the capitalist market relations that were determinative of class.[20] However, he has little to say about how gender domination may be determinative of obstacles to self-development once such feudal legal impediments are removed, or of how liberation from gender oppression may involve factors that can only be understood at the level of internal affect and self-perception. Macpherson does not contribute to our understanding of how transforming gender relations may be a project as fundamental as—or, as many feminists believe, even more fundamental than—transforming relations between the owners of capital and those who must sell their labor. He considers how the latter transformation might involve changed personalities and aspirations. "Man as maximizing consumer" would be replaced by "man as exerter and developer of his human capacities."[21] However, there is no indication of the sorts of comparable transformations that would be needed in gender characteristics and aims to overcome the oppression of women.

Macpherson briefly considers the question of "internalized impediments," the phenomenon of "men hugging their chains," or becoming "slaves of their own possessions."[22] He acknowledges that his recommendations for judging how impediments are to be reduced has dealt entirely with external impediments. His response to possible criticism along these lines is to suggest that the impediments "were external before they were internalized," and to hope that the gradual reduction of external impediments will contribute to a reciprocal "breakthrough of consciousness."[23] But this can hardly be an adequate suggestion for handling the sorts of considerations that a feminist view of the requirements for liberation brings to light. It has been no accident that, repeatedly, and in one context after another, "consciousness-raising" has been the beginning of feminist actions, not the by-product. This does not mean that consciousness-raising is a solitary flash of awareness. Although it can be that, it is typically a shared and participatory practice. But it involves changing internal ways of thinking and feeling. What this changed consciousness first affects seem to be the internal springs of empowerment, even before any external expression of resistance or exercise of power is possible, and certainly before the external impediments have actually been removed or even reduced. The power to give voice to one's aspiration to be heard is not so much the removal of an external impediment as the beginning of internal empowerment. The latter fits awkwardly into Macpherson's analysis, yet it is an essential component of feminist theory and practice.

A truly democratic society, in Macpherson's view, will require equal access to the means of life and the means of labor, which will require an end of class inequalities.[24] While feminists often share this view of one set of needed changes, they also point out that the end of class inequalities may leave gender inequalities relatively intact. That racial antagonisms may also outflank a diminishment of class conflict has also been demonstrated.

Further, Macpherson's account of how class inequalities might be overcome does not provide the insights needed to grasp the more subtle forms of capitalist hegemony—the ways, for instance, in which media images of the rich and famous turn aspirations, as well as false hopes of reaching them, into greater and more resilient obstacles than are usually recognized. This is an enormous topic to which, in my view, social philosophers should pay far more attention than they have. I have begun to consider it in a number of papers, but will not do so further here.[25] In any case, it seems even clearer in the case of gender inequalities than in the case of class inequalities that a focus on the external impediments which Macpherson examines can hardly be adequate for understanding oppression and how it might be overcome.

What we can conclude, then, is that the range of what must be attended to in removing obstacles to self-development must be greatly expanded beyond that of Macpherson. It must include many false images and distorted feelings by which oppressed persons are disempowered. It must also include many lacks which women suffer as women, not only as members of a class from whom, as Macpherson explains it, power is extracted by the owners of capital. We can conclude, in addition, that the revisions in Macpherson's view must go deeper still, so that attention is paid much more explicitly and fully to how the provisions of internal empowerments is to proceed. The removal of external obstacles—even when the range of the latter has been expanded appropriately—is surely part of the process, but the process may be vitiated by inattention to other parts.

THE PERSONS OF DEMOCRATIC SOCIETIES

Let's turn now to another question: What kinds of beings are those for whom full development and making the best of themselves is to be facilitated by social arrangements? Macpherson argues convincingly that they need not be the insatiable consumers or the egoistic economic agents of traditional liberal theory. But does he see these persons in ways that coincide with feminist views of persons?

In his discussion of how our concepts of property ought to be revised, he argues for rights to property as rights of access to the means of life and labor, and as rights not to be excluded. "The concept of property," he writes, "as solely private property, the right to exclude others from some use or benefit of something, which is already a concept of individual right to a revenue, will have to be broadened to include property as an individual right not to be excluded from the use or benefit of the accumulated productive resources of the whole society.[26] He recognizes the ways in which the productive resources of a society should be thought of as collective and socially achieved capacities to provide persons with what they need, not as the mere privately and individually owned results of individual efforts and transactions. The rights of access to the means of life and labor should, in his view, be assured by new conceptions of property and adequate understandings of the kinds of institutions needed for such rights to be protected in a truly democratic society. However, these rights remain, for Macpherson, individual rights. Those who are to be the bearers of these rights, while not merely consumers and egoists, are still individuals of a fairly isolated kind conceptually. Their self-development is not seen as intimately tied to the development of any other persons. Macpherson's requirement is only that the development of any one individual not be at the expense of any other. The power of a person is measured by an absence of impediment to his or her individual development. The class-less society sought by Macpherson will free individuals from the impediments which they now suffer as a result of their membership in an exploited class. Once freed from class membership, however, they will not be defined inherently by any other social group or by ties to any other persons.

From the point of view of much feminist theory, this degree of individual isolation is rather suspect. Even if the oppression brought about by class divisions would be a thing of the past, and even if gender domination would be overcome, we would all still be persons with ties to other persons. We would still be at least partly constituted by such connections; they would be part of what we are as persons. For instance, we would still be the daughter or son of given parents, and probably the mother or father of given children. We would still have racial or ethnic or other ties that, at least in part, would make us the persons we would be. If we look, for instance, at the realities of the relation between the mothering person (who can be male or female) and the child, we can see that what we value in the relation cannot be broken down into individual gains and losses for the individual members in the relation. Self-development apart from the relation may be much less important than the satisfactory development of the relation. What matters may often be the health, the growth, and the development of the relation and its members in ways that cannot be understood in the individualistic terms of the liberal tradition, even as reinterpreted by Macpherson. His individualism is the individualism of John Stuart Mill rather than that of Hobbes or Bentham. However, it still seems little touched by the types of feminist doubts to which I have referred.[27]

Of course, the objection may be raised that such intimate relations are irrelevant for the construction of democratic society or of the "public" institutions with which Macpherson and the traditions of political and social theory have been concerned. Yet this is where feminist theory may most importantly depart from traditional political and social theory, whether liberal or other. Feminist theory insists on reconsidering the concept of the person that is to enter into the public life of government or economic activity. There are not two separate

147

entities here—a public or working person, and a private person. There is only one person, involved in and affected by both public and private social reality, however they might be understood. If we must rethink the liberal concept of *person* to acknowledge how artificial and male-biased is the individual of classical liberal theory, who springs full-blown out of nowhere into a self-sufficiency from which the individual considers entering into social relations, then, of course, we must rethink the social and political theory built around this concept of *person*. Also, if we must rethink the concept of the *person* who sells his or her labor—recognizing that it, too, has been constructed without adequate regard for the labor of those who have created, brought up, and continue to care for this worker—then again, we must also rethink the social and political theory built around this concept of *person*.

Feminist theory asks why the relationships between people in what has mistakenly been relegated to a "private" sphere beyond "public" concern should not be considered in the construction of broader social arrangements. Certainly we reject arguing from the patriarchal family to the patriarchal, monarch-headed society, or to a paternalistic workplace. Certainly we can agree that Locke's vision represented progress over Filmer's and that Marx's represented progress over Locke's. But if we look at the postpatriarchal relations of care and concern that we expect to be possible in family relationships—or in relationships among friends—it is not unreasonable to suggest that some perhaps weaker, but still analogous, versions of these should characterize social relations generally.[29] In place of the development of individual powers that, at best, do not diminish the powers of others—the sort of self-development at which Macpherson's democracy would aim—we might aspire to the development of social relations, relations of trust for instance.[30] Or relations of care and concern, of mutually appreciated expression, of shared enjoyment. It is not at all utopian to consider the sorts of political and social institutions that can foster such relations—and they might be rather different from those that Macpherson would recommend—those that would, in his words, "maximize men's developmental powers."[31]

Macpherson does consider how "membership in a national or cultural community which has defined itself historically is part of what it means to be human," and how "the right to national self-determination may be humanly more important to its claimants than any of the individual rights" on the usual lists of human rights.[32] However, he does not pursue this challenge to his own notions of individual self-development. The difficulties which the latter—and individual human rights—are bound to encounter with a capitalist economic system are, for him, problems enough.

In *The Life and Times of Liberal Democracy,* he briefly considers how participatory democracy "brings with it a sense of community," and how "the enjoyment and development of one's capacities is to be done for the most part in conjunction with others, in some relation of community."[33] Yet he immediately moves on to the vicious circle in which we seem to be: "We cannot achieve more democratic participation without a prior change in social inequality and in consciousness [away from man as maximizing consumer] but we cannot achieve the changes in social inequality and consciousness without a prior increase in democratic participation."[34]

He then examines where loopholes may occur, and how roadblocks to participation may be reduced. No version of participatory democracy could develop or, in his view, last without a strong commitment to "the equal right of every man and woman to the full development and use of his or her capacities."[35] It is this conception of self-development that remains at the heart of Macpherson's hopes for the future.

As I interpret him, Macpherson values collective enterprises only instrumentally, and in terms of the contribution they may make to individual self-development. If individual self-development includes a need or desire to work cooperatively with others, institutions should fully permit such activity. However, there seems to me to be no way, on Macpherson's scales, to appreciate the value of shared, relational activity in itself.

Certainly a society should resist excessive collectivism. It should not promote shared feelings and activities at the expense of all privacy and unshared self-development. But we ought to be able to evaluate how a society is doing at both levels—that is, in terms of both the fostering of social trust and shared concern for community projects, and the fostering of individual self-development. Macpherson has a much more satisfactory view of the latter than has most of the liberal tradition. But his ontology and his ethics seem to make little room for the former.

SHARED EXPERIENCE

Let us consider these issues in a different domain than that of the family—namely, the domain of expression. Clearly, the developmental power of someone who learns to play a musical instrument better, and to play more songs, can be increased without decreasing the developmental powers of anyone else, once the material needs of the expression —the instrument, the leisure, music lessons, and the like—have been made possible. Macpherson would emphasize that, for many activities, providing such material means would not be especially difficult, and individuals can gain great satisfaction from such pursuits in place of the market contests which require that for some to be winners, others must be losers. Now consider the difference between playing music as an expression of individual achievement, and playing music as a social, shared activity. On Macpherson's view of self-development, we would have no reason to value an experience of shared enjoyment, as when those who listen to a song are moved by it or participate in singing in addition to the experience of an individual demonstrating to his satisfaction and on his own criteria that he has mastered a given level of difficulty. While we may hesitate to subscribe to any general claim that shared aesthetic experiences are always, or even in general, to be preferred to individualistic ones, it does seem that social arrangements which foster interpersonal, intergroup, intercultural aesthetic experiences may be worth striving for, and that they cannot be evaluated in terms that measure only the development of expressive monads.

This is not to deny that much artistic creation is a lonely task. The point here is about the wide range of cultural experiences engaged in by anyone or everyone. Even if it is not intuitively clear whether shared cultural experiences that foster relationships of trust or concern between persons, or whether more purely individualistic cultural experiences are of greater value, we can recognize that the former can have value not reducible to the latter. Not all shared cultural experiences are morally admirable. Many express nationalistic xenophobia, racial intolerance, or sexist reaction. However, many others express care and concern among persons, and nourish the bases for social trust. It certainly makes sense to evaluate shared cultural experiences and to ask what social arrangements should be developed or maintained to foster morally admirable forms of such experiences.

A serious shortcoming of Macpherson's ideal of democracy is that with it, as with traditional liberal theory, the adequate evaluation of shared experience and of collective endeavors is impossible. Only if the shared experience or the collective endeavor would contribute to the maximization of individual self-development would it be, on Macpherson's account, of value. This seems misguided. Even if we hesitate to compare shared, collective progress with individual self-development, or reject a comparison ascribing greater value to either, we should at least be able to ask of a social theory that it ascribe appropriate values to social relationships between persons in ways distinct from its evaluations of gains and losses to individuals in isolation from one another.

Some will suggest, of course, that neutral political institutions should permit but not promote such shared aesthetic experiences as those to which I have alluded, and that it is no proper function of government to take sides about what may be thought to be alternative conceptions of the good life.[36] But if this conception of government in fact leads to a privatization of activity and to individualistic persons pursuing private gains, while such shared concerns as schools, parks, transportation systems, protection of the environment, and public culture become increasingly impoverished, then institutions built on this conception of government must be evaluated on these grounds among others.

FEMINIST MORAL THEORY AND ITS IMPLICATIONS

Ever since the psychological studies made by Carol Gilligan and others suggested that women tend to interpret moral problems somewhat differently from the way men tend to interpret them, feminist moral philosophers have found apparent empirical support for what many have supposed: that feminist moral theory will be significantly different from nonfeminist moral theory.[37] While a consensus is not yet possible, and while we should all be keenly on guard against the misuses to which claims of difference have traditionally been put, it nevertheless seems likely that feminism will require a fundamental transformation of moral theory, as well as of social, political, economic, and legal theory. From a feminist point of view, radical changes are needed in, for instance, our standard conceptions of reason and emotion, of the public and the private, and of persons and their relationships.[38] The implications for theory of these changed conceptions are obviously enormous.

It may also be that it is our historically located, and thus changeable, circumstances that have led women to interpret moral problems more in terms of social relationships between actual persons and less in terms of either abstract rules or individual interests. It may also be that, on reflection, we will insist on seeing feminist concerns as the framework for moral theory within which other approaches—such as the fair treatment of persons thought of as individuals in a political system—must be fitted. Then, of course, with a feminist approach to what morality requires, we may also have views of what it is that social arrangements should facilitate or foster which will be quite different from any of the currently leading candidates from the liberal or Marxist traditions.

While we can acknowledge that the Marxist tradition enables us to see the realities of class oppression that the liberal tradition obscures, we can also recognize that the Marxist tradition may obscure as well as over-look the realities of gender oppression. Although the liberal tradition's respect for individual rights provides some moral guidelines that we too will strive to preserve, we can recognize that, without social ties of a deeper kind than offered by liberal theory, there may be no society within which to respect individuals.

We can suggest that imagining a society without gender oppression involves imagining persons inherently in social relationships acting together to foster human development. This will involve such issues as protecting the environment, defusing intergroup violence, and caring enough about the children of future generations to summon the political will to now do what is essential. The "preservative love" that Sara Ruddick[39] sees as guiding the activity of mothering may need to have analogues well beyond the family if we are to have a chance of preserving the life of humanity. Ruddick argues from the practices of mothering to political strategies for the peace movement. It is not only in the household and the marginal community that human relationships of trust and concern must be sought, but at the level of the global future.[40]

NOTES

1. Alison Jagger, *Feminist Politics and Human Nature* (Totowa, N.J.: Rowman & Allanheld, 1983).
2. C. B. Macpherson, *Democratic Theory: Essays in Retrieval* (Oxford: Clarendon Press, 1973), 51. I draw no special conclusions from the exclusive use of masculine pronouns. Macpherson did modify the practice in his later work.
3. Ibid., 54.
4. Ibid., 54-55. See also Nancy Hartsock, *Money, Sex, and Power* (New York: Longman, 1983).
5. For further discussion, see Virginia Held, *Rights and Good. Justifying Social Action* (Chicago: University of Chicago Press, 1989), esp. chap. 8.
6. See ibid.

7. See Gerald MacCallum, "Negative and Positive Freedom," *Philosophical Review* 76 (July 1967): 312-34.

8. Macpherson, *Democratic Theory*, 60.

9. The phrase is Husseen Abdilahi Bulhan's. He uses it in *Franz Fanon and the Psychology of Oppression* to characterize slaves and oppressed persons of color. Citing the work of Orlando Patterson and Chester Pierce, he means by it a status in which, in the words of Bartky's summary, "one's person lacks integrity, worth and autonomy, and in which one is subject to violations of space, time, energy, mobility, bonding and identity." In Sandra Lee Bartky, *Femininity and Domination: Studies in the Phenomenology of Oppression* (New York: Routledge, 1990), 133 n. 6.

10. Sandra Bartky, *Femininity and Domination*, 85.

11. Ibid., 86.

12. Ibid., 87.

13. Ibid., 85.

14. Ibid., 97.

15. See Roberta M. Hall and Bernice R. Sandler, "The Classroom Climate: A Chilly One for Women?" Project on the Status and Education of Women (Washington, D.C.: Association of American Colleges, 1982).

16. Ann Ferguson and Nancy Folbre, "The Unhappy Marriage of Patriarchy and Capitalism," in Lydia Sargent, ed., *Women and Revolution* (Boston: South End, 1981), 317. See also Ann Ferguson, "On Conceiving Motherhood and Sexuality," in Joyce Trebilcot, ed., *Mothering. Essays in Feminist Theory* (Totowa, N.J.: Rowman & Allanheld, 1984).

17. Ann Ferguson and Nancy Folbre, "The Unhappy Marriage," 319.

18. Defined by Macpherson as a man's "ability to use other men's capacities ... power over others, the ability to extract benefit from others." C. B. Macpherson, *Democratic Theory*, 42.

19. See C. B. Macpherson, "Pluralism, Individualism, and Participation," in *The Rise and Fall of Economic Justice, and Other Papers* (New York: Oxford University Press, 1985).

20. C. B. Macpherson, *The Life and Times of Liberal Democracy* (New York: Oxford University Press, 1977), 19-20.

21. Ibid., 100.

22. C. B. Macpherson, *Democratic Theory*, 76.

23. Ibid.

24. Ibid., 74.

25. See, for example, Virginia Held, "Access, Enablement, and the First Amendment," in *Philosophical Dimensions of the Constitution*, ed. D. Meyers and K. Kipnis (Boulder, Colo.: Westview Press, 1988); and "Culture or Commerce: On the Liberation of Expression," in *Philosophical Exchange* (SUNY Brockport) (1988-89), 73-87. For an introduction to these issues, see Ian Angus and Sut Jhally,

eds., *Cultural Politics in Contemporary America* (New York: Routledge, 1989); James Curran, Michael Gurevitch, and Janet Woollacott, eds., *Mass Communication and Society* (London: Arnold, 1977); Michael Gurevitch et al., eds., *Culture, Society, and the Media* (London: Methuen, 1982).

26. C. B. Macpherson, *Democratic Theory*, 133.

27. See especially C. B. Macpherson, "Pluralism, Individualism, and Participation."

28. One of the best examinations along these lines of classical liberal theory is Christine Di Stefano, "Masculinity as Ideology in Political Theory: Hobbesian Man Considered," *Women's Studies International Forum* (Special Issue: *Hypatia*) 6, no. 6 (1983): 633–44.

29. See, for example, Virginia Held, "Non-Contractual Society: A Feminist View," in *Science, Morality and Feminist Theory*, ed. Marsha Hanen and Kai Nielsen (Calgary: University of Calgary Press, 1987).

30. See Virginia Held, *Rights and Goods*, chap. 5, and Annette Baier, "Trust and Anti-Trust," *Ethics* 96 (1986): 231–60.

31. C. B. Macpherson, *Democratic Theory*, 50.

32. C. B. Macpherson, "Problems of Human Rights in the Late Twentieth Century," in *The Rise and Fall of Economic Justice*, 23.

33. C. B. Macpherson, *The Life and Times of Liberal Democracy*, 99.

34. Ibid., 100.

35. Ibid., 114.

36. On the conception of government as neutral arbiter, see the work of John Rawls and Ronald Dworkin; see also Charles Larmore, *Patterns of Moral Complexity* (Cambridge: Cambridge University Press, 1987).

37. See Carol Gilligan, *In a Different Voice: Psychological Theory and Women's Development* (Cambridge: Harvard University Press, 1988); Joan C. Tronto, "Beyond Gender Difference to a Theory of Care," *Signs* 12, no. 4 (Summer 1987): 644–63; see especially Eva Feder Kittay and Diana Meyers, eds., *Women and Moral Theory* (Totowa, N.J.: Rowman & Allanheld, 1987); and see also Marsha Hanen and Kai Nielsen, eds., *Science, Morality, and Feminist Theory* (Calgary: University of Calgary Press, 1987). For a comparison of feminist medical ethics with nonfeminist medical ethics, see *Hypatia* 4, no. 2 (Summer 1989), special issue, "Feminist Ethics and Medicine."

38. See Virginia Held, "Feminist Transformations of Moral Theory," *Philosophy and Phenomenological Research* 1, Suppl. (Fall 1990); and Alison M. Jaggar, "Feminist Ethics: Some Issues for the Nineties," *Journal of Social Philosophy* 20, nos. 1 and 2 (Spring/Fall 1989).

39. Sara Ruddick, *Maternal Thinking: Towards a Politics of Peace* (Boston: Beacon Press, 1989).

40. See, for example, Adrienne Harris and Ynestra King, eds., *Rocking the Ship of State: Toward a Feminist Peace Politics* (Boulder, Colo.: Westview Press, 1989).

Chapter 7
Macpherson's Neglect
of the Political

Jane Mansbridge

I will argue in this chapter that C. B. Macpherson's understanding of democracy makes few specifically political claims for the democratic process. His stress on harmony leaves little room for either the legitimate exercise of coercive power or political deliberation, and his stress on the economic requirements for full human development leaves little room for the role of political participation in developing human faculties.

THE LEGITIMATE EXERCISE OF COERCIVE POWER

For a generation raised on too narrow a definition of power, Macpherson's greatest contribution may have been his stress on the subservience of much democratic politics to economic power. His phrase *extractive power* aptly characterizes the processes by which the powerful extract benefits from the less powerful—those made less powerful primarily, in his view, through not owning capital. Few contemporary theorists write as if economic power were irrelevant to democracy, and most explicitly consider, somewhere in their work, the effects of economic arrangements on democracy. Macpherson played an important role in making the economic-political connection now almost a philosophical truism.

Macpherson also expanded the contemporary understanding of power further by returning to the root concept of general capacities from the focus, predominant in the 1950s, on power over others.[1]

In his concern for delegitimating extractive power and relegitimating a broader understanding of power as capacity, Macpherson saw his task explicitly as directing political thought away from the collective action problem that Hobbes and later twentieth-century rational-choice theorists posed, of whether some coercion might not be a useful social tool in bringing about the collective good. This endeavor, as we shall see, led him never to ask what circumstances, if any, might legitimate the political use of coercive power among equals.

In the second half of the twentieth century, collective action theorists had begun to say that collective coercion can be collectively useful whenever goods are indivisible (meaning that once created, they must be freely available to all—like national defense or a public park). Returning to an analysis of Hobbes much like that of Macpherson himself,[2] these theorists pointed out that atomistic (and possessive) individuals, calculating their own costs and benefits, and realizing that with an indivisible good they need not pay in order to benefit, would find it economically rational not to contribute to the provision of that good, even if they wanted it enough to be willing to pay if paying were required to enjoy it. Because with indivisible goods each individual finds it economically rational to "free ride" on the others' efforts—and will, as a consequence, not contribute to providing the good—each will end up, through an interactive process in which others act the same way, having less of the desired good than he or she would have been willing to pay for.

Later theorists pointed out that the public goods problem, first formulated this way by Mancur Olson,[3] was only one instance of a larger "prisoners' dilemma" problem, in which individual actions designed to minimize personal costs and maximize personal benefits can, in interaction with others acting the same way, produce lower benefits for each individual than a more cooperative strategy.[4]

In social dilemmas such as this, the motivations of love and duty (that is, empathy with others and commitment to principles such as sharing, equity, and honesty) can often solve the collective action problem by inducing people to cooperate, even when doing so requires forgoing the greater individual payoffs for noncooperation. Political process, including face-to-face deliberation, can create and maintain both love and duty.[5] To protect those who want to act cooperatively from being "suckered" by potential defectors, however, and in circumstances where the dynamics that induce love and duty are weak, a collective can also use coercive power to change the payoffs for each individual so that, even in the short run, each individual sees more benefit in cooperating than in exploiting the others' cooperation. In these circumstances, individuals will often be willing to subject themselves to potential coercion in order to increase the likelihood that they, and others, will act cooperatively. Given the difficulty of acting unanimously on every issue, they might even be willing in some circumstances to be coerced by the majority.

The foregoing is, briefly, the traditional liberal case for government, updated in collective action language. It is the case for the legitimate use of coercive power, its questions involving when coercive power is legitimate, and why. The formulation presumes a possessive individualist human nature. Moreover, while it remains formally silent on economic power, by analogizing real politics to a prisoners' dilemma game, it implies both an actually existing equality among the players and a "bottom up" construction of political life, beginning with an uncoerced agreement to play among the players themselves. Macpherson dedicated his life to making political thinkers aware of what formulations like this left out of consideration. He played a critical role in moving theorists of his generation away from what had been an almost exclusive preoccupation with politics narrowly conceived, and toward the exploration of existing economic domination and the potential human capacities that could be released in a better economic system.

Much of Macpherson's work had the goal of exposing the interpenetration of economic and political power, with economic power in his analysis having the primary effects on people's lives, and political power maintaining and reinforcing those effects. John Rawls, he pointed out, was unable to see that inequality in the market system will always allow one class to dominate another. Rawls's opposition to domination in principle was thus vitiated by his acquiescence to domination in practice.[6] Similarly other liberal theorists, while reducing the meaning of power to "power over others," did not recognize the most important forms of power over others, which they relegated to an economic and nonpolitical realm.

Macpherson was keenly aware both of the inherent top-down power of government—which he distrusted and disliked—and of the interpenetration of government power with economic power. Liberal democracy, he wrote,

> like any other system, is a system of power; ... indeed, again like any other, a double system of power. It is a system by which people can be *governed*, that is, made to do things they would not otherwise do, and made to refrain from doing things they otherwise might do. Democracy as a system of government is, then, a system by which power is exerted by the state over individuals and groups within it. But more than that, a democratic government, like any other, exists to uphold and enforce a certain kind of society, a certain set of relations between individuals, a certain set of rights and claims that people have on each other both directly, and indirectly through their rights to property. These relations themselves are relations of power—they give different people, in different capacities, power over others.[8]

This suspicion of top-down power in both economic and governmental realms kept Macpherson from discarding, in the name of a broader understanding of power as human capacity, the narrower understanding of power as "power over," or, to use another of his favorite words, "control." At one point, he stated firmly that "No one will deny the importance of power as control over others. It will, and should, remain a central concern of political science."[9] Less frequently, Macpherson referred approvingly to power exercised from the bottom up—that is, by the people over their representatives. In his treatment of one-party states, to certain of which he gave a "genuine" claim to democracy,[10] Macpherson based that claim not only primarily on political outcomes,[11] but also secondarily on political processes, meaning structures of power over others. Considering potential bottom-up power in the internal workings of one-party states, Macpherson wrote that, in the "narrow or strict sense [of being] a system of government, ... democracy surely requires that the majority should really control those who do rule."[12] Finally, in Macpherson's own ideal model of participatory democracy in *The Life and Times of Liberal Democracy,* power appears fleetingly as the direct bottom-up control of the people over their representatives.[13]

Macpherson's insights on the nature of power—whether within liberal democracies, one-party systems, or participatory democracies—have, however, one critical limitation. They apply only to vertical power among implied unequals, not to horizontal power among equals. In Macpherson's writing, power works either from the top down (bad) or from the bottom up (good). Of top-down power, from the more powerful over the less, Macpherson wrote, with implicit disapproval, that "political power, being power over others, is used in any unequal society to extract benefit from the ruled for the rulers."[14] Of bottom-up power, from the less powerful rank and file over the more powerful representatives, Macpherson wrote occasionally and approvingly in his discussions of democratic one-party states and participatory democracy. But of horizontal power among equals—the legitimate coercing of some in the polity by others—Macpherson wrote only once, never using the phrase *majority rule*, with its connotations of power. In this one sentence he suggested, with words almost administrative in their implication that power is not at work, that a computer "could easily deal with the...incompatibilities [of "opposed interests"] by ascertaining the majority position."[15]

Yet if the rule of a majority is to play its traditional role in liberal democratic theory, power over others among equals must be legitimate. Normative democratic theorists must ask the liberal question of what conditions, if any, can legitimate the extraction of benefits by equals from equals. Thinking of power only as exercised up or down among unequals makes Macpherson's theories realistic in most actual political situations, but incomplete as ideal theory. Macpherson's ideal theory spends little time on legitimate control, coercion, or power over others.

Macpherson does not address this question of the normatively legitimate uses of horizontal power among equals for three reasons: his concern for understanding power as human capacity rather than as power over others, his goal of moving from a narrow political definition of democracy to a broader social one, and, most importantly, his belief in potential harmony.

First, Macpherson wanted power to retain its original meaning of human capacities, and saw the development of those capabilities as the ultimate moral end.[16] As a consequence, he strongly opposed the "reduction of power to power over others."[17] Reporting on the liberal conception of power, Macpherson commented, "Power, because it is seen as control over others, is certainly not seen as something whose increase or maximization is desirable in itself."[18] The "because" clause in this sentence reveals that Macpherson himself saw no justification for increasing or maximizing power over others. In his eyes, such increase could be only a negative value. Yet Arnold Tannenbaum, an organizational sociologist, has concluded that organizational effectiveness is greatest and member loyalty strongest in organizations in which both members and officers report having a great deal of control over one another, not in organizations where the total amount of control reported is low.[19] Mutual power over others may be a sign of a healthy collectivity, providing that the power meets certain criteria of legitimacy.[20]

Second, Macpherson wanted to move theorists from understanding democracy as "merely a mechanism of choosing and authorizing governments" or "simply a system of government" to understanding it as a "kind of society—a whole complex of relations between individuals."[21] By extension, therefore, "the egalitarian principle inherent in democracy requires not only 'one man, one vote' but also 'one man, one equal effective right to live as fully humanly as he may wish.'"[22] This move, deemphasizing strictly political relations in favor of social relations, was central to all his work.

Finally, as John Keane points out in this volume, Macpherson's "postulate of the nonopposition of essentially human capacities"[23] led him, following one interpretation of Marx, to an ideal vision of social life without important sources of contention—and therefore without politics as contestation or power.

> [That] men, if freed from scarcity and from ... the ideologies inherited from ages of scarcity ... would live together harmoniously enough that their remaining contention would be only creative tension ... is basic to any demand for or justification of a democratic society. The case for democratic *government* ("one man, one vote") can indeed be made sufficiently on the opposite assumption: in a thoroughly contentious society everyone needs the vote as a protection. But the case of a democratic *society* fails without the assumption of potential substantial harmony.[24]

Such a society "is only possible when both genuine and contrived society have been overcome."[25]

THE ROLE OF POLITICAL PARTICIPATION IN HUMAN DEVELOPMENT

Like several other leading political theorists of the early 1970s, Macpherson made human development central to his normative scheme. Unlike many others, he examined at length the potential meanings in the concept, using his considerable verbal skill to revivify for the next generation of theorists the ideal of the "maximization of human powers." His influential essays on the maximization of powers did not, however, make a central claim that political participation helped develop human powers. Rather, he stressed again and again that no political system can "maximize individual powers" in the absence of a socialist, or at least a noncapitalist, economic system.[26]

Macpherson may have believed that participation in democratic procedures in the absence of socialism could at least improve (as opposed to maximize) human powers. In his essays on human development he did not express himself on this point. He argued simply that, because a capitalist market economy will always compel a continual transfer of power from some to others, liberal democracy under capitalism can never fulfill its claim to maximize all individual powers.[27] In Macpherson's eyes, the key to individual development was not political participation, but capital and other material resources. "Without access to them, one cannot use one's skill and energy in the first business of life, which is to get a living, nor therefore, in the real business of life, which . . . is to enjoy and develop one's powers."[28] In his two central essays on this subject, Macpherson focused his analysis only on the important and, until then, much neglected effects on human development of the economic system. He never mentioned human development through political participation.

Macpherson wrote on human development at a time when that value had begun to flourish again after a period of neglect. Philosophical interest in *paideia*–human education or development, broadly speaking–probably began in ancient Greece, waned during Christian dominance in the Middle Ages, was revived by Jean-Jacques Rousseau (who seems to have coined the phrase *the development of the faculties*), and was fully embraced by the German Romantics of the next generation. When, in the midnineteenth century, Alexis de Tocqueville reported his observation that participation in the democracy of the New England town meetings seemed to enlarge the character of its citizens, J. S. Mill combined this empirical insight with the Romantic "obsession"[29] with self-development to create a new normative theory of democracy.[30] In this new theory, Mill argued that participation in democratic decisions improves the character of the citizenry and, in turn, creates a better state.

Mill's theory did not play a major role in twentieth-century democratic theory until, in 1960, Arnold Kaufman, coining the term *participatory democracy*, argued that the "main justifying function" of a democracy of participation is and always has been "the contribution it can make to the development of human powers of thought, feeling, and action."

161

Ten years later, Carole Pateman argued forcefully that "the experience of participation ... will develop and foster the 'democratic' personality,"[32] which she briefly described as involving autonomy and a resistance to hierarchy. Kaufman did not detail the specific powers of thought, feeling, and action that he thought democratic participation would produce. Pateman suggested that participation would produce political efficacy (the most important outcome), a sense of cooperation, commitment to collective decisions, and democratic character. In her analysis, these traits all had value because they helped democracy function.

In two essays written just before and after Pateman's book, Macpherson addressed himself more specifically to what individual development might mean, and argued for certain forms of development on the grounds that they were "uniquely human." Exerting and developing any human capacity were for Macpherson "ends in themselves."[33] In his view, the

> uniquely human capacities include the capacity for rational under-standing, for moral judgment and action, for aesthetic creation or contemplation, for the emotional activities of friendship and love, and, sometimes, for religious experience.[34]

In the second essay, he specifically excluded human characteristics whose development prevents other humans from using and developing their capacities: *"Human* capacities are taken to be only . . . the non-destructive ones."[35]

These two essays are among the few in which a major contemporary thinker has addressed the content of the much-discussed goal of individual development. Yet the claim that what is human, or essentially human, is necessarily good in itself is problematic. One need not subscribe to the Christian doctrine of original sin to entertain as a plausible alternative hypothesis that human beings have developed the capacity for evil far beyond that of other animals. Although some animals play with their prey, and many animals enforce behaviors of subordination, the human is the only species to have developed the practices of sexual sadism, slavery, and genocide. Simply defining the destructive aspects of human nature as not genuinely or essentially human risks neglecting these essentially human attributes. Macpherson's argument requires introducing standards of destructiveness and non-destructiveness that extend beyond simply belonging to the human species.[36]

Five years after his essays on the maximization of human powers, Macpherson's *Life and Times of Liberal Democracy* ended by advocating participatory democracy—an ideal then promoted by other political theorists almost entirely on the grounds of the potential for human development in the political process. A few passages in the *Life and Times* did give political participation an independent role in human development. Macpherson's discussion of J. S. Mill and Marx, for example, concluded that "only by actual involvement in joint political action can people transcend their consciousness of themselves as consumers and appropriators."[37] For Marx, a sharpened class consciousness "would lead to various kinds of working class political action, which would further increase the class consciousness of the working class."[38] For Mill, a broadened franchise "would lead to more widespread political participation which would in turn make people capable of still more political participation and would contribute to a change in consciousness."[39] Macpherson pointed out that class consciousness seemed, in Western societies, to have declined rather than increased, and the broadened franchise had not produced the result Mill had hoped for, but he took hope in the potential for cumulative change stemming from increases in either participation or consciousness.[40] This expression of hope—plus one paragraph on how "an appetite for participation, based on the very experience of it, may well carry over from the workplace to wider political areas"[41]—exhaust Macpherson's analysis of the effects of political participation on human development. One cannot say that the political process per se figured importantly in his understanding of the maximization of human powers.

POLITICAL DELIBERATION

John Keane's essay in this volume points out how Macpherson's postulate of the nonopposition of human values made it difficult, if not impossible, for him to conceive of the political process as one of continuing contestation. Macpherson focused not on the political process, which might transform preferences, but on the underlying structure of interests rooted in economic relations and related to the political process as base to superstructure. Therefore, in spite of his convictions regarding underlying harmony, Macpherson did not ask through what kinds of transformations of individuals the political process might produce harmony. Nor did he ask what effect public, as opposed to private, deliberation might have on individuals' conceptions of their interests.

Keane's own vision of the democratic process is deliberative. Avoiding the suggestion of some deliberative theorists that deliberation has the implied goal of agreement on a common good, Keane conjures up instead a constantly replenished plurality of voices, each pressing for ways of seeing not fully commensurate with the others. Other postmodern theorists also stress the unsettled quality of democratic politics.[42] Each settlement, they argue, creates a set of procedures and outcomes that benefits some more than others, or fits more comfortably with the principles of some than others. Democracies must not only allow but encourage those most discomfited by the process to reopen the question. Democracy is, in this view, not only the potential for reopening, but the process of constant reopening itself.[43]

Every postmodern theorist I can think of has absorbed from Macpherson and others of his generation the lesson that political power is interpenetrated by, and sometimes no more than a manifestation of, economic power. The lesson now taken for granted, such theorists have gone on to analyze the politically process as, ideally, unsettled in principle—a line of inquiry that directly challenges Macpherson's reliance, through most of his work, on the potential in reduced scarcity and class division for generating underlying harmony.

A different group among today's deliberative theorists sees the political process as an opportunity to create commonalities, including a common understanding of a common good, out of individuality. Unlike the deliberative theorists who stress continual destabilization, writers such as Benjamin Barber and Joshua Cohen stress the processes within deliberation that can turn "I" into "we."[44] This group complements Macpherson's analysis rather than directly challenging it. Recognizing implicitly or explicitly the need for economic structures compatible with widespread equal resources and equal respect, these theorists then investigate the ground that Macpherson himself hardly touched: the political process of deliberation.

Deliberation is a critical ingredient in the political process. In contrast to coercive power, by which one actor gets another to do something the other would not otherwise do through force or the threat of sanction,[45] in deliberation an actor gets others to act differently through persuasion.[46] Deliberation changes selves as well as preferences. Deliberation involves conflict and commonality, reason and emotion, self-interest and altruism, and the probing both of what one wants for oneself and what others want. Ideally, deliberation should help participants better understand the bases of their conflicting interests and their potential for common interest.[47]

When Macpherson turned to Third World forms of democracy that postulated what he called a general will,[48] he had the opportunity to ask in more detail which forms of political deliberation were likely to foster a genuine good will, and which were likely to stifle, or masquerade as, a general will. In a 1966 essay, he described "prepolitical" society as one in which "the local, community-centered society traditionally made its decisions by discussion among equals."[49] This ideal he called *the indigenous traditional idea of democracy.*[50] But he did not explore the potential forms or content of discussion in this traditional ideal,[51] which he believed had evolved into one-party democracy. Nor did Macpherson discuss the deliberative possibilities in one-party democracies, judging these on external outcomes—that is, on whether or not the results of political decisions benefited the "common people"—and on a criterion of internal process focused not on deliberation but on power, that is, on whether the rank and file controlled the leaders of the party.[52]

In *The Life and Times of Liberal Democracy,* Macpherson touched briefly on the role of deliberation in politics, mentioning discussion once each in his descriptions of J. S. Mill[53] and John Dewey,[54] and in his conclusion that while "no doubt something could be done with two-way television to draw more people into active political discussion," some government body would inevitably have to decide what questions would be asked, thus vitiating genuine, bottom-up direct democracy.[55] However, in his television example, as in his treatment of intraparty democracy, Macpherson treated the political process per se as one concerned centrally with power (in the sense of power over others), not with deliberation.

For Macpherson, in short, the subject of political deliberation was of no great interest. Those who come after him and who have reintroduced the deliberate political process as a subject of study have nevertheless been deeply influenced by his work. Of none of the new deliberative theorists could one say, as Macpherson said of the deliberative theorists of the prewar period, that they wrote "as if the democratic process were an arrangement whereby rational, well-intentioned citizens, who had, of course, a whole variety of different interests, could adequately adjust their differences in the peaceful, rational, give-and-take of parties and pressure groups and the free press. They allowed themselves to hope that the class issue would go away...."[56] The new deliberative theorists, whether postmodern or communal, take differ-

JANE MANSBRIDGE

ences in economic power heavily into account. Then they turn to the
subject Macpherson left relatively untouched: the political process itself.

THE MEANING OF "DEMOCRACY"

The degree to which Macpherson saw democracy not as a political
process—whether coercive or deliberative and developmental—but as a
substantive end appears in the meanings and normative loadings he
gave to the word *democracy.* When he assigned, for example, different
meanings to democracy in three periods of history, he favored in each
case the meaning that was substantive, not procedural; a matter of ends,
not means; and societal rather than political.

Macpherson's "pre-liberal" period (Greek, Roman, medieval, and
Rousseauist) gave birth to what he called the "original" understanding of
democracy. Although this original understanding had a partial meaning
of "rule by and for the oppressed people,"[57] which we may call "semiprocedural" (it included rule *by* as well as for the oppressed), Macpherson
favored its other partial meaning of "the realization of the humanity of
all men,"[58] which was purely substantive. Macpherson argued that the
substantive meaning of the realization of the humanity of all men was
the meaning of democracy held by the common people, as opposed to
the semiprocedural meaning held by the ruling classes.[59] The substantive
meaning was also immanent in the semiprocedural meaning so that it
emerged, over time, with the help of certain perceptive thinkers.[60] Most
importantly, the substantive meaning differed from the semiprocedural
in emphasizing, in Macpherson's words, "ends, not means."[61] "[T]he classic,
pre-liberal idea of democracy," he wrote, makes "the criterion of
democracy the achievement of ends which the mass of the people
share."[62] In its classic or original meaning, therefore, democracy described
not a political process but a social state in which each individual could
fully develop his or her capacities. Democracy was a matter of ends, not
means; it was substantive, not procedural; and it was societal, rather than
political.

To state institutions in what he called the "liberal" period (the seventeenth through eighteenth centuries), Macpherson did not grant the title
of democracy. In one essay, he wrote that "democratic principles and
institutions did not amount to anything before the nineteenth century."[63]
In another, he concluded that there was "nothing democratic about [the
liberal state],in any sense of equality of real right."[64]

166

In his comparison of the "liberal" and the later "liberal-democratic" periods, Macpherson gave only the second the title to the word *democracy*. While in some of his paragraphs, the democracy in liberal-democracy seems to be procedural and derived from a franchise extended to most adult men,[65] in the paragraphs that meant most to Macpherson's theory, the democracy in liberal-democracy is entirely substantive, derived from returning to the substantive preliberal meaning of the development of human powers. "It was," he wrote, "the ethical concept of man's powers that was reintroduced into the Western tradition in the nineteenth century, and its reintroduction was what converted the liberal into the liberal-democratic theory."[66] He further argued that the principle of seeing democracy "as a kind of society—a whole complex of relations between individuals—rather than simply a system of government" was "*the* principle introduced into predemocratic liberal theory in the nineteenth century to make it liberal-democratic."[67] The key element in liberal-democracy, like the key element in original democracy, was substantive, not procedural. It was a matter of ends, not means, and societal rather than political.

CONCLUSION: MACPHERSON'S NEGLECT OF THE POLITICAL

Contemporary philosophers owe a great debt to C. B. Macpherson for broadening the meaning of democracy, exposing the political power inherent in the control of capital, pointing out how political systems maintain the power relations inherent in economic systems, and reinvigorating the ideal of the full development of human powers. These contributions inevitably led him away from the procedural aspects of democracy, or what he called the "narrow" view of democracy as a "system of government," rather than as a kind of society.

Contemporary theorists cannot, therefore, turn to Macpherson for much help on questions concerning the political processes of deliberation or the exercise of power among equals. While he touched on the process of discussion, he did not ask what kinds of discussion, in what contexts, and in what political forms might produce good decisions, the potential for reopening questions, or the transformations of self that help people understand their own interests or reconstruct their preferences in the light of a common good. While he wrote at some length on power, he did not ask when some members of a collective might legitimately coerce other equal members of that collective into doing what they do not want to do or what undermines their interests. In both matters of common interest and matters of conflict, therefore, Macpherson's project of broadening the horizons of contemporary philosophy led him to neglect the elements of common life that are most distinctively political.

The task for the next generation is to integrate into their descriptions of contemporary reality the fundamental facts of structural inequality in market systems, while asking what independent contribution the political process can make in these or in more equal circumstances, either to deliberative understanding or to legitimate decision making in matters of irresolvable conflict.

NOTES

1. C. B. Macpherson, "Problems of a Non-Market Theory of Democracy," in *Democratic Theory: Essays in Retrieval* (Oxford: Oxford University Press, 1973), 45, referring to Robert Dahl and David Easton, and to Harold Lasswell's repudiation of Bertrand Russell. William Connolly also repudiated "power over" ("Power and Responsibility," in *The Terms of Political Discourse* [Lexington, Mass.: D. C. Heath, 1974]), as did some feminists (see Nancy Hartsock, *Money, Sex, and Power* [New York: Longman, 1983]), after the early lead of Mary Parker Follett's *Dynamic Administration* (New York: Harper, 1940) and Dorothy Emmett, "The Concept of Power," *Proceedings of the Aristotelian Society* 54 (1953-54): 1-26.

2. C. B. Macpherson, *The Political Theory of Possessive Individualism: Hobbes to Locke* (Oxford: Oxford University Press, 1962).

3. Mancur Olson, *The Logic of Collective Action* (Cambridge: Harvard University Press, 1971); see also Paul A. Samuelson, *The Foundation of Economics* (Cambridge: Harvard University Press, 1955).

4. Russell Hardin, *Collective Action* (Baltimore: Johns Hopkins University Press, 1982).

5. See my "On the relation of altruism and self-interest," in J. Mansbridge, ed., *Beyond Self-Interest* (Chicago: University of Chicago Press, 1990).

6. "Revisionist Liberalism" in Macpherson, *Democratic Theory*, 92.

7. "Problems," in Macpherson, *Democratic Theory*, 46.

8. C. B. Macpherson, *The Real World of Democracy* (Oxford: Oxford University Press, 1966), 4; emphasis in original. See also pp. 39 and 42, especially "If men were angels, government would not be necessary. Since they are not, government is necessary, and government must mean that the governors have power to compel the governed" (p. 39).

9. "Problems," in Macpherson, *Democratic Theory*, 48.

10. These nations "therefore have genuine claim to be called democratic" (Macpherson, *Real World,* 29, also 3), and are "in a genuine sense democratic" ("Revolution and Ideology in the late Twentieth Century" in Macpherson, *Democratic Theory,* 162).

11. E.g. "fulfilling democratic aspirations" ("Market Concepts in Political Theory" in Macpherson, *Democratic Theory,* 190), with "democracy" being defined as producing the "conditions for the full and free development of essential human faculties" (Macpherson, *Real World,* 37). See generally pp. 29–33, 36, and 58 of *Real World* for an emphasis on ends, not means.

12. Macpherson, *Real World,* 18. See also p. 22: "If there is only one party, there must be, within it, effective means for those at the bottom to control those at the top," and p. 27: "Whether the expression of this will through a single party be called democratic in the strict sense depends on how much control there is of the leaders by the rank-and-file within the party, that is, how much intra-party democracy there is, and beyond that, on how open membership in the party is, and how strenuous a degree of activity is required as the price of membership in the party." But see "Market Concepts" in Macpherson, *Democratic Theory,* 191 n. 3 for equivocation on the necessity of intraparty democracy for making a "genuine" claim to the label of *democracy.*

13. C. B. Macpherson, *The Life and Times of Liberal Democracy* (Oxford: Oxford University Press, 1977), 109–10.

14. "Problems," in Macpherson, *Democratic Theory,* 47.

15. Macpherson, *Life and Times,* 96.

16. Macpherson, *Real World,* 37 and 58; Macpherson, *Life and Times,* 2; "Democratic Theory: Ontology and Technology" in Macpherson, *Democratic Theory,* 32.

17. "Problems," in Macpherson, *Democratic Theory,* 42.

18. Ibid., 48.

19. Arnold S. Tannenbaum, *Control in Organizations* (New York: McGraw-Hill, 1968).

20. Although my *Beyond Adversary Democracy* (Chicago: University of Chicago Press, 1983) argues primarily that important forms of democracy presume common interest, it also suggests criteria for legitimate democratic decisions in instances of conflict.

21. "Problems," in Macpherson, *Democratic Theory,* 51.

22. Ibid.

23. Ibid., 55.

24. Ibid. Emphasis in original.

25. Ibid. See also pp. 71 and 74. But see *per contra* his conclusion, five years later in *The Life and Times of Liberal Democracy,* 96–97 and 112–13, that opposing interests and differing convictions on important matters would persist even as material scarcity became less pressing and class differences diminished or were eliminated.

26. "The Maximization of Democracy" in Macpherson, *Democratic Theory*, 3ff.

27. Ibid., 10. Macpherson remained agnostic on whether socialist systems could fulfil this claim.

28. Ibid., 11. See also 59-70 on the impediments to using one's human capacities. These impediments are all material. None has to do specifically with impediments to participation in politics.

29. The word *obsession* is Mill's. See John Stuart Mill, *Autobiography* (1873; reprint: New York: Columbia University Press, 1960).

30. See my "On the Idea that Participation Makes Better Citizens," in *Political Theory* (forthcoming), for evidence that this theory was new with Mill. Aristotle, Machiavelli, and Rousseau did not argue that interactive participation in the making of decisions helps develop citizens' character. Rousseau did argue that human character improves when we give a law to ourselves, and that the political process helps us see what the law should be. However, his understanding of politics involved neither deliberation nor power.

31. Arnold S. Kaufman, "Human Nature and Participatory Democracy," in Carl J. Friedrich, ed., *Responsibility: NOMOS III* (New York: Liberal Arts Press, 1960), 266-89, reprinted in William E. Connolly, ed., *The Bias of Pluralism* (New York: Atherton Press, 1969), 184, 188, 190, 198.

32. Carole Pateman, *Participation and Democratic Theory* (Cambridge: Cambridge University Press, 1970), 64. Also, "The major function of participation in the theory of participatory democracy is . . . an educative one, educative in the very widest sense . . . " (p. 42).

33. "Maximization," in Macpherson, *Democratic Theory*, 4-5.

34. Ibid. He later expanded his list of uniquely human capacities to include the capacities for wonder or curiosity, for laughter, and for "controlled physical/mental/aesthetic activity, as expressed for instance in making music and in playing games of skill." "Problems," in ibid., 54.

35. "Problems," in ibid., 55.

36. On this issue, see also Kai Nielsen, "Alienation and Self-Realization," *Philosophy* 48 (1973): 21-33, and Mary Midgley, *Beast in Man* (Ithaca, N.Y.: Cornell University Press, 1978).

37. Macpherson, *Life and Times*, 100.

38. Ibid.

39. Ibid., 101.

40. Ibid.

41. Ibid., 104.

42. I use the term *postmodern* to describe political philosophical, literary, and sociological analyses that celebrate difference.

43. William Connolly, *The Politics of Ambiguity* (Madison: University of Wisconsin Press, 1987); Bonnie Hoenig, "Declarations of Independence: Arendt and Derrida on the Problem of Founding a Republic," *American Political Science Review* 85 (1991): 97-114.

44. Benjamin Barber, *Strong Democracy* (Berkeley: University of California Press, 1984); Joshua Cohen, "Deliberation and Democratic Legitimacy," in Alan Hamlin and Phillip Pettit, eds., *The Good Polity* (Oxford: Basil Blackwell, 1989). See also Hanna Fenischel Pitkin and Sara M. Shumer, "On Participation," *democracy* 2 (1982): 43-54.

45. Peter Bachrach and Morton Baratz, "Decisions and Non-Decisions: An Analytical Framework," *American Political Science Review* 57 (1963): 632-42.

46. Steven Luke's *Power: A Radical View* (London: Macmillan, 1974) generates a fourfold table combining the two methods of coercive power and persuasion with the two situations of conflicting and common interests. Coercive power is appropriate to situations of conflicting interests, and may be legitimate if each actor has equal power. Persuasion is appropriate to and legitimate in situations of common interest. The off-diagonal cases are less legitimate. Coercive power in situations of common interest is paternalism, sometimes necessary but usually suspect and incorporating unequal respect. Persuasion in situations of conflicting interests is manipulation, illegitimate in any version of democratic theory.

47. See Jane Mansbridge, "A Deliberative Theory of Interest Representation," in Mark P. Petracca, ed., *The Politics of Interest: Interest Groups Transformed* (Boulder, Colo.: Westview Press, 1992).

48. Macpherson, *Real World,* 26.

49. "Revolution," in Macpherson, *Democratic Theory,* 161.

50. Ibid., 162.

51. Ibid.

52. See below, in text accompanying notes 57-68, discussion of the meaning of democracy.

53. Macpherson, *Life and Times,* 51.

54. Ibid., 74.

55. Ibid., 95.

56. Ibid., 71, referring to Ernest Barker, A. D. Lindsay, R. M. MacIver, and John Dewey, among others.

57. Macpherson, *Real World,* 24. See also: in "its original meaning" democracy meant "government by or for the common people, by or for the hitherto oppressed classes" (*Real World,* 5); and, "rule by or in the interest of the hitherto oppressed class" (*Real World,* 12). Contemporaneously with these lectures, Macpherson also postulated a somewhat different form of original democracy. As we have seen, he described prepolitical society as one in which "the local, community-centered society traditionally made its decisions by discussion among equals" ("Revolution," in Macpherson, *Democratic Theory,* 161). This form of democracy he called "the indigenous traditional idea of democracy" (p. 162). Although this phrase implies a single traditional meaning of democracy, the words *indigenous* and *prepolitical* perhaps indicate a pre-Greek context, while "original" democracy may be thought to have begun with the Greeks.

58. Macpherson, *Real World,* 13.

JANE MANSBRIDGE

59. "Democracy, as seen from the upper layers of class-divided societies, meant class rule, rule by the wrong class" (Macpherson, *Life and Times*, 10). Also: "Democracy appeared as a class thing mostly to upper-class eyes. It was mainly ruling-class spokesmen, who had always thought and spoken in terms of class politics, who treated the claims of the democrats as class claims.... To the people at the bottom, or even half-way up, democracy was never entirely or essentially a class thing. For them, it had always been not just a way of freeing themselves from oppression, but of freeing the whole of humanity, of permitting the realization of the humanity of all men" (Macpherson, *Real World*, 13). It is unclear to which historical period Macpherson is referring here. The extension of normative ideals to "the whole of humanity," including in some nonpolitical respects women, came in the West about the time of the Stoics and Christianity. In the earlier Athens of the fifth century B.C., democratic normative ideals generally applied only to free adult men born in that city. The idea that women, as part of all humanity, should be free from oppression probably did not become a concern of "the people at the bottom" until the twentieth century, if then.

60. In *The Real World of Democracy*, Macpherson described first a sequential, and then an immanent, process by which what one might call the "universal substantive meaning" (the meaning held by the Greek common people) emerged from the partial semiprocedural meaning. Describing the sequential process, Macpherson argued that the Soviet countries and the "newly independent under-developed countries" thought of themselves as democratic in "something like its original meaning, government by or for the common people, by or for the hither-to oppressed classes." "Yet here too the meaning has changed ..." These countries now thought of democracy "not in its original meaning as rule in the interests of a class, but as rule in the interests of the whole people, transcending classes" (*Real World*, 5). "It has changed from a primarily class concept to a humanistic concept transcending class. Let us see how this has happened" (*Real World*, 12). Describing the immanent process, he wrote, "The Marxian idea of democracy ... started from the age-old notion of democracy as class rule but gave it a new turn by making it more precise. The old notion had been rather vague about how the liberation of a class was to be the liberation of humanity. Marx gave it a new precision.... [The rule of the working class] would be democratic because it would comprise the great majority of the population, and because its purpose would be the humanization of the whole people" (*Real World*, 15).

61. "Democratic Theory," in Macpherson, *Democratic Theory*, 29.

62. Ibid. In this passage he argues that "the classic formulator of this democratic doctrine was Rousseau." Considering Rousseau as reintroducing ancient Greek ideals makes this passage more consistent with his other statements on the historical sources of the "original" pre-liberal meaning.

63. Ibid., 24.

64. Macpherson, *Real World*, 8.

65. See comments on the franchise becoming democratic ("Democratic

Theory," in Macpherson, *Democratic Theory,* 26); "the demands of the common people for a political voice" and the "fully democratic franchise" ("Post-Liberal-Democracy?" in Macpherson, *Democratic Theory,* 174); and on the addition of the democratic franchise (Macpherson, *Real World,* 36); e.g., "the liberal-democratic state is essentially the liberal state with a democratic franchise added" (Macpherson, *Real World,* 44). Substance also seems subsidiary to procedure in the statement that "the democratic principle" in the transition to the "liberal-democratic" system was "the equal entitlement of every man to a voice in choosing government and to some other satisfactions" ("Post-Liberal" in Macpherson, *Democratic Theory,* 172).

66. Macpherson, *Democratic Theory,* 10. It was reintroduced with a more egalitarian component. Now each individual was equally entitled to opportunity to realize his or her human essence (ibid.; see also p. 21).

67. "Problems," in ibid., 51; emphasis added.

Chapter 8
Liberalism and
Modern Democracy

Chantal Mouffe

In 1964, an essay entitled "Post-Liberal-Democracy?" by C. B. Macpherson argued that we need to elaborate a theory of democracy that would sever the links that had been established between the liberal ethical principle of human self-realization and the capitalist market economy. He wrote, "Fifty years ago the world was almost the preserve of the Western liberal-democratic capitalist societies. Their economies were triumphant, and so were their theories. Since then, two-thirds of the world has rejected the liberal-democratic market society, both in practice and in theory."[1] Alas, almost thirty years later, the wind seems to be blowing in the opposite direction. From Latin America to Eastern Europe, the market is increasingly presented as a necessary condition for a successful democratization, and it has become the central symbol of those who are struggling for the creation of a "post-Communist democracy."

Of course, this does not mean that Macpherson was mistaken in calling for the development of what he referred to as a "liberal-democratic socialism." I believe that, today, such a theory is more necessary than ever before. At a moment when we are witnessing the beginning of a new political configuration of left-liberals and post-Marxists entering into a promising dialogue, Macpherson is undoubtedly appearing as an important point of reference. His thesis that the ethical values of liberal democracy provide us with the symbolic resources to carry through the struggle for a radical-liberal-democracy is now being accepted by many forces on the left whose objectives are the extension and deepening of the democratic revolution. Indeed, his belief in the radical potential of the liberal-democratic ideal is shared by those of us who want to redefine socialism in terms of radical and plural democracy.

There are, nevertheless, some problems with Macpherson's approach, and I intend to bring them to the fore by contrasting his position with that of a fellow liberal-democratic socialist, Norberto Bobbio. Bobbio and Macpherson share a commitment to the tradition of liberal democracy that both try to extend in a more radical direction. They want to defend liberal principles while expanding the scope of democratic control, and they consider that the crucial issue for the Left is how to achieve a socialism compatible with liberal democracy. However, there are important differences in the ways they visualize such a liberal-democratic socialism.

Although Bobbio agrees that a greater degree of participation is needed, his model is not one of participatory democracy, and he does not put as much emphasis as Macpherson on direct democracy. Bobbio also does not believe that scarcity could ever be overcome, or that we could go beyond the individualistic premises of liberalism. For him, the solution consists in linking those premises with the notion of distributive justice as in the Rawlsian type of social contract in which the social rights provide the basis for the equality required by a modern democratic polity.[2] Macpherson defends the ideals of liberal democracy and its ethical principles, but he is very critical of its institutions. On the other hand, Bobbio defends those institutions, and his aim is to adapt them to make possible more equality and a greater democratic accountability.

At first sight the difference between the two could appear to be the classical one between some Eurocommunist form of democratic socialism and social democracy. However, we have increasingly come to recognize that once the reform/revolution dichotomy has been abandoned, such a distinction is not very useful. If the commitment to the liberal-democratic framework is really taken seriously, there can only be different strategies for democratization, each to be judged according to its objectives.

From that point of view, Bobbio often appears much more radical than Macpherson, who puts a too exclusive emphasis on economic class relations to the detriment of the demands of the "new social movements." For that reason, Macpherson did not adequately grasp the wide range of social relations in which relations of domination had to be challenged so that the liberal principle of equal rights of self-development could be realized. Bobbio, on the contrary, recognized that the process of democratization had to spread from the sphere of political relations to the whole sphere of social relations, encompassing gender, family, workplace, neighborhood, school, and so on.

Therefore, the problem for Bobbio is to combine the democratization of the state with the democratization of society. He states, "Nowadays, if an indicator of democratic progress is needed it cannot be provided by the number of people who have the right to vote, but the number of contexts outside politics where the right to vote is exercised. A laconic but effective way of putting it is to say that the criterion for judging the state of democratization achieved in a given country should no longer be to establish `who' votes, but `where' they can vote."[3]

The problem with Bobbio is that, while I believe he is right in saying that the process of democratization is not to be conceived exclusively as consisting in the transition from representative democracy to direct democracy, I think that he goes astray when he presents representative democracy as the privileged type of democratic institution. For instance, he asserts, "In short, we can say that the way modern democracy is developing is not to be understood as the emergence of a new type of democracy but rather as a process in which quite traditional forms of democracy, such as representative democracy, are infiltrating new spaces, spaces occupied until now by hierarchic or bureaucratic organizations."[4] To me, this is clearly unsatisfactory.

There are many social relations in which representative forms of democracy would be completely inadequate and forms of democracy should therefore be plural and adapted to the type of social relations in which the democratic principles of liberty and equality are going to be implemented. Representative democracy is better suited to some and direct democracy to others. We should indeed also imagine new ones.

Nevertheless, Bobbio is basically correct to call our attention to the fact that we should not expect the emergence of a completely new type of democracy and that liberal institutions are here to stay. In that respect, he presents a useful corrective to Macpherson, whose views on that matter are rather ambiguous. Of course, Macpherson does not propose to get rid of liberal political institutions, but he often seems to accept them as a *pis-aller,* a second-best that we must tolerate because of the weight of tradition and the actual circumstances in Western societies. This is why, in *The Life and Times of Liberal Democracy,* he presents the model 4B of participatory democracy—the one that combines a pyramidal direct/indirect democratic machinery with a continuing party system—as the more realistic one.[5] But he does not disqualify model 4A, the pyramidal councils system that, according to him, would be in the best tradition of liberal democracy, despite the fact that the framework of liberal political institutions would have disappeared. This is, to my view, a highly dangerous notion of participatory democracy that does not take account of the crucial importance of liberal political institutions for modern democracy.

To take seriously the ethical principle of liberalism is to assert that individuals should have the possibility of organizing their lives as they wish, of choosing their own ends, and of realizing them as they think best. In other words, it is to acknowledge that pluralism is constitutive of modern democracy. The idea of a perfect consensus, of a harmonious collective will is, therefore, to be abandoned, and we must accept the permanence of conflicts and antagonisms. Once the very possibility of the realization of a substantial homogeneity is discarded, the necessity of liberal institutions becomes evident. Far from being a mere cover-up for the class divisions of capitalist society, as many participatory democrats seem to believe, they provide the guarantee that individual freedom would be protected against the tyranny of the majority or the domination of the totalitarian party/state.

In a modern democracy, there is no longer a substantive idea of the good life on which all rational persons could agree. This is the pluralism that the fundamental liberal institutions of separation of church and state, division of powers, and limitation of state power help to secure. Under modern democratic conditions, characterized by what Claude Lefort calls "the dissolution of the landmarks of certainty,"[6] the interconnection between liberal institutions and democratic procedures is the necessary condition for the extension of the democratic revolution into new areas of social life. This is why political liberalism is a central component of a project of radical and plural democracy. Bobbio is indeed right to affirm that modern democracy must be a pluralistic democracy.[7] He is also right to urge us to acknowledge that socialist goals can be achieved, and that they can only be achieved acceptably within the liberal-democratic framework.

I believe that democracy must come to terms with pluralism because, under modern conditions in which one can no longer speak of the people as if it were a unified and homogeneous entity with a single general will, the democratic logic of identity of government and the governed cannot alone guarantee respect for human rights. The logic of popular sovereignty can avoid descending into tyranny only by virtue of its articulation with political liberalism. This is a danger that we can better understand when we examine critiques of liberal democracy coming from the Right. I want to show where the rejection of pluralism can lead by discussing Carl Schmitt's challenge to parliamentary democracy.

CARL SCHMITT ON PARLIAMENTARY DEMOCRACY

Carl Schmitt is usually known for a few very provocative theses, one of these being that liberalism negates democracy and that democracy negates liberalism. In the preface to the second edition of *The Crisis of Parliamentary Democracy* published in 1926, he argues that liberalism and democracy must be distinguished from one another, and that once the characteristics of the two are specified, the contradictory nature of modern mass democracy becomes evident. Democracy, declares Schmitt, is the principle that equals are to be treated equally. This necessarily implies that unequals will not be treated equally. According to him, democracy requires homogeneity—a homogeneity that exists only on the basis of the elimination of heterogeneity. Thereby, all democracies have always excluded what threatened their homogeneity. He considers the liberal idea of the equality of all persons as persons to be foreign to democracy. It is an individualistic humanitarian ethic, not a possible form of political organization. The idea of a democracy of mankind is, for him, unthinkable because an absolute human equality—an equality without the necessary correlate of inequality—would, he says, be an equality robbed of its value and substance and perfectly meaningless.[8] We can only understand universal and equal suffrage within a given circle of equals, because it is only when homogeneity exists that equal rights make sense. This is why, in the different modern democratic states where universal human equality was established, equality has always meant the exclusion of those who did not belong to the state.

Schmitt concludes that modern mass democracy rests on the confusion between the liberal ethics of absolute human equality and the democratic political form of identity of governed and governing. Its crisis results, therefore, from

> the contradiction of a liberal individualism burdened by moral pathos and a democratic sentiment governed essentially by political ideals. A century of historical alliance and common struggle against royal absolutism has obscured the awareness of this contradiction. But the crisis unfolds today ever more strikingly, and no cosmopolitan rhetoric can prevent or eliminate it. It is, in its depths, the inescapable contradiction of liberal individualism and democratic homogeneity.[9]

This is not the only problem that Schmitt sees with parliamentary democracy. He also criticizes it for being the union between two completely heterogeneous political principles: the one of identity proper to the democratic form of government, and the one of representation proper to monarchy. Such a hybrid system is the result of the compromise that the liberal bourgeoisie has managed to establish between absolute monarchy and proletarian democracy by way of combining two opposite principles of government. Schmitt affirms that the representative element constitutes the nondemocratic aspect of such a democracy and that, as far as parliament provides the representation of political unity, it is in opposition to democracy:

> As democracy, modern mass democracy attempts to realize an identity of governed and governing, and thus it confronts parliament as an inconceivable and outmoded institution. If democratic identity is taken seriously, then in an emergency, no other constitutional institution can withstand the sole criterion of the people's will, however it is expressed.[10]

Schmitt announces that the unnatural alliance established in the nineteenth century between liberal parliamentary ideas and democratic ideas has reached its moment of crisis. The parliamentary regime has lost its rationale because the principles on which it justified itself are no longer credible under the circumstances of modern mass democracy. According to him, the essence of the liberal parliament is public deliberation of argument and counterargument, public debate and public discussion. The claim is that, through such a process of discussion, truth will be reached. This is, he says, a typical rationalist idea that can be grasped only within the context of liberalism understood as a consistent, comprehensive, and metaphysical system. He argues that

> normally one only discusses the economic line of reasoning that social harmony and the maximization of wealth follow from the free economic competition of individuals, from freedom of contract, freedom of trade, free enterprise. But all this is only an application of a general liberal principle. It is exactly the same: That the truth can be found through an unrestrained clash of opinions and that competition will provide harmony.[11]

According to Schmitt, the following is what has happened: The liberal parliamentary order was based on confinement to the sphere of the private of a series of important divisive issues like region, morality, and economics. This was required in order to create the homogeneity that was the necessary condition for the working of democracy. Parliament could, in that way, appear as the sphere where individuals, separated from their conflicting interests, could discuss and reach a rational consensus. With the development of modern mass democracy came the "total state," which the democratic pressures for the extension of rights pushed to intervene into more and more areas of society. The phenomenon of depolitization characteristic of the previous phase was then reversed and politics began to invade all the spheres. Not only did parliament increasingly lose its importance, because many decisions concerning crucial issues started to be taken through different procedures, but it also became the arena where antagonistic interests were confronting each other. This, for Schmitt, marked the end both of the liberal state and of democracy.

He claims that, in such conditions, the view that openness and discussion were the two principles which legitimated parliamentarism has been left without any intellectual foundation.

> There are certainly not many people today who want to renounce the old liberal freedoms, particularly freedom of speech and the press. But, on the European continent, there are not many more who believe that these freedoms still exist where they could actually endanger the real holders of power. And the smallest number still believe that just laws and the right politics can be achieved through newspaper articles, speeches at demonstrations, and parliamentary debates. But that is the very belief in parliament. If in the actual circumstances of parliamentary business, openness and discussion have become an empty and trivial

formality, then parliament, as it developed in the nineteenth century, has also lost its previous foundation and its meaning.[12]

Schmitt was, of course, writing those lines in 1923, and his analysis refers particularly to the situation of the Weimar Republic, but his point is still relevant today. Current liberal democracies are certainly not on the verge of collapse; however, the enormous literature on the crisis of legitimacy in recent decades and the growing preoccupation with the massive disaffection from politics indicate that the problems pointed out by Schmitt have not yet found a solution.

To be sure, many things have changed in liberal political theory. Any attempt to give an ethical and philosophical justification of parliamentary democracy has been abandoned in favor of what Macpherson has called an equilibrium model of democracy. He shows that such a model does not pretend to have any ethical component and treats citizens simply as political consumers. Its main tenets are

> first, that democracy is simply a mechanism for choosing and authorizing governments, not a kind of society nor a set of moral ends; and second, that the mechanism consists of a competition between two or more self-chosen sets of politicians (élites) arrayed in political parties, for the votes that will entitle them to rule until the next election.[13]

Many consider today that it is this "pluralist elitist" conception of democracy that explains the lack of interest and participation in the democratic process, and that we must recover the ethical appeal that was present in the political theory of liberals like J. S. Mill, MacIver, or Dewey. This is an important point to which I will return. For the moment, I want to indicate only that, if this is to be done successfully, we must come to terms with Schmitt's critique of parliamentary democracy.

Far from having become irrelevant due to the posterior transformations in liberal democracies, such a critique is as pertinent as ever and, in many cases, the phenomena that he was describing have been reinforced. For instance, many of Bobbio's current preoccupations with the danger of invisible power confirm Schmitt's predictions. Bobbio denounces the reappearance of the *arcana imperi* and the increasing role played by secrecy, in which he sees "a trend completely at variance with the one that inspired the ideal of democracy as the apotheosis of visible power on the part of the citizens, but on the contrary towards the maximum control of the subjects on the part of those in power."[14]

Obviously, evaluations of that phenomenon by Bobbio and Schmitt differ, but they both recognize that it creates a problem that can undermine the legitimacy of the parliamentary system.

LIBERALISM AND THE NEGATION
OF THE POLITICAL

I think that we can learn much from Schmitt's critique of parliamentary democracy without having to follow him in his rejection of liberal democracy. He allows us to become aware of the shortcomings of liberalism that must be remedied if we want to develop an adequate liberal democratic political philosophy. Reading Schmitt in a critical way can also help us to realize the crucial importance of the articulation between liberalism and democracy, and the dangers involved in any attempt to renounce liberal pluralism.

Indeed, Schmitt's main target is not democracy but liberalism, whose pluralism he violently opposes. The intellectual core of liberalism resides for him "in its specific relationship to truth, which becomes a mere function of the eternal competition of opinions."[15] For a conservative Catholic like Schmitt, such a view is absolutely inadmissible, as is the liberal belief in the openness of opinions and its vision of law as *veritas* and not *auctoritas.* This is what Schmitt objects to rather than democracy per se, which he sees as perfectly compatible with an authoritarian regime. For example, he states that "Bolshevism and Fascism by contrast are, like all dictatorships, certainly antiliberal but not necessarily antidemocratic."[16] He personally advocates replacing parliamentary democracy by a plebiscitary democracy. This is, for him, a type of possible regime nearer to the ideal model of democratic identity, and he asserts that, through the democratic plebiscitary procedure of acclamation, it would be possible in a mass democracy to reestablish a more authentic public sphere.[17]

The crucial issue concerns the very nature of modern democracy. Schmitt refuses to accept that a new form of society has emerged from the disintegration of the theologico-political model. He does not want to acknowledge that under modern conditions, with the disappearance of a substantive common good and the impossibility of a single homogenous collective will, democracy cannot be conceived on the ancient model of identity of rulers and ruled. Not only must it be of a representative sort, but it also necessitates institutions to guarantee the protection of individual rights. His profound hostility to the effects of the democratic revolution and the fact that, as Claude Lefort has shown, power now "is linked to the image of an empty place, impossible to occupy, such that those who exercise public authority can never claim to appropriate it,"[18] prevent him from seeing any value in liberal political institutions. Such a rejection of liberal pluralism and the political institutions that accompany it can have very dangerous consequences and open the door to totalitarianism. In the case of Schmitt, this needs no demonstration.

I am not arguing here that his work prior to his joining the Nazis in 1933 was already tainted by their ideology. It is clear to me that it was not, and it is incontestable that Schmitt did his best to impede Hitler's legal rise to power. But his antiliberal conception of democracy also made it possible for him to accept Nazi rule later. I believe that this should be understood by people on the left who are aiming for the realization of a perfect democratic homogeneity and see liberalism only as an obstacle to such an ideal.

We do not have to accept Schmitt's thesis that there is an inescapable contradiction between liberalism and democracy. Such a contradiction is the result only of his inability to grasp the specificity of modern democracy. Yet there is certainly a tension between liberalism and democracy, and between its two constitutive principles of liberty and equality. They can never be perfectly reconciled, but for me this is precisely what constitutes the principle value of liberal democracy. It is this aspect of nonachievement, incompleteness, and openness that makes such a regime particularly suited to modern democratic politics. Unfortunately, this aspect has never been properly theorized, and liberal democracy does not have the political philosophy that could provide it with adequate principles of legitimacy. Schmitt is certainly right to argue that those principles are very unsatisfactory and in great need of reformulation.

Ironically enough, while Schmitt himself believed that such a reformulation is doomed because of the basic contradiction between liberalism and democracy, he still can be very useful for such a task. His uncompromising critique of liberal rationalism and universalism—and its complete lack of understanding of the political—is particularly illuminating and must be taken into account if we want to provide liberal democracy with the philosophy it needs.

In *The Concept of the Political,* Schmitt argues that the pure and rigorous principle of liberalism cannot give birth to a specifically political conception. Every consistent individualism must indeed negate the political, since it requires that the individual remain *terminus a quo* and *terminus ad quem.* In consequence,

> there exists a liberal policy in the form of a polemical antithesis against state, church, or other institutions which restrict individual freedom.

> There exists a liberal policy of trade, church and education, but
> absolutely no liberal politics, only a liberal critique of politics. The
> systematic theory of liberalism concerns almost solely the internal
> struggle against the power of the state.[19]

Liberal individualism is unable to understand the formation of collective identities and it cannot grasp the collective aspect of social life as
being constitutive. This is why, according to Schmitt, liberal concepts
move between ethics and economics, which can be conceived in individualistic terms. But liberal thought evades state and politics. It attempts to
"annihilate the political as a domain of conquering power and repression."[20] For Schmitt, the political is concerned with the relations of friend
and enemy. It deals with the creation of a "we" opposed to a "them." It
is the realm of "decisions," not free discussion. Its subject matter is conflict and antagonism, and these indicate precisely the limits of rational
consensus—namely, the fact that every consensus is, by necessity, based
on acts of exclusion.

The liberal idea that the general interest results from the free play
of private interests, and that a universal rational consensus could emerge
from free discussion inevitably blinds liberalism to the phenomenon of
the political, which, for Schmitt, "can be understood only in the context
of the ever-present possibility of the friend and enemy grouping, regardless of the aspects which this possibility implies for morality, aesthetics
and economics."[21] Liberalism believes that, by confining the divisive
issues to the sphere of the private, agreement on procedural rules should
be enough to regulate the plurality of interests in society. But this liberal
attempt to annihilate the political is bound to fail. The political can never
be domesticated or eradicated since, as Schmitt indicates, it can derive its
energy from the most varied of human endeavors. "Every religious,
moral, economic, ethical or other antithesis transforms itself into a political one if it is sufficiently strong to group human beings effectively
according to friend and enemy."[22]

I believe that Schmitt is right to point out the deficiencies of liberal
individualism with respect to the political. Many of the problems facing
liberal democracies today stem from the fact that politics has been
reduced to an instrumental activity, to the selfish pursuit of private
interests. The limitation of democracy to a mere set of neutral procedures, the transformation of citizens into political consumers, and the
liberal insistence on a supposed neutrality of the state have emptied
politics of all its substance. It has, indeed, been reduced to economics and

stripped of all its ethical components. This, of course, was in part the result of a positive phenomenon: the separation between church and state, and the distinction between the public and the private. But if the separation between the private domain of morality and the public domain of politics was a great conquest for liberalism, it also led to the relegation of all normative aspects to the domain of individual morality. Thus, a real gain in individual freedom also made it possible for an instrumentalist conception of politics to become dominant later with the progressive disqualification of political philosophy and the growth of political science. There is an increasing awareness among political theorists of the need to revive political philosophy and to reestablish the link between ethics and politics. Unfortunately, the different approaches are unsatisfactory, and I do not think that they can provide an adequate political philosophy for modern democracy.

TOWARD A RADICAL-LIBERAL-
DEMOCRATIC POLITICAL PHILOSOPHY

The present revival of political philosophy is dominated by the debate between Kantian liberals and their communitarian critics. In a sense, both aim at recovering the normative aspect of politics which had been cast aside by the dominance of the instrumentalist model. Deontological liberals like John Rawls and Ronald Dworkin want to infuse politics with morality. Following the model set by Kant in *On Perpetual Peace,* they are advocating a view of politics bound by norms and guided by morally defined goals.

The communitarians on the other side attack liberalism on account of its individualism. They denounce the ahistorical, asocial, and disembodied conception of the subject that is implied by the idea of an individual endowed with natural rights prior to society. They also reject the thesis of the priority of the right over the good that is at the core of the new liberal paradigm established by Rawls. They want to revive a conception of politics as the realm in which we recognize ourselves as participants in a community. Against the Kantian inspiration of rights-based liberals, the communitarians call upon Aristotle and Hegel. Against liberalism, they appeal to the tradition of civic republicanism.

The problem is that some of them, like Michael Sandel and Alasdair MacIntyre, seem to believe that a critique of liberal individualism necessarily implies the rejection of pluralism. So, they end up by proposing to return to a politics of the common good based on shared moral values.[23] Such a position is clearly incompatible with modern democracy, because it leads to a premodern view of the political community as organized around a substantive idea of the common good. I do agree that it is important to recover notions of civic virtue, public spiritedness, common good, and political community that have been discarded by liberalism. However, they must be reformulated in a way that makes them compatible with the defense of individual liberty.

The solution proposed by the Kantian liberals is not satisfactory either. Independent of the fact that their attempt to provide political liberalism with a new political philosophy does not put into question liberal individualism or its rationalism, what they present as political philosophy is nothing more than a public morality to regulate the basic structure of society. In other words, they do not see any real difference in nature between moral philosophy and political philosophy. For them, the issue is only a matter of field of application. For instance, Rawls asserts that "the distinction between political conceptions of justice and other moral conceptions is a matter of scope; that is the range of subject to which a conception applies, and the wider content a wider range requires."[24]

The problem with Rawls is that, by not distinguishing properly between moral discourse and political discourse and by using a mode of reasoning which is specific to moral discourse, he is unable to recognize the nature of the political. Conflicts, antagonisms, and relations of power disappear, and the field of politics is reduced to a rational process of negotiation among private interests under the constraints of morality. This is, of course, a typically liberal vision of a plurality of interests that can be regulated without the need for a superior level of political decision, and in which the question of sovereignty is evaded. For that reason, Rawls believes that it is possible to find a rational solution to the question of justice, establishing in that way an undisputed and "publicly recognized point of view from which all citizens can examine before one another whether or not their political and social institutions are just."[25]

Against such rationalist denials of the political, it is useful to remember, with Carl Schmitt, that the defining feature of politics is struggle, and that "there always are concrete human groupings which fight other concrete human groupings in the name of justice, humanity, order, or peace."[26] Therefore, there will always be a debate about the nature of justice, and no final agreement can ever be reached. Politics in a modern democracy must accept division and conflict as unavoidable, and the reconciliation of rival claims and conflicting interests can only be partial and provisional. To present, with Rawls and the Kantian liberals, the basis of social unity as consisting in a shared rational conception of justice is certainly more commendable than to see it as a *modus vivendi* secured by a convergence of self- and group-interests. Still, it is not such an attempt to establish moral limits to the pursuit of private egoism that is going to provide liberal democracy with an adequate political philosophy.

What is at stake is our ability to think the ethics of the political. By that, I mean the type of interrogation that is concerned with the normative aspects of politics, the values that can be realized through collective action and through common belonging to a political association. It is a subject matter that should be distinguished from morality, which concerns individual action. Under modern conditions, in which the individual and the citizen do not coincide because the private and the public have been separated, a reflection on the autonomous values of the political is required. This is precisely the task of political philosophy, which must be distinguished from moral philosophy.

I consider that such a reflection on the ethics of the political calls for the rediscovery of a notion that was central in classical political philosophy: the notion of *regime* in the Greek sense of *politeia,* which indicates that all forms of political associations have ethical consequences. Therefore, the elaboration of a liberal-democratic political philosophy should deal with the specific values of the liberal-democratic regime, its principles of legitimacy, or, to use Montesquieu's term, its "political principles." Those are the principles of equality and liberty for all. They constitute the political common good which is distinctive of such a regime.

Yet, there will always be competing interpretations of the principles of liberty and equality, the type of social relations in which they should apply, and their mode of institutionalization. The common good can never be actualized. It must remain a *foyer virtuel* to which we must constantly refer, but which cannot have a real existence. It is the very characteristic of modern democracy to impede such a final fixation of the social order and to preclude the possibility for a discourse to establish a definite suture. Different discourses will indeed attempt to dominate the field of discursivity and creative nodal points, but they can only succeed in temporarily fixing the meanings of equality and liberty.

To put it in another way, while politics in a liberal democracy aims at creating a *we*, and at constructing a political community, a fully inclusive political community can never be achieved because, as Schmitt tells us, in order to construct a *we* it must be distinguished from a *them*, and that means establishing a frontier, defining an enemy. Therefore, there will permanently be a "constitutive outside," as Derrida has shown us—an exterior to the community that makes its existence possible. On this point, Schmitt's ideas converge with several important trends in contemporary theory which affirm the relational character of every entity, the unavoidable link identity/difference, and the impossibility of a positivity that would be given without any trace of negativity.[27]

To be useful for the elaboration of a modern political philosophy, the concept of regime must make room for the ideal of division and struggle, for the friend/enemy relation. Schmitt's analysis of the concept of *Verfassung* or constitution is particularly helpful here, especially when he refers to the "absolute" concept of the constitution. For him, this indicates the unity of the state understood as political ordering of social complexity. It presents the social not as an ensemble of relations exterior to the political, or something on which neutral political procedural rules are imposed, but as something that can exist only through a specific mode of institution that is provided by the political. Any *Verfassung* always determines a certain configuration of forces, both with respect to the outside by distinguishing one form of political society from another, and with respect to the inside by providing the criteria to distinguish between the friend and the enemy among the different social forces.[28]

To present Schmitt as having a simplistic, one-sided view of politics—as Habermas does—is a complete misreading of his work.[29] Schmitt was very much concerned with the role of values in understanding politics, and he criticizes liberalism precisely for ignoring it. He rightly stresses the need for common political values in a democracy. Of course, his solution is unacceptable because he believes in the necessity of a substantive normative and social homogeneity. However, if we cannot embrace his solution, he can still help us to grasp the complexity of the task which faces us. The rationalist longing for an undistorted rational communication and a social unity based on rational consensus is profoundly antipolitical, because it ignores the crucial place of passions and affects in politics. Politics cannot be reduced to rationality because it indicates precisely the limits of rationality.

Once we recognize that, we can begin thinking about democratic politics and political philosophy in a different way. What we should aim toward in a modern democracy is a politically created unity through common identification with a particular interpretation of its political principles, and a specific understanding of citizenship. Political philosophy has an important role to play here, not in deciding the true meaning of notions like justice, equality, or liberty, but in formulating different interpretations of those notions. In that way, it will provide diverse and always competing languages to construe a range of political identities, modes of conceiving our roles as citizens, and ways of visualizing what kind of political community we want to constitute.

Envisaged from that point of view of a postmetaphysical political philosophy, the influence of Macpherson has been decisive. He has provided many of us on the left with a language that allowed us to recognize the importance of political liberalism at a time when it was, unlike today, very unfashionable. For that reason, and despite all the critiques that can be addressed to his work, I consider that our debt to him is incontestable, and I see the project of a radical liberal democracy as his real legacy.

NOTES

1. Crawford Brough Macpherson, *Democratic Theory: Essays in Retrieval* (Oxford: Oxford University Press, 1973), 183.
2. Norberto Bobbio, *The Future of Democracy* (Oxford: Oxford University Press, 1987), 131-37.
3. Ibid., 56.
4. Ibid., 55.
5. C. B. Macpherson, *The Life and Times of Liberal Democracy* (Oxford: Oxford University Press, 1977), 112.
6. Claude Lefort, *Essais sur le politique* (Paris: Seuil, 1986), 26.
7. Bobbio, *Future of Democracy*, 59. I use the term *pluralism* here to indicate the end of one single substantive conception of the common good to be accepted by all, and not in the way it is used in American political science, as in the pluralist-elitist model.
8. Carl Schmitt, *The Crisis of Parliamentary Democracy* (Cambridge: M.I.T. Press, 1985), 11-12.
9. Ibid., 17.
10. Ibid., 15.
11. Ibid., 35.
12. Ibid., 50.

13. Macpherson, *Life and Times of Liberal Democracy*, 78.
14. Bobbio, *Future of Democracy*, 97.
15. Schmitt, *Crisis of Parliamentary Democracy*, 97.
16. Ibid., 35.
17. Ibid., 16.
18. Claude Lefort, *The Political Forms of Modern Society* (Oxford: Oxford University Press, 1986), 279.
19. Carl Schmitt, *The Concept of the Political* (New Brunswick, N.J.: Rutgers University Press, 1976), 70.
20. Ibid., 71.
21. Ibid., 35.
22. Ibid., 37.
23. Michael Sandel, *Liberalism and the Limits of Justice* (Cambridge: Cambridge University Press, 1982), and "Morality and the Liberal Ideal," *New Republic*, 7 May 1984. For a more detailed critique of Sandel, see my article "American Liberalism and Its Critics: Rawls, Taylor, Sandel, and Walzer," *Praxis International* 8, no. 2 (July 1988).
24. John Rawls, "The Priority of Right and Ideas of the Good," *Philosophy and Public Affairs* 17, no. 4 (Fall 1988): 252.
25. John Rawls, "Justice as Fairness: Political Not Metaphysical," *Philosophy and Public Affairs* 14, no. 3 (Summer 1985): 229. This critique of Rawls is developed in my article "Rawls: Political Philosophy without Politics," *Philosophy and Social Criticism* 13, no. 2 (1987).
26. Schmitt, *Crisis of Parliamentary Democracy*, 67.
27. For a development of those theoretical considerations and their consequence for understanding the political, see Ernesto Laclau and Chantal Mouffe, *Hegemony and Socialist Strategy: Towards a Radical Democratic Politics* (London: Verso, 1985), and Ernesto Laclau, *New Reflections on the Revolution of Our Time* (London: Verso, 1990).
28. Carl Schmitt, *Verfassungslehre* (Berlin: Duncker and Humbolt, 1980), 204-34.
29. Jurgen Habermas, "Sovereignty and the *Führerdemokratie*," *Times Literary Supplement*, 26 September 1986.

William E. Connolly

MODELS OF DEMOCRACY

C. B. Macpherson was a democrat and an idealist, with each of these terms constituting a precondition of the other. His contributions to democratic theory, written mostly between 1966 and 1977, provide a wonderful opportunity for self-reflection and critical renewal for those who were his students and colleagues during this period. In reviewing Macpherson's writings, I also enjoy the opportunity to reconsider my own thinking during the decade of the New Left, without having to identify myself too closely as an object of critical reflection. I was fortunate enough to attend a six-week colloquium in Irvine, California, in 1969, where Brough Macpherson and Arnold Kaufman, author of *The Radical Liberal,* presented seminars on democratic theory, often arguing against Joel Feinberg and Joseph Tussman, who also presented seminars on allied topics.

The affinity between Kaufman and Macpherson can be marked by a seminar which I took with Kaufman in the early 1960s entitled

"Human Nature and Participatory Democracy." The course was also attended by Tom Hayden, and it set much of the agenda for the Port Huron Statement. Both in its delineations and its critiques, the organization of that seminar tracked closely the four models of democracy presented by Macpherson several years later.

I was aligned with Macpherson and Kaufman during the Irvine Conference and came to their defense—although it was unnecessary—whenever a smart-assed young conservative named George Will intervened to tame the "excesses" of democracy. I confess (if that is the right word) that the three of us met a few times to chart our strategy for the next day's debates, with Tussman and Will providing our central targets. We took considerable pleasure in these exchanges, partly because these other guys were squirming under the pressure of life during the late 1960s and partly because we were pretty confident that the track of the democratic left was preferable to the utopian realism peddled by our opponents. I wouldn't mind seeing Tussman and Will—or their functional equivalents—squirm again, and that little surge of anticipatory pleasure, however unlikely it is to be realized, reminds me how indebted my thinking remains to the critical spirit of Kaufman (who died in a plane crash two years after the conference) and Macpherson.

Macpherson's explorations of the democratic ideal occurred in the context of several debates that have been translated and displaced today but not eliminated. The pluralist-elitist debate, the role of apathy in supporting or undermining democracy, the debate between participatory and representationalist ideals of democracy, the relation between equality and democratic citizenship, the issue of the superiority of capitalism or socialism, the question of the United States as an imperial power or defender of the free world, the relation of facts to values in political inquiry, and the relationship between Marxist and liberal theory—these issues crossed and crisscrossed, so that a theorist concerned with one would be compelled to engage the others eventually.

The pluralist-elitist debate has been translated today into the liberal-communitarian debate, and the latter has shifted from a debate between political theorists and researchers in American politics to a debate within political theory. Broadly associated with this shift are issues about the primacy of justice (or rights) over the good, the primacy of hermeneutics over universal models of rationality, the extent to which genealogy exposes hidden affinities between hermeneutics and universal codes of rationality, the decline of the American empire (having lasted about twenty years), the deflation of socialist idealism, the attenuation of democratic idealism in late-modern states, the role of post-Nietzschean thought in political theory, the danger of nihilism, and the insufficiency of the sovereignty problematic.

It is easy to discern continuities flowing through these discontinuities. More significantly, perhaps, it is possible to discern losses submerged within these shifts in the terms of political discourse. Lodged within the first set of issues, Macpherson linked issues of apathy, participation, freedom, and realization in democratic politics to the structure and performance of the political economy. More specifically, he pressed the question of the essential relation between political democracy and economic equality. This latter issue has not altogether disappeared into the folds of new debates. However, it has receded, as the abilities of communitarians and individualists to articulate ideals of selfhood and commonality have surpassed the abilities of either to specify the mode of political economy that best protects and nourishes its idealism. The demise of socialist idealism, however, may soon engender a corollary return to criticism of capitalist idealism. Certainly the latter is needed in the aftermath of Reaganism, and Macpherson would help to identify the pertinent issues were he writing today.

These contemporary shifts in the dominant terms of academic discourse correlate with a certain displacement of democracy itself from the center of theoretical controversy. There are many democrats in theory but fewer theorists organizing their thinking around visions of democracy appropriate to the end of the twentieth century. We need Macpherson today.

Macpherson's four models of democracy reveal the centrality of class inequality in his analysis. Each of the first three models—presented in order of their chronological appearance in the modern West—is defined by the problematic relation it bears to class inequality in capitalism. Protective democracy, formulated by Jeremy Bentham and James Mill, presupposed the hegemony of a market economy. It sought regular elections to advance market interests and to protect against the tyranny of the state within this setting. Its problem was to "produce governments which would establish. . .a free market society and protect citizens from rapacious governments."[2] It thereby sought to regulate and restrain interests already established in civil society rather than to become a "morally transforming force."[3] Its acceptance of class inequality inclined it to exclude several constituencies from effective citizenship and to restrict the rights of citizens; but its commitment to democracy required it to equivocate with respect to these restrictions. Macpherson quotes James Mill to illustrate this "seesaw." "The business of government is properly the business of the rich ... (we have finally enacted that ideal in the United States.) If they obtain it by bad means, the government is bad. If they obtain it by good means, the government is sure to be good. The only good means of obtaining it are the free suffrage of the people."[4]

Developmental democracy represents a notable advance in democratic idealism. Its best representatives were John Stuart Mill and T. H. Green. The key problem was to elevate working-class men into rational beings" because they "can no longer be governed or treated like children ... "[5] In the Millian conception, the "model of man" as a possessive individualist—that is, of people as "conflicting, self-interested consumers and appropriators"—is compromised by the conception of man as "a being capable of developing his powers or capacities."[6] Democratic participation also becomes the central route to self-development. Mill was confounded, in Macpherson's reading, by the incompatibility between "the claims of equal human development and the existing class inequalities of power."[7] He did not develop an effective theoretical strategy for responding to this problem, instead treating it as a temporary residue from the past.

> Mill had seen the contradiction between his developmental ideal and the class-divided and exploitive society of his own time. [But] he did not see that it was a contradiction between capitalist relations of production as such and the developmental ideal.[8]

Those who follow Mill in this tradition—including John Dewey, Robert MacIver, and John Findlay—saw the structural contradiction even less clearly than did Mill. Moreover, unlike him, they thought the perfection of democratic education and institutions would suffice by itself to reduce the contradiction to workable terms.

Equilibrium democracy, otherwise known as "pluralist democracy," was enunciated by Joseph Schumpeter in 1942 and elaborated by a constellation of American political scientists—mostly from Yale, it seems—in the 1950s and early 1960s. It enhances the realism of democratic theory by resubmerging its developmental dimension. Its realism—situated ambiguously between a description of actual arrangements through the vocabulary of democracy and an idealization of established modes of representation as the best form of governance available to modern life—depreciates the value of participation and appreciates the functional importance of apathy. Apathy among a majority of citizens now becomes functional to democracy, because intensive participation is inefficient to rational individuals. Participation activates the authoritarianism already latent in the masses, and it overloads the system with demands which it cannot meet. The equilibrium model sinks participation and development under three waves, with the visibility of the first and third waves concealing the crucial role played by the second: first, by treating democracy as the institutional means to register "the desires of people as they are" rather than a process which contributes "to what they might be or wish to be";[9] second, by condensing the desires and interests of citizens into the vocabulary of possessive individualism; and third, by legitimizing institutional and ideological bulwarks against pressures that overflow the terms of interest representation.

Democracy now becomes a vehicle of social legitimacy and rational policy within the priorities of the class system. Chiming in with other critics of pluralist theory in his choice of a contemporary exemplar of the equilibrium ideal, Macpherson quotes Robert Dahl to seal his case:

> If the democratic system depended solely on the qualifications of the individual voter, then it seems remarkable that democracy has survived through the centuries . . . but when one considers the data in a broader perspective—how huge sections of the society adapt to political conditions affecting them or how the political system adjusts itself to changing conditions over long periods of time—he cannot fail to be impressed . . . Where the rational citizen seems to abdicate, nevertheless angels seem to tread.[10]

Macpherson contends that these angels tread heavily on democratic ideals of equality and development. "The equilibrium it produces is an equilibrium in inequality; the consumer sovereignty it claims is to a large extent an illusion . . ."[11] Social inequality engenders political apathy. It is an apathy of resignation and hostility among excluded members rather than one reflecting a rational allocation of time among contented "satisficers." The equilibrium model protects against tyranny, but it performs poorly when measured by the standards of developmental democracy.

Macpherson then endorses participatory democracy, although neither with the unfettered enthusiasm of many of its supporters during the 1960s nor with great confidence that it would become installed in Western states. The problem is that structural changes in the political economy are needed to transcend class inequality, and the transcendence of class inequality is needed to make participatory democracy possible. Macpherson inscribes his own version of Rousseau's paradox of politics into the fabric of modern democracy when he says,

> We cannot achieve more democratic participation without a prior change in social inequality and in consciousness but we cannot achieve the changes in social inequality and consciousness without a prior increase in democratic participation.[12]

Macpherson finds it difficult to envisage an institutionalization of participation that speaks to the issues most fundamentally relevant to the life of the entire society and the welfare of its citizens. He thus is drawn to a reluctant endorsement of representative institutions, holding out some hope that they may wither away under the weight of participatory institutions in the murky future.

I hope this summary brings out connections between the development of capacities and the conquest of class inequality in Macpherson's delineation of models of democracy. I now want to think further about these two standards.

DEMOCRACY AND EQUALITY

The reduction of inequality is surely crucial to robust democracy, but it must be pursued in ways which do not undermine other crucial elements in democracy. It must also be viewed not as an end in itself, but as a support to effective citizenship. If these conditions are granted, it is probably neither necessary nor feasible to remain as attracted to command economies as Macpherson tended to be. If markets are included (but not treated as exclusive) as a means of organizing capital, determining production, and organizing work, then a compromise in the ideal of economic equality may also be unavoidable. However, it also seems to me that the standard of equality demanded by democracy now becomes both less stringent than that intimated by Macpherson and more demanding than that reached today either by operative democracies or most liberal visions of democracy.

If the standard is one in which every citizen is provided with sufficient opportunity for work, income, and security to enable active participation in the life of education, consumption, culture, and politics sustained by the culture, then the goal of equality becomes the less demanding, but still difficult, objective of reducing the established scope of inequality. If one adds the more controversial requirement that no class receive so much income that it can manufacture private escapes from the collective issues of ecology, military service, maintaining peace, maintaining a viable housing stock, public education, and the like, then the demands become more difficult to meet. However, perhaps they are still not so categorical that meeting them requires that the corollary democratic virtues of diversity, openness, and cultural variety be squeezed.

There are two goals then: First, there is the goal of lifting the floor below which no one is allowed to fall because it enables everyone to be a participant in the common life if he or she is inclined to do so; second, there is the goal of establishing a ceiling that disables a rich minority from so distorting priorities in the political economy that the political prospects of responding democratically to collective issues is undermined. When private escapes to pressing collective issues are too readily available to a significant minority, structures of compensatory consumption are built up that intensify the collective evil and make it even more difficult to respond to it politically in the future. This can be discerned today, in the United States and elsewhere, in the fields of transportation, education, military service, medical practice, ecology, and suburbanization, with a large portion of tax dollars going to provide infrastructural support for practices that exclude large constellations of people from their effective use. This also impairs public support to sustain a viable system of public education, curtail military adventurism, maintain a housing stock within the financial reach of all members, establish universal medical care, forestall urban decay, and protect the integrity of the environment. A democracy adopts practices of public representation and participation that reach the most fundamental issues impinging upon the society; and it responds to such issues in ways that sustain the coalitions of democratic citizenship into the future.

Thus, my version of Rousseau's paradox for contemporary politics is this: rough equality is a prerequisite for effective democracy, but effective democracy is a prerequisite for rough equality.

How could a Western democracy institutionalize rough equality if it found the will to address this paradox? It seems to me that the best prospect is to combine a more highly progressive tax system with evolution to modes of consumption that are inclusive rather than exclusive in form.[13] The two must advance together if either is to succeed.

The evolution of inclusive modes of consumption might increase public support for a more progressive tax system, one which discernibly provides common benefits that appear neither to working-class whites to be restricted to the urban poor (that is, to blacks), nor to the underclass to be beneficial primarily to white professional classes.

An exclusive item of consumption is one which cannot be extended broadly without (a) decreasing the private value of the good to those who received it first, (b) increasing the private costs of its use, (c) accentuating the adverse social effects of its use, and (d) increasing the costs borne by the state in subsidizing this good and rectifying the adverse social effects of its use. Few staples of consumption fit all of these criteria perfectly, although many come close.

A transportation system built around highways and cars, a housing system centered around single-family suburban units, a high-technology system of medical care built around doctors who set private fees, and a private health insurance system—all approximate exclusive goods. Once the social infrastructure of consumption—that is, enabling laws, tax subsidies, governmental grants, architectural design, established materials of construction, governmental highway programs, and the organization of medical research—becomes defined around the production of such exclusive goods, it becomes increasingly difficult for even middle-class households to make ends meet while participating in available forms of transportation, housing, education, and medical care. Such a system of production and consumption intensifies inequality, requiring the state to increase the subsidies of those at the lower end of the income scale at the risk of alienating middle-class taxpayers already squeezed by the established universe of consumption, or to discipline and punish those forcibly excluded from established patterns of the good life.

The American political economy is built around the illusory goal of universalizing exclusive goods, and this objective helps to erode one of the economic preconditions of democratic citizenship.

An inclusive good reverses these effects. It is susceptible to universalization because its private value is increased as it is extended more generally to the populace; its unit social costs are reduced through its extension; and state support for its development and extension reduce the total social costs of meeting consumption needs in its domain.

A single example must suffice here. If the sizable state subsidies for health care in the United States were shifted from established programs and state subsidies to enabling legislation and subsidies for the universalization of HMOs, the exclusionary/inflationary effects of the present medical system could be curtailed. As successful experiments with such programs have shown (before they were emasculated in the United States by the Reagan administration), the system of salaries for physicians, preventive health care, enhanced patient involvement in self-care, reduced recourse to surgery, and generalized incentives within health care units to reduce high-technology expenditures while protecting patients from serious and expensive diseases, fosters inclusion, cost reduction, local control, and self-reliance.

A reduction in economic inequality is a key condition of democratic citizenship in late-modern states, but the fear of many liberals is that these very reductions will stifle the cultural diversity and individuality also important to a democratic ethos. The changes in the social infrastructure of consumption proposed here, though, might reduce inequality while also supporting cultural diversity.

One further effect should also be noted. I believe—as did Macpherson, I think—that the goal of constant economic growth in pursuit of private affluence is increasingly running into conflict with the end of constitutional democracy to which it has been joined historically. New forms of discipline, regulation, surveillance, and exclusion are introduced to support growth, and these forces threaten to erode some of the social preconditions of democratic citizenship and governance. If the end of growth is now becoming an imperative of the civilization of productivity, while the promise of the universalization of private affluence is receding as a credible hope for the future, then a democratic program to reconstitute the infrastructure of consumption could also help to relax some of the electoral pressures on behalf of the growth imperative. As exclusive goods are extended into more areas of the economy and to new constituencies striving to participate fully within it, the effective costs of participating in the common economic life are increased. A variety of households find that they can only hope to participate in the costs of education, housing, transportation, health care, retirement, security against crime, and cultural life by pressing for large increases in their wages and salaries. The enlargement of difficulties in meeting the imperative of growth is matched by a generalized insistence that growth must be pursued to support the next cycle of wage and salary demands of workers striving to make ends meet within the established universe of consumption.

On my reading, then, it is possible to be both an affluent society marked by the proliferation of consumption possibilities and one in which a majority of households finds it difficult to participate in the established universe of consumption. But such a combination is deadly for the prospects of democracy, if by that one means a society in which most people have the effective opportunity to participate in politics and no segment of the society finds itself effectively excluded from engagement in these practices. It is deadly because it closes whole classes of people out of the established life of the society, because it creates constituencies whose suffering constitutes a danger to everyone else, and because the predictable response by powerful and privileged constituencies to that threat is to deploy the institutions of democratic representation to exclude, punish, and discipline dangerous and disaffected elements.

I believe that my perspective on the economic conditions of democratic practice has much in common with the spirit of Macpherson, even though there is considerable divergence between us over how this spirit is to be expressed, balanced, and activated.

DEMOCRACY AND NORMALIZATION

Things become more complicated when considering the link between democracy and the realization of human powers or capacities in Macpherson's theory. Macpherson distinguishes between extractive power and developmental power.

Extractive power involves the ability to command benefits for oneself from the labor or actions or others, usually by controlling resources to which they need access. Developmental power is the ability to realize and exercise human capacities. The former divides people, while the latter can unite them—once each individual and group accepts the principle that the development of itself is not to occur at the expense of anyone else. Let Macpherson speak in his own voice about the latter power.

> But this leaves open the question, what are these human capacities? . . .
> [They] include the capacity for rational understanding, for moral judgment and action, for aesthetic creation or contemplation, for the emotional activities of friendship and love, and, sometimes, for religious experience.[14]

How are these capacities to relate to each other within the self and among selves in a democratic society conforming to the Macpherson ideal?

The further assumption which is at first sight a staggering one, is that the exercise of his human capacities by each member of a society does not prevent other members exercising theirs: that the essentially human capacities must all be used and developed without hindering the use and development of all the rest. . . .

Now to describe as essential human characteristics only those ones which are not *destructively contentious* is of course to take a fundamentally optimistic view. That view has been at the root of the democratic vision, and indeed of the liberal vision . . . That men if *freed from scarcity* and from *intellectual error* (i.e., the ideologies inherited from the ages of scarcity) would live together *harmoniously* enough, that their remaining contention would only be creative tension, cannot be proved or disproved except by trial. But such a proposition is basic to any demand for or justification of democratic society . . . [T]he case for a democratic *society* fails without the assumption of potential *substantial harmony* . . . In any case the postulate of non-opposition of essentially human capacities cannot be said to be contradicted from experience, for it is asserted of the capacities that would be held to be human in a society as yet nowhere realized.[15]

A few points deserve notice here. First, Macpherson not only emphasizes economic equality as an essential precondition of democracy, but he further postulates that once equality is introduced and contrived scarcity overcome, it will be possible for each to realize his capacities in harmony with everyone else and for the general democratic ethos to exude a consensual harmony that eliminates destructive contention. Class inequality is not only an impediment to democracy for Macpherson, but it comes close to constituting the problem of evil and the key to its solution. Second, Macpherson, specifies this fundamental conviction, however, as a postulate to be acted on rather than something that is known to be true. Third, the level of generality reached in the formulation is so high that it is not perfectly clear just how warm, harmonious, consensual, unalienated—the early Marx haunts these passages—and communitarian a realized democracy is projected to be.

I agree with Macpherson in the judgment that every political theory —whether realistic or idealistic, individualistic or communitarian, egalitarian or inegalitarian, democratic or aristocratic—contains, somewhere in its structure, contestable postulates or projections. I also agree that the most crucial postulates in Macpherson's theory, and others too, have not been proven through historical experience, scientific evidence, or reason. Macpherson is salutary in striving to articulate key postulates underlying his most important contentions while emphasizing their contestability. The democratic theorists whom he reviews and criticizes—particularly those who pride themselves on their realism about "human nature" as it always has been and always will be—are often less reflective on this score.

I do not agree that one set of postulates (say, Macpherson's as opposed to those governing the equilibrium model) is automatically more optimistic than an alternative set. Standards of what counts as instances of optimism and pessimism are already entangled in a set of prior convictions concerning the character of the good life and the range of possibilities within which it can be sought. For example, the realist or equilibrium theory of democracy is optimistic about the degree to which Western capitalistic states can approximate the ideal of democracy as they conceive it. When judged from their perspective, Macpherson is more pessimistic on this score. These are intratheoretical judgments which are often presented as if they were objective standards of assessment *between* theories.

Macpherson restricts the future contestability of his postulates, suggesting that the right set of social trials may allow us in the future to reach definitive judgment about the most fundamental issues. I treat such postulates as unavoidable and contestable projections. They are unavoidable because no theory can dispense with some such set, and they are contestable because, while subject to a variety of historical and speculative tests, the most fundamental ones are unlikely to be susceptible to *definitive* settlement now or in the future.

I find Macpherson's postulates, indeed, to be dangerous in some ways and to be at odds with some elements in the vision of democracy I subscribe to. Within my perspective, they are too "optimistic" about the pursuit of coherence and harmony, and too "pessimistic" about the creative role to be played by political disturbance, even in the most democratic society.

Balanced against this latter judgment, however, is a sense that the very generality of his most fundamental theoretical formulations may well make them compatible with some of the postulates and ends intrinsic to my idealism. So, instead of trying to pin the meaning of his generalities down more specifically, I will elaborate on a few ingredients in the conception of democracy that I endorse.

If someone finds my vision to be compatible with hers and—however unlikely this may be—finds the combination to be appealing, I urge her to endorse the tropes through which I idealize. The play of rhetorical configurations in political reflection is important to the sensibility and direction of practical judgment. All political theorists actually take contests of rhetoric seriously when they impinge on the domains of personal identity, the value of community, the importance of the individual, the significance of gender, the role of equality, and the character of democracy. I merely add that there are excellent reasons for doing so.

Macpherson theorizes democracy within a three-tiered problematic of alienation, repression, and collective realization. People are alienated from a harmonious identity. This alienation is maintained by institutions that repress the self, and a correct institutional arrangement will enable individuals to flourish within a more harmonious collective identity.

Because it would be unfair to reduce Macpherson to a cultural stereotype without doing the same to myself, you can say that my problematic contains three corollary components: normalization, depoliticization, and politicization.

Enunciating these two problematics in this way exaggerates the distance between them. But these two caricatures bring out salient differences in emphasis.

Those who find alienation to be the most fundamental defect in an order tend to divide between those who think that things are falling apart into relativism, nihilism, anarchism or narcissism, and those who think things are held too tightly together by repressive institutions which keep a lid on possibilities for harmonious community that might otherwise emerge. Both alienation perspectives oppose realist, pluralist, and equilibrium readings of established politics. We can, then, discern a three-way debate between an alienation/loss perspective, an alienation/ repression perspective, and a realist/equilibrium perspective.

However, the parties to this three-way debate often coalesce when confronting the stance I endorsed. All discern it to embody irrationality, nihilism, anarchism, or withdrawal of the capacity for ethical concern. These proponents tend to judge the implications of this alternative from the vantage point of the general problematic in which they are entangled together, and then they tend to attribute these implications to the internal structure of the alternative itself. That is why it is wise to begin elaboration of my vision of democracy with a rough delineation of the general problematic in which it occurs.

To say that modern societies are, among other things, normalizing societies is not only to say that they bestow institutional privilege on a restrictive set of identities and then apply intensive institutional pressures to establish those identities as the norms against which a variety of modes of otherness are defined and treated. It is also to say that these norms are touted as standards that the self will endorse for itself, once it understands its true nature. To couch this equation in the language of normalization is not to gesture toward an order in which no norms exist, but to contest the terms of this implicit equation between cultural norm and self-realization, and to expose the politics of self-policing that it enforces.

Everyone does not become the same in a normalizing society. The *opposite* is more likely to occur. In a normalizing society, selves who differ from the norms are shuffled into categories of personal abnormality, perversity, incapacity, irrationality, sickness, irresponsibility, personal defect, and the like. These abnormalities themselves vary across domains (for example, medical practice and sexual customs); degree of severity (eccentricity, a sick sense of humor, or paranoid schizophrenia); and importance to the identity of the entire civilization (a welfare freeloader or a terrorist). A normalizing society, then, proliferates abnormalities, treating a broad array of conduct to be in itself in need of punishment, help, love, self-correction, and improvement.

All societies elaborate boundaries, restrictions, standards, and limits, and every order devises penalties for the infractions that it identifies. A normalizing society proliferates detailed norms of individual identity. It establishes them more through the abnormalities it identifies than through affirmative proofs of its standards of normality. It interprets deviations to be psychological defects among its members, and it devises complex strategies of therapy, self-confession, and self-policing to situate its standards of normality more deeply into the identity of the self and the culture. It treats, say, gender duality as a complex constellation of norms defining an abnormal constellation of homosexuals, lesbians, hermaphrodites, bisexuals, the sexually impotent, and the like, who are deemed to be in need of surgery, therapy, or punishment. To the extent that a normalizing society succeeds in installing these standards within the psyche of the abnormals, to that extent it succeeds in getting them to treat themselves as somehow the source of the difficulties they encounter. Its proponents debate whether the source of each abnormality is in the perverse choice of the abnormals or a defect within them for which they are not responsible, more than it debates the extent to which the structural characteristics of the order and its ideals of community spawn a perverse politics of normalization.

To call a society a "normalizing" society is to call attention to the violence within it from the vantage point of a critical assumption. The assumption: There is no single identity which is intrinsically true in the sense that it, if attained, would create an internal harmony within the self that would still competing drives, possibilities, and tendencies; would enable a variety of selves who realized it together to enter into a harmonious consensus; and would enable the collectivity to achieve an unconstrained consensus binding its members together into a community.

A normalizing society subjugates difference in the name of individual self-fulfillment and/or common realization. Individualist and communitarian ideologies of normalization diverge in where they locate the site of normalization, but they embody complementary strategies of normalization when conceptualized from this perspective. One inscribes its norms on the universal individual and the other on the realized community. Each treats one set of socially established identities as if it were intrinsically true, and each defines competing identities and ulterior dispositions operating below the threshold of identity as intrinsically abnormal. Either in their idealizations of the future or their descriptions of the present, they treat too many norms in the society that they endorse as if they harmonized with the intrinsic identity of the individual or the community. This is typically done not at the level of explicit argumentation, but through a failure to contest or problematize a culturally established set of abnormalities. A normalizing society treats too many of its own limits as intrinsically true rather than as dictates that it is pressed to enforce to maintain itself. It insinuates too many of these codes too unambiguously into the self-identification of its members, often fostering self-loathing in those who internalize the norm while encountering dispositions in themselves that diverge significantly from it.

The perspective advanced here is wary of postulates about true identity and true community whenever the language of the universal individual, harmony, identity, realization, capacity, essentiality, commonality, fulfillment, civic virtue, and participation is not problematized or ambiguated even as it is being advanced. The objection is not to the projection of an ideal against which actuality is appraised, but to the suggestion that the ideal is not itself to be problematized and ambiguated in its formulation of the relation between social order and self-identity. One might problematize one's own ideal, for instance, by treating it as an inherently contestable projection to which one is devoted. Or one might adopt a stance in which its very assertion is compromised by gestures which call it into question, even for oneself, or one might legitimize points of contestation between identities supported by the order that one admires and the claims of those whose contingent formation of self differs from those standards. To put the point perhaps too briefly, to theorize through the vocabulary of normalization is to presumptively endorse the politicization of socially established unities implicitly taken by the culture to be reflective of a natural harmony within the self or between the self and the true order.

Macpherson shares something with equilibrium theorists of democracy here. While he tends to think that the true identity requires introduction of a new institutional framework, they tend to think that the established institutional framework already expresses and enables the true self as a self-interested agent, ignoring the extent to which this latter formation of self is also a highly organized formation.[16] Macpherson and realist democrats vary in their theories of identity, but not in the unequivocal hegemony they give to the problematic of identity. Against Macpherson and his realist opponents I do not say that no preference can be defended between one standard of identity and another. Nor do I say that life can be lived outside the medium of an identity which provides a self with its preliminary dispositions and bearings. I do say that identities and norms are ambiguous formations and that a democratic ethos, properly formed, responds best to this ambiguity.

THE AMBIGUITY OF DEMOCRACY

I treat identity, not as the independent unity of a self or collectivity, but as a contingent, relational formation laced with dissonances and ambiguities. Those contingencies branded mostly deeply, say, into the self form the core of its identity. Those differences most threatening to its self-certainty are likely candidates to be defined as abnormalities, if those sharing this identity have the power to do so and have not engaged genealogical strategies to undercut this drive. The paradox of personal or collective identity is that, while it requires differences to receive definition, some of the very differences it requires represent threats to its self-assurance. A democratic politics is, thus, one which enables a people to participate in its own governance while it also generates political means to fend off the sacrifice of difference to preserve the stability of identity. Democratic politics, then, is properly the site of a tension or productive ambiguity between governance and disturbance of naturalized identities. It thrives only while this tension is kept alive.

This perspective projects the expectation that every organization of identity/difference—because it is established upon human beings not predisposed to coalesce entirely with any particular mode of selfhood and society—will engender elements of resistance and curtail alternative possibilities of being that exceed it. It is from these latter sources that energies to destabilize the dogmatism of identity are generated. This is not to say, then, that every order subjugates difference to the same degree, which allows the theorist to return comfortably to familiar debates on the grounds that no critical perspective can be sustained by this perspective. A democratic order that politicizes intersections between the demands of identity and the claims of order already constitutes an improvement over those that do not.

Within this ethical problematic, there is always a presumptive need to express such resistances and possibilities in a language that seeks to distance itself from the circumscriptions of established identity. This counterbalances a corollary drive—which most of us, most of the time, are more predisposed to enact—to enclose actuality within the folds of a unified identity (realist democratic theory) or to juxtapose against it the ideal of a unified identity (Macpherson's democratic idealism).

It is difficult to detach ourselves experimentally from the identities in which we are enclosed, because we all swim in this sea of normalities and abnormalities. A genealogical sensibility is needed to make progress on this front to make progress toward defamiliarization of internalized standards of normality and distantiation from the drive to balance criticism of actuality against a harmonious idealization of possibility.

We have, then, isolated one set of tendencies in late-modern society under the heading of "normalization." This has also been joined to the assertion that late-modern societies are not simply, or unequivocally, normalizing societies. They possess counterdispositions and possibilities within them. One of these counterdispositions resides within the ambiguous practice of democracy.

Among the key components in the agonistic ideal of democracy is the way in which its practices of politicization subject established identities, norms, conventions, and ideals to denaturalization. Democracy is ambiguous on this score. So, let us pursue a little further the dimension that is deemphasized within the Macpherson ideal.

If operative identities and norms are entrenched contingencies that tend to present themselves as deep truths through the definition of that which deviates from them, then democratic contestation can compromise and attenuate these tendencies. Democratic contestation can unsettle naturalized settlements, disturb customary judgments of abnormality, and expose contingent elements in fixed standards lodged below the threshold of explicit articulation. Such a perspective on democracy gives priority to life over identity, treating identity not as the deepest truth in the self one seeks to realize but as a contingent formation drawn from a pool of life never exhausted by it. A particular identity is a social construction that enables some possibilities of life by disabling others, and that realizes itself by containing, concealing, regulating, and denormalizing that in life which runs over and under it. Because democracy contains the possibility of heightening the experience of contingency, it is through democratic politics that the care for difference can become more generally inscribed in the culture.

Representative democracy constitutes its members as more than role-bearers with a station and a set of assignments and as more than citizens who ratify collective programs. It constitutes them as agents who can question, interrogate, doubt, dissent, protest, organize, resist, disturb, prod, and disrupt fixed cultural priorities, as well as obey and mandate collective purposes. Moreover, the capacity of the self as a dissident citizen informs and energizes its other roles within bureaucratic institutions, career organizations, erotic engagements, family life, gender relations, class relations, and interstate relations. This disruptive and denaturalizing dimension of a democratic ethos must be prized and idealized. It is essential to effective contestation of pressures for normalization lodged in the psychic needs for self-reassurance, the inertia of settled vocabularies, the forgetfulness of habituation, the consolidation of abnormalities through institutional organization, and the communal pressures for collective coordination.

While some ideals of political democracy celebrate it as the consummate medium of legitimation and social coordination, as the embodiment of a general will, this alternative gives equal and opposing weight to its contribution to the experience of contingency in standards of normality. Politics is idealized here specifically because it is a medium of ambiguity. It is at once the means through which general purposes become crystallized and enacted, and the medium through which previous settlements sedimented into fixed arrangements are unsettled and interrogated. It is when democracy maintains tension between these interdependent antinomies that it functions as the perfection of politics.

Two kinds of democratic theory lend too much legitimacy to the drives to unity and consensus. Those individualist and collectivist theories of democracy organized around *mastering* the natural environment so that maximum productivity, affluence, and control over contingency can be realized share a lot with those individualist and communal theories seeking *attunement* to a higher harmony in being more or less discernible to those who seek it.

The first legitimates too much discipline by treating it as appropriate to the end of mastery it supports. The second legitimizes too much discipline on behalf of its ideals of consensus, harmony, and integration. Both play down the *celebration* of politics as a medium through which to unsettle naturalized settlements and to contest injuries done to those placed on the wrong side of normal/abnormal dualities.

From my perspective, both the mastery and the attunement problematics—each with individualist and collectivist versions—underplay the ambiguity of achievements they admire the most. Both, although not in the same ways, give too much weight to discipline and normalization in politics. Both, although at different points in their ideals, diminish the importance of contestation, disturbance, and denaturalization to late-modern life.

Now, of course, everything said here can be pressed back into the currency of identity, realization, fulfillment, and so on—as long as one conventional dimension of those terms (the emphasis on unity and internal integration) is stretched beyond its usual valence, while another dimension (how these terms function to identify the fundaments or "postulates" of a theory) is wheeled out for emphasis. For surely this critical appraisal of a normalizing society rests on certain presumptions about the fundamental character of being. I will not resist too much the familiar effort to show how I presuppose *some version* of the conceptions I modify, if the masters of conceptual enstretchment promise not to contract those terms back into their conventional range once the polemical point has been made. It is doubtful, I imagine, that we will be able to sustain this agreement for more than a few sentences.

I will try to press these meta-agents of coherence to join me in tilting the balances they now give to the textual politics of democratic theory. I take some comfort in the probability that this game of metathrust and parry can go on indefinitely, with neither side likely to make a clinching move that will silence the other for more than a couple of weeks. It meshes with my vision of democratic politics. It fits Nietzsche's recommendation in his presentation of the "spiritualization of enmity" to seek adversaries whom you wish to maintain in contestation, rather than to conquer or eliminate.

In a series of interviews conducted by Charles Taylor, Paul Rabinow,

Martin Jay, Richard Rorty, and Leo Lowenthal in April 1983, Michel Foucault was asked—it may not be too difficult to guess by whom—about his orientation to the pursuit of consensus.

Interviewer(s):
There is a vision of politics associated in America with Hannah Arendt, and now Jurgen Habermas, which sees the possibility of power as acting in concert, acting together, *rather than* power as a relation of domination. The ideal that power can be a consensus, a realm of intersubjectivity, common action is one that your work seems to undermine. It is hard to find a vision in it of alternative politics. Perhaps, in this sense, you can be read as anti-political.

Foucault:
The idea of a consensual politics may indeed at a given moment serve either as regulatory principle or better yet as a critical principle with respect to other political forms; but I do not believe that liquidates the problem of the power relation. . . .

Interviewer(s):
If one can perhaps assume that the consensus model is a fictional possibility, people might nonetheless act according to that fiction in such a way that the results might be superior to the action that would ensue from the rather bleaker view of politics as essentially domination and repression. . . . [I]t might in some sense be better, healthier, freer, whatever positive value one uses, if we assume that the consensus is a goal still to be sought rather than one we simply throw away and say it's impossible to achieve.

Foucault:
Yes, I think that is, let us say, a critical principle . . .

Interviewer(s):
As a regulatory principle?

Foucault:
I perhaps wouldn't say regulatory principle, that's going too far, because starting from the point where you say regulatory principle, you grant that it is indeed under its governance that the phenomenon has to be organized, within limits that may be defined by experience or the context. I would say, rather, that it is perhaps a critical idea to maintain at all times: to ask oneself what proportion of nonconsensuality is necessary or not, and then one may question every power relation to that extent. The furthest I would go is to say that perhaps one must not be for consensuality, but one must be against nonconsensuality.[17]

It seems to me that Macpherson could have been an interrogator of Foucault in this exchange. I pretty much concur with Foucault in the distributive emphasis and nuance of his response. His point can be placed positively on the register of democratic theory, I think, by saying that a democratic culture is one in which a productive tension is maintained between, on the one hand, ruling, governance, hegemony, and consensus, and on the other, disturbing the naturalization of those formations. Unlike the suggestions advanced by the question(s) about the unidimensionality of Foucault's conception of power, I also do not find this response to be at odds with the range of concerns philosophically available to him prior to that interview. I suggest it is possible to construct a democratic theory appropriate to late-modern states that combines a critique of consent and consensus when they are absent with critical engagement of both when they are present. These points are only reinforced when we recall how such a complex condition as consent or consensus is never fully "present" and how likely it is that the consent we offer at some levels to practices and standards are qualified by resistances and dissent at others. Only those who yearn for a world governed by an intrinsic harmony-of-being would dismiss, out of hand, this ambiguous orientation to consent and resistance.

An idealization of democracy as an ambiguous medium through which the absence of consensus is interrogated, and the presence of consensus is interpreted as a sign of danger, generates its own paradoxes. Thus, I earlier endorsed the reduction of inequality as an important precondition of democratic politics. It is conceivable that the standard could—someday, somewhere—become part of the institutionalized background of democratic life. If the consensualization of equality were to become established, I might strive to call the terms behind the consensus into question. Equality may be both a precondition of democracy and a danger to it, as well as an economic condition that enables the dual functions of citizenship along some dimensions and curtails it along others.

However, what if a democratic culture embodying agonistic respect among its members were itself to form the consensual background of late-modern life? Is this, finally, a consensus to be treated unambiguously? Is it time, at last, to be reasonable?

So many conditions of life push in the direction of consensualizing hegemonic identities—including the inertia of shared vocabularies, the pressures of social coordination to make each self calculable, and the persisting tendency toward transcendental narcissism in which we strive to translate what we are into that which conforms to an intrinsic order of being—that I am tempted to worry about this particular paradox only if and when its time comes. Democracy is the practice that enables participation in collective decisions while contesting sedimented settlements from the past. To achieve cultural consensus on this ambiguous practice of democracy would be to achieve a world in which criticism of the politics of nonconsensuality is enabled, while the comforts of stable consensuality are periodically disturbed. This constitutes my ideal of democratic equilibrium, or, if you prefer, democracy as the ambiguous medium of politics.

A vibrant democratic culture maintains dissonant interdependence between the politicization of difference and collective action through democratic means. Such a theorization of democracy denies a fundamental purpose or harmony-in-being to which we can become attuned. It projects an abundance of life and energies. That projection, in turn, is to be problematized *within the theory* by treating it as contestable, and by calling attention to the role it plays in guiding political interpretation. It is to be problematized *in relations between theories* by entering into relations of agonistic respect with theorists who, explicitly or implicitly, project alternative fundaments into their interpretations of the actual and the possible. The respectful agonism between theoretical perspectives in intellectual life recapitulates the ideal of agonistic respect in democratic life.

Such a vision of democracy can draw from Macpherson in its appreciation of equality as a critical principle; in its acknowledgement of the indispensable role of projection (or "postulates") in political reflection; in its recognition of the uncertain relationships between academic discourse and political practice; in its appreciation of the need to attend to possible uses and misuses of its thought in future and unanticipated contexts; and in its commitment to the adventure of speculative reflection amidst these risks and uncertainties.

DEMOCRACY AND SOVEREIGNTY

The preceding reflection proceeds roughly within the sovereignty problematic. That problematic treats the state as the territory within which democracy occurs, and treats things outside as beyond the reach of democratic practice or, alternatively, construes the globe itself as a place to be organized along the lines of a sovereign democracy. Realists, again very roughly, adopt the first perspective, and idealists accept the second, with Macpherson making gestures in the second direction.

But reflection about democracy within the problematic of sovereignty can no longer suffice. The world of politics is too globalized. We have witnessed the globalization of capital, labor, and contingency, with the last effect being the most important one facing political democracy.

By the globalization of contingency I mean the contemporary production of a whole series of dangerous possibilities of global significance that emanate from the state system but strain the inclination or ability of any single state or traditional constellation of state alliances to respond to them. Such possibilities include the greenhouse effect; the destruction of natural resources essential to every region of the world, such as fertile soil, clean water, sufficient food, fresh air, or energy; the degeneration of the state system into a world of strife and insecurity flowing under and through boundaries between states; or a series of nuclear exchanges that destroys civilization.

The globalization of contingency defines late-modernity as a distinctive *time* without a commensurate political *place*. In this time, we can pose questions about the global effects of this network of interdependencies and the legitimacy or illegitimacy of the practices that produce them. However, there is no institutionalized territory large enough to define and respond to these issues within the terms of democratic accountability.

A realist might treat this as a tragic condition that can best be tended to by supporting modest democracy within states, and the traditional web of diplomacy, war, conquest, and subversion between states. An idealist might respond by dreaming of a sovereign place corresponding to the global reach of these contingencies. It could be argued that, in both instances, the relation between late-modernity as a time and the absence of a corollary space of political action fosters de-democratization of the most fundamental issues facing the contemporary world. The key issues tend to be shuffled outside the electoral discourse of territorial democracies because dramatization of them inside would reveal how many effects escape the control of state institutions of representation, participation, rights, and citizenship. Attempts to confront the issues through supranational institutions also tend to be resisted within states as it becomes clear how circumscribed the territorial politics of democratic representation would become if supranational institutions acquired more power in these domains.

Democratic political theorists and realist international theorists

215

typically don't have much to say to each other, each group thinking that the other makes wild assumptions about the world outside its domain of inquiry. At another level, however, we have reached a certain accommodation. Each type justifies is own place in the academic division of labor by treating the state as the locus of a fundamental boundary between internal and external politics. The former concentrate on life inside the state, where debates over membership rights, participation, representation, justice, community, and individuality can occur. The latter treat relations between states as an anarchical system of conflicts and alliances engaged by state leaders properly insulated from intensive democratic accountability and unmoved by too many concerns about legitimacy in relations between states. In both cases, the globalization of contingency becomes submerged as an active theme of democratic politics.

These terms of academic accommodation must now be contested. Democratic political theory must extend itself into the global domain or deteriorate into a quaint form of nostalgia for a world where people pretended that fundamental issues of life were resolvable within the confines of a territorial state. Today's state is becoming a conduit for the translation of global pressures into disciplines, sacrifices, imperatives, and demands applied to its domestic populace according to the relative degree of domestic vulnerability possessed by each internal constituency. This effect compromises internal structures of democratic citizenship and accountability. It also reveals the poverty of democratic theories which either restrict themselves to the confines of the territorial state or soar to the ideal of a global sovereign place where world democracy could be institutionalized.

If late-modernity is a time without a commensurable democratic place, the concern for democracy cannot proceed by extending to the world stage categories of democratic citizenship and representation forged within the problematic of sovereignty. That would be like endorsing the traditional family while saying its members can no longer reside in the traditional home or celebrating the traditional novel while eliminating the role of a plot within it. Perhaps the contemporary need is to supplement territorial democracy in its application to the interior politics of states, with a politics of nonterritorial democratization of global contingencies.

I have not explored this nonterritory with the attentiveness required, but one dimension seems clear to me. What is needed, today and tomorrow, is the formation of cross-national, nonstatist democratic movements focusing upon particular global contingencies, challenging ways in which the normal operation of internal state politics and external state relations can depoliticize global issues. The participants would not give highest loyalty to their own state, to the normal individual, to an internal ideal of community, or even to timeless truths about existence itself. They would compromise these loyalties and obligations by the aspiration to represent—through publicity, exposés, boycotts, and the like—global issues arising within the time in which they live. They would aspire to ventilate global issues by venturing beyond the confines of democratic politics as an established structure of accountability within sovereign states, generating new internal *and* external pressures upon states to respond to these conditions. They would supplement the politics of territorial democracy with cross-national, nonstatist democratization of global issues.

The drive is toward the democratization of issues rather than the formation of a global, democratic state. It is toward supplementary democratization of global issues so that territorial states and alliances of states are pressed to respond to a new set of pressures. The aspiration is to politicize global issues so that they become debated more publicly within states, and so that states are under greater pressure to legitimize their priorities to external constituencies affected by them. It is to foster a democratization of global issues without aspiring to a global democratic state.

The imperative of nonterritorial democratization is utopian. It also compromises the traditional line of correspondences among sovereignty, belonging, democratic accountability, and the territorial state. It reflects traditional theory in its quest to expose and contest submerged issues that deeply impinge upon life, but it breaks with it in projecting a course of democratization that exceeds the terms of electoral accountability in a sovereign state. It exudes an aura of unreality because of the absence of a sovereign place in which it could be institutionalized and through which a certain correspondence could be established between the scope of the troubles it identifies and institutionalized terms of accountability within which it proceeds. Moreover, the powers of mobilization it strives to draw upon pale by comparison to the hold that traditional self-identities of the citizen, the voter, the taxpayer, and the loyal dissenter exert over members of territorial states. It is doubly unrealistic.

However, traditional categorizations of democracy also exude their own aura of unreality as the institutional terms of internal state accountability increasingly fall short of the most profound issues facing the late-modern time. The complex machinery of democratic representation will run idle with respect to the most fundamental issues of the day unless the territorial politics of democratic accountability is supplemented and challenged by the politics of nonterritorial democratization.[18]

Perhaps the question today is which dimension of unreality to attack and which to accept. Nonterritorial democratization must either ambiguate and stretch established assumptions, boundaries, and priorities of the sovereign state, or the internal politics of the sovereign state in a globalized economy will increasingly curtail democratic effectiveness. Perhaps a series of disparate developments—such as divestment movements aimed at international corporations investing in South Africa, the formation of Greenpeace, Amnesty International, Foucault's defense of the boat people as a constituency floating outside the protection of rights bestowed by states, and recent movements in Europe to foster arms reduction among major powers might be explored to see how each reconfigures this discrepancy between territorial democracy and the globalization of late-modern life.

I suspect that Macpherson might be drawn to this last abstract and preliminary reflection, although it diverges from the direction that his own reflections took on the same terrain. It tracks with his insistence upon broadening the sphere of democratic action to match the scope of issues confronting the times. At least, my thinking it has been stimulated by reengagement with his texts within a changed context of democratic practice.

The following injunction marks an issue in need of further reflection: The traditional territorialization of democratic practice must be contested and supplemented if the globalization of contingency is not to reduce established structures of democracy to statist ghettoes.

NOTES

1. Arnold S. Kaufman, *The Radical Liberal: The New Man in American Politics* (New York: Atherton Press, 1968).

2. C. B. Macpherson, *The Life and Times of Liberal Democracy* (New York: Oxford University Press, 1977), 34.

3. Ibid., 43.

4. Ibid., 42.

5. John Stuart Mill, quoted by Macpherson in ibid., 45.

6. Ibid., 51, 48.

7. Ibid., 49.

8. Ibid., 70.

9. Ibid., 79.

10. Macpherson, quoting Robert Dahl, in ibid., 82.

11. Ibid., 86.

12. Ibid., 100. Rousseau's own version of the paradox is: "In order for an emerging people to appreciate the healthy maxims of politics, and follow the fundamental rules of statecraft, the effect would have to become cause; the social spirit, which would be the result of the institution, would have to preside over the founding of the institution itself; and men would have to be prior to the laws what they ought to become by means of laws." Rousseau, *On the Social Contract: With Geneva Manuscript and Political Economy,* edited by Roger Masters and translated by Judith Masters (New York: St. Martin's Press, 1978), 69. I have built an interpretation of Rousseau around this quotation in chapter 3 of my *Political Theory and Modernity* (Oxford: Basil Blackwell, 1988).

13. This distinction between exclusive and inclusive goods is discussed in Michael Best and William E. Connolly, *The Politicized Economy,* 2d ed. (Lexington, Mass.: D. C. Heath, 1982). It is elaborated further in terms of its implications for the Democratic party in the United States in my "Civic Disaffection and the Democratic Party," in *Politics and Ambiguity* (Madison: University of Wisconsin Press, 1987), 31-41.

14. C. B. Macpherson, *Democratic Theory: Essays in Retrieval* (Oxford: Clarendon Press, 1973), 53-54.

15. Ibid., 54-55; emphasis added.

16. In *Political Theory and Modernity,* I give a reading of Hobbes in which the self-interested self is a social construction rather than simply the datum upon which society is built. This social construct is designed to convert an unruly, irascible, and volatile being into a calculable, predictable, and governable individual, so that the individual is not simply the problem a sovereign must cope with nor the restraint to sovereign power the individualist can celebrate. It is also a construct designed in the service of order and governance. See chapter 2 and the first interlude. Macpherson, I want to say, becomes diverted from seeing, amid their significant differences, certain affinities between his position and that of Hobbes.

17. Foucault, "Politics and Ethics: An Interview," in Paul Rabinow, ed., *The Foucault Reader* (New York: Pantheon Books, 1984), 377-79; emphasis added.

18. The rhythms of writing and presentation do not correspond neatly to those of publication. This essay was first presented in 1989. It embodies an initial effort to think about, first, the relation between identity/difference and democracy, and, second, sovereignty and democracy. It sets the agenda, then, for the last couple of chapters of *Identity\Difference: Democratic Negotiations of Political Paradox* (Ithaca, N.Y.: Cornell University Press, 1991); and "Democracy and Territoriality," *Millennium,* December 1991, 463-84.

Chapter 10
The Signifiers of
Democracy

Ernesto Laclau

The most lasting legacy of C. B. Macpherson will probably be the radical contextualization that he introduced in the consideration of the question of democracy. He showed the contingent character of the articulation existing between democracy and liberalism, the unexpressed assumptions that lie at the heart of liberal theory and that govern its discursive sequences, and, finally, the other ways in which democracy, as a world phenomenon, could be conceived and articulated to totalizing discourses other than those of Western liberalism. Thus, Macpherson opened the way to a radical historicization of the categories of political theory. By showing that the links between the various components of a theoretical structure or a worldview are not necessary or logically required, but are contingent—and consequently always reversible—constructs, he helped to considerably widen the field of what requires a *historical* explanation.

In this chapter, I move further in the direction opened by Macpherson. I show, through the analysis of what is involved in the process of political representation, the complexity of the question of democracy in the contemporary world, and both the dangers and the new possibilities that the present situation opens. But let me first summarize the main lines of Macpherson's argument in the 1960s concerning the three types of democracy that he found operating in the world arena: liberal democracy, Soviet democracy, and the democracy of the under-developed countries.

"Democracy has become an ambiguous thing, with different meanings—even apparently opposite meanings—for different peoples."[1] In the case of liberal democracy, the important fact to be taken into account is that the two terms were, for a long while, opposed to each other. Democracy was identified with mob rule and had a mainly pejorative meaning. At the same time, liberalism—in the sense of representative government—had existed for a long while without being democratic in any possible sense of the term. It was only through a long process, which embraced the whole nineteenth century and the beginning of the twentieth century, that the articulation between liberalism and democracy was progressively established.

> In our Western societies, the democratic franchise was not installed until after the liberal society and the liberal state were firmly established. Democracy came as a top dressing. It had to accommodate itself to the soil that had already been prepared by the operation of the competitive, individualist market society, and by the operation of the liberal state, which served that society through a system of freely competing, though nondemocratic, political parties. It was the liberal state that was democratized, and in the process, democracy was liberalized.[2]

In the case of Communist states, we find a first example of non-liberal democracy. By the latter, Macpherson understands "rule by or in the interests of the hitherto oppressed class."[3] The period of proletarian dictatorship was called "democracy" by Marx, and this denomination is justified insofar as the term *democracy* is used in its original and normal sense. Thus, democracy is a class rule (rule by the oppressed). It will come to an end when the abundance attained by economic transformation makes class rule unnecessary. With Leninism, we do not have class rule but vanguard rule. However, this vanguard rule does not involve abandoning the goal of a classless society.

> For it is now clear that even if there were nothing at stake but the continued maintenance of the Soviet system, and the maintenance of their leaders in positions of power, they would be compelled to move towards the original goal. For with the new stage that military technolo-

gy has reached, the Soviet system can only hope to make its way in the world, or even hold its place in the world, by influence rather than by might. And its influence, both within the working class in advanced countries, and in the underdeveloped nations of Asia and Africa, depends entirely on the progress it can make towards the goal of a classless society.[4]

As for the question of whether a vanguard-ruled state can be considered democratic, everything depends on whether we are speaking of a system of government or of a type of society. Macpherson is prepared to accept that a one-party system could be democratic, providing that three conditions are met: that there is an effective measure of intraparty democracy; that there is an open membership; and that participation in party activities does not require efforts more strenuous than those that normal citizens are prepared to give. On the whole, Macpherson thinks that Communist states have been wrong in claiming that they are democratic, both in the narrow and in the broader sense.

In the case of the underdeveloped countries which have experienced anticolonial revolutions, Macpherson sees an even clearer attachment to the traditional conception of democracy as rule by the oppressed, and also clear patterns at work which tend to make very problematic any simple articulation between liberalism and democracy. In the first place, the market mechanisms and the possessive individualist ideology which accompanies them have not played as predominant a role as in Western societies. In the second place, the illiberal tendencies are accentuated by a set of circumstances that move in the direction of consolidating the one-party system—the enormity of the tasks confronting the new state, the need to accumulate large amounts of capital for economic development, and other needs. Consequently, the claim to democracy rests entirely on the presence of a popular collective will. To what extent a collective will expressing itself through a single party can be called "democratic" depends entirely on the degree of control of that party by the rank and file. Here the three conditions mentioned for the Communist parties apply also to those of the underdeveloped countries. On the whole, Macpherson believes that these conditions are more nearly met in the underdeveloped countries than in the Communist ones. While in the Communist cases the vanguard "was separated from the rest of the industrial working class by its degree of class consciousness, and from the mass of the people by its different class basis," in the case of the underdeveloped countries the political class consciousness of the vanguard has been national rather than class consciousness. The vanguard has typically been at one remove, rather than two removes, from the mass of the peasantry, the one remove being in educational advantage, zeal and ability, more than anything else. They can therefore properly claim to represent a general will more fully, or at least more immediately after the revolution, than where the vanguard was more separated from the masses.[5]

In various aspects, Macpherson's vision of the real world of democracy in the 1960s is clearly dated today. The degree of interpenetration between liberalism and democracy in Western capitalist societies is, today, clearly less than it was in the two decades which followed the end of World War II. The decline of communism as a totalizing model has been accompanied in the societies of the Eastern bloc by an eruption of antagonisms, new forms of struggle, and fragmented identities which have destroyed any image of a transparent, homogeneous, and classless society. Finally, the discredit of the bureaucratic forms of political management, which presided over the aftermath of the process of decolonization in the Third World, has put increasingly into question the credentials of those forms of bureaucratic ruling to be considered as democratic in either of the two senses distinguished by Macpherson. Nevertheless, there are, in Macpherson's approach to the question of democracy, some fundamental intuitions that make his vision more contemporary today than, perhaps, at the time in which it was originally formulated. This basic intuition turns essentially around this point: the chasm that he established between the underdog and his or her demands, on the one hand, and the politico-institutional forms of their expression and articulation, on the other. By prolonging the logic implicit in Macpherson's argument beyond the point that he did, we can obtain a perfectly contemporary picture of some of the crucial problems that democratic societies confront today. In this chapter I concentrate on four aspects.

FIRST ASPECT

If we look at the three varieties of democracy described by Macpherson, we will find that there is a fundamental asymmetry between variant one and variants two and three. While both the Soviet and the underdeveloped countries' types of democracy are grounded in a dichotomization of political spaces and in the construction of the underdog—whether in class or in populist terms—as a pole of power, liberal democracy is not. Even more, the democratization of liberalism or the process through which democracy was incorporated as a "top dressing" of a fully fledged liberal state can be described as a conscious effort to blur the marks of social division. If the first half of the nineteenth century was the era of democracy or the people as a social pole antagonistic to the status quo, the liberalization of democracy can be described as a process of differential absorption of social demands, which tends to dissolve their discursive articulation around a popular pole. The other two types of democracy, on the contrary, tend to reassert the moment of social division and popular power.

This distinction is important because it points to the basic fact that democratic demands are not given but constructed, and that social agents who must be represented in the democratic process have to be created by that very process. By showing the contingency of the link between liberalism and democracy, Macpherson's analysis makes it possible for us to think of different types of historical constructions and articulations than those that were considered in the 1960s. If at that time—the heyday of the welfare state and of the process of decolonization and the last stages of the Cold War—the world looked fixed in three different types of democracy that presented the closed character of matrices, today the rigid distinction between those types tends to become more and more blurred. We can, from this perspective, recognize a double movement.

On the one hand, since the late 1960s the ability of liberal democracies to absorb social demands in the classical differential way has decreased. There has been, over the last two decades, a great deal of talk about the "crisis of governability" in Western democracies. This has given place to a proliferation of new social movements whose demands could not easily be channeled through the existing institutional apparatuses and, consequently, to the emergence of democracy as an ensemble of demands outside and against the system. This is certainly a new type of democracy—given that the constituencies do not naturally tend to coalesce around a popular pole—but it is, nevertheless, as antisystem as the radical democracy of the past. On the other hand, and as a second movement both in the Soviet world and in the underdeveloped countries, the themes of liberal democracy tend increasingly to be part of the political agenda. The de-ideologization that is accompanying the decline of totalizing worldviews is increasingly leading to the emergence of fragmented demands of various sections of the populations whose fulfillment requires the establishment of the civic and political rights associated with liberalism. If, in Western societies, there are emerging strong forces pushing for a further democratization of society, in the Eastern bloc and, to some extent, also in the underdeveloped countries, there is a tendency of popular and democratic forces to demand reforms of a liberal type. Thus, there is an approximation in the experiences of various types of society, which are likely to face political problems of an increasingly similar type. Consequently, there is the chance that democracy could become a more universal political language, organized around common themes and common values.

In this new possible world of democracy, the articulation between various social and political elements will be far more contingent than in the past. Here is the point at which Macpherson's analysis must be radicalized, pushing further in the direction pointed out by him. It is not only that there is no necessary articulation between liberalism and democracy; it is also that the various components of the classical liberal ideology have no necessary link between them.

Let me give an example. Both in the Soviet world and in the underdeveloped one, we are witnessing an increasing reinforcement of the market mechanisms. Unless we accept from the beginning the simplistic conclusion that these countries are on the way to becoming full-fledged capitalist societies, the real question from a democratic and socialist perspective should be: Is the operation of market mechanisms necessarily linked to capitalist control and to possessive individualism? What type of market operation is compatible with a democratic and socialist society? There is a whole theory of socialist regulation that requires formulation here, and it can only start from a radical deconstruction of the necessary links that traditional socialism had established between social elements.

Two further conclusions follow from this analysis. The first is that, if social elements have no other forms of unity than the contingent articulation that hegemonic practices are able to construct, politics in the future is likely to be less doctrinaire and more pragmatic, less oriented to long-term teleologies and more to building medium-term political projects. This mainly applies, of course, to radical politics.

The second conclusion is that, if we are conceiving our political engagements in increasingly pragmatic terms, we have to stop speaking about "matrices of society." Possessive individualism has, no doubt, been an immensely pervasive force in the molding of the cultures in which we live, but it is not a matrix, simply because societies do not have matrices. Consequently, the history of the increasing articulation between liberalism and democracy in the West should not be pictured as the progressive adaptation and incorporation of democratic demands to an unchanged core constituted by the possessive individualism of capitalist societies, but rather as an uneasy tension in which the dislocations resulting from capitalist expansion generated social struggles which led, partly to concessions from the system, partly to its reform, and also partly to adaptation to it. Hegemony means exactly that: recognition of an outside that is not reducible to the logic of the hegemonizing force, and establishing a grammar of social action in which the outside—even in its opposition to the inside—becomes part of the latter. The history of the relation between liberalism and democracy becomes in this way a more complex and ambiguous process than the one that a story in terms of a simple absorption could lead us to believe.

SECOND ASPECT

It is important to realize the fragility that is inherent in the historical terrain from which democracy emerges. This relates to the fact that the identity of the underdog is not a fully realized identity but is, on the contrary, an identity constituted in opposition, as the negation of the forces that deny it and that prevent its full constitution. The unity of the people is only the negation of what opposes it, said Saint-Just. The primary terrain of constitution of democracy is not one of fully acquired identities, but of the failure in constituting them. Consequently, the primary terrain of democracy is that of an original dislocation. There is no common measure between the negated identity and the political discourse that is going to reconstitute it at the level of the political imaginary. The negation of an identity does not involve within it the forms of identification that are going to open the way to a culture of resistance—that is to say, of those discursive forms that are going to provide a principle of reading that restores the intelligibility of the whole situation. If the peasants are expelled from the land by the landowners, the nature of the antagonism is not immediately transparent to the agents intervening in it. They must discursively create both the enemy and their own identity as a pole of the conflict. In this process of discursive construction, various discourses can compete, such as a reading of the situation in terms of a cosmic struggle (millennialism), or in terms of popular oppositions (the underdog against those at the top),

227

or in terms of class struggle. In any case, the availability of certain discourses is what ultimately decides what reading is going to prevail. Discourse is often accepted not because it is particularly liked, but because it is the only one that ensures a certain intelligibility of what would otherwise be an entirely irrational situation. It is here that Macpherson's three types of democracy can be seen as three different discursive surfaces, articulating the demands of the underdogs. They can be differentially articulated within a continuous and homogeneous institutional system in the case of liberal democracy. Alternatively, they can be unified around an entity—class—and confrontationally opposed to power conceived as the domination of other classes (as in the Soviet case). Finally, we can maintain this confrontational model but conceive it in the opposition between the nation, or the people, and the colonial powers (as in the case of the underdeveloped countries).

The important point here is that there is no necessary connection between the experiences of dislocation from which the democratic demands emerge and the ideological forms that are going to give them discursive presence. Macpherson's list cannot stop with his three types, given that Shiite fundamentalism or the various forms of European totalitarianism do exactly the same: appeal to the common man, and present themselves as plebeian discourses opposed to the dominant sectors. What is important to realize is that totalitarianism emerges also from a terrain of the democratic revolution—that is, from a terrain in which the dislocations inherent in the constitution of a capitalist world economy open the way to democratic demands of equality. In a traditional hierarchical society, both radical democracy and totalitarianism would have been impossible. The order of the world could not be changed because it was immanent in a social order that was not threatened by any internal or external dislocation.

The complexity of the situation increases further when we move from the totalizing discourses which operate as surfaces of inscription of the different democratic demands to the relations between these demands, because it is fairly obvious that no natural unity among them can be presupposed. How should one put into question the fact that many democratic demands of the Iranian masses found their surface of inscription in Islamic fundamentalism? There can be no doubt that many other demands that we would spontaneously tend to consider democratic are excluded from that discourse. The real world of democracy is consequently becoming not a world in which three conceptions of democracy dispute the historical arena among themselves, but a world in which there is an increasing interpenetration between these conceptions, in which many discourses that we would have never called "democratic" nevertheless hegemonize democratic demands and in which we have a plurality of underdogs who do not tend to establish any form of unity among their various struggles.

THIRD ASPECT

Are we in a better position if, instead of maintaining a broad concept of democracy as rule by the oppressed, we try to restrict ourselves to the narrow conception of democracy that is linked to the notion of democratic control? But here again, matters are far from clear.

At the heart of the notion of democratic control we find the paradoxes inherent in the notion of representation. The category of representation presupposes the *fictio iuris* that somebody is present in a place from which he or she is materially absent. But let us take an extreme case, one in which there is apparently no representation at all—that is, one in which the same social agent whose basic identity is constituted in point A of society has to be present in point B in order to defend his or her interests. We would tend to say that here there is no representation at all, given that there is no duality representative/represented. Nevertheless, we cannot avoid the impression that something such as a representation is taking place, even in this extreme case. The interest of the agent in situation B cannot simply be read off from the mere consideration of the starting point A. It requires a new interpretation that redefines the meaning of both A and B. So, even in a case in which the same agent acts at the level of both A and B, he or she is not simply the same agent. He or she is representing himself or herself, which is something very different, because the whole situation must be reinterpreted, and, in this sense, his or her identity must be reconstructed, taking into account the new dimensions of the terrain in which the representation takes place. The representation is never a passive process in which an identity, constituted at one point, transmits its interests to different points. It involves an active process of constituting a new identity. This is even more evident if we move from our extreme case to more normal cases of representation, those in which representatives and the represented are different agents. In those cases, the representatives have an even clearer role in defining the interests that they represent. We should also notice that here we are not dealing with a perverse distortion of the process of representation, but with something that belongs to its very essence—that is, the representative cannot betray an interest that did not exist in the first place. Of course, there are cases of actual perversion and distortion. All I am saying is that distortion is a special and extreme case within a continuum in which the two terms of the alternative construction/representation shade into one another.

Let us consider the cases of dislocated identities that we discussed earlier. It is clear that, in them, identities that had been shattered at the level of their everyday life were reconstructed through political discourses that proposed a new reading of their situation. The representative is the one who constitutes the identity of the represented. We cannot avoid the feeling that there is something deeply democratic in a Third World nationalistic military regime that carries out structural anti-oligarchical reforms, and that gives the masses a new sense of their dignity and of their place in society. Here we are back to the broader conception of democracy and to all the problems concerning the role of enlightened vanguards that Macpherson discusses. What I am suggesting is that the distinction between the narrow and the broader senses of democracy is not an absolute one, because the unevenness that is inherent in the concept of representation pervades all forms of democratic control. Consequently, the problem of democratic control is not one of making the relation of representation transparent, so that it fully expresses the will of the represented, because that will was not there in the first place. Rather, it consists in making the represented participate as much as possible in the formation of a new will, to ensure as much as possible their complicity in all the impurities and unevenness that the process of representation presupposes.

FOURTH ASPECT

Operating deconstructively within Macpherson's text has led us to a set of conclusions:

1.   Democracy, in the broader sense of people's rule, cannot be limited to the three types described by Macpherson, because it embraces—if this is the only criterion—various forms of fundamentalism and totalitarianism.

2.   Democracy in the narrow sense is an essentially impure phenomenon that participates in all the ambiguities of the process of representation.

3. We are far from being in a hopeless situation, given that the very state of fragmentation of the various democratic demands requires more freedom—in the classical liberal sense—for their expression and defiance.

The double movement of democratization of liberalism and liberalization of democracy—far more radical than the similar processes that took place in the Western societies of the nineteenth century—contains the promise of a new universalism.

It is important to understand the pattern of this process of universalization. This is not a process of peaceful spread of principles that impose themselves as a result of their intrinsic moral value. Rather we are dealing with a process of hegemonization that takes place through protracted struggles. I would argue that all processes of hegemonization involve the production of empty signifiers that unify a certain politico-ideological field.

Let us take a case that is very common in Third World countries: the new function that values and symbols of a rural origin take when they are transplanted to an urban context. The new migrants from the rural areas bring with them to the cities an ensemble of cultural values and, when confronted with the new hostile environment—problems of housing, police violence, new discipline of the factory, and so on—they transform those values into the basis for a new culture of resistance that dichotomizes the social space. Every new demand, every new grievance, is inscribed as a new link in the chain of equivalences unified by those symbols. Then, when other groups in society initiate a process of mobilization and social protest, they incorporate in their discourse those symbols of the rural migrants, because they are the only available ideological raw materials in that society that express feelings radically against the status quo. In this process, those symbols tend to lose all specific content and to become empty or floating signifiers. In order to be the overdetermining element of a large chain of social demands, they have to dispossess themselves of any determinate meaning. Let us just think of the imprecision that the term *democracy* had for the demonstrators at Tiananmen Square. Because of this imprecision, it could operate as the surface of inscription for practically any social demand.

The conclusion that follows from this would be that the more the political imaginary is organized around empty signifiers, the more democratic that society will be—or, to put it in a slightly different way, democracy increases as far as its values are more indeterminate. However, this is not entirely so. It is true that if the democratic logic

231

operated to its last limits, we would have total indeterminacy. But in that case we would also have a total disintegration of the social fabric. Thus, the sliding of the political signified under the democratic signifiers has to be arrested at some point. This is why a society cannot be entirely democratic. Even the most democratic of societies is a system of power and is partly based on force and exclusion.

This element of exclusion is what gives to a certain social and political configuration its only principle of unity. Social negativity and exclusion is the condition of any social objectivity. That we are prepared to include in the chains of democratic equivalences the rights of some groups, and not those of others, defines the kind of society that we consider acceptable in positive terms, not in the terms of indeterminacy characteristic of democracy. This act of exclusion is, obviously, an act of power, and all power involves force. As I have argued elsewhere, force does not necessarily mean physical force—it can be just the force of persuasion, which is a force nevertheless. As the frontiers between what is *in* and what is *out,* between what is accepted and what is excluded, are essentially unstable, the answer to the question, What is democracy? cannot be given outside of any context. We can only try to hegemonize the democratic chains of equivalences for the type of social arrangement that we defend. Naturally, this can only result in a hegemonic struggle around the signifiers of democracy that would make them even more ambiguous.

Radical democracy is a political project that has emerged in the capitalist West and that makes sense only in terms of chains of equivalencies between democratic demands that have only emerged in the West. But for the reasons previously given, it would be wrong to attribute to radical democracy a purely ethnocentric value and to assume that different cultures and different peoples constitute separate universes totally uncontaminated by the principles of equality and freedom that have been constructed by our culture. On the contrary, the dislocations of the world system are generating increasing tensions and imbalances in the Soviet and in the underdeveloped world that cannot be dealt with any longer in terms of the totalizing ideologies that have long been dominant in those societies. This makes the latter susceptible to receiving the impact of the discourses of freedom and equality that a project of radical democracy presupposes. As I have pointed out, the same dislocations are operating in the West, and making possible in this way a further deepening of the democratic revolution. The chains of democratic equivalence in societies other than the West will be different from those of the latter because the democratic demands that constitute them are different. But some core of democratic values can be common to all of them and can create the basis for the universalism to which I referred previously.

The complexity of this new world of democracy is the historical terrain from which any radical political project today has to start. The lasting significance of the work of C. B. Macpherson is to have started exploring its true dimensions.

NOTES

1. C. B. Macpherson, *The Real World of Democracy* (Oxford: Oxford University Press, 1966), 2.
2. Ibid., 5.
3. Ibid., 12.
4. Ibid., 17.
5. Ibid., 28.

Mihailo Marković

Editor's Note by Joseph H. Carens

As I write this note early in 1993, yet another story has appeared in today's newspaper describing the deliberate use of rape by Serbian forces in Bosnia to impregnate Muslim women. The rape, torture, and murder of innocent people, the deliberate shelling of civilians, the use of detention camps, the destruction and expropriation of homes, and the forced movement of whole populations—all these are the now familiar components of "ethnic cleansing."

What has this to do with a book on the intellectual legacy of C. B. Macpherson? Just this. I feel obliged not to pass over in silence the apparent contradiction between the theory that one of the contributors—Mihailo Marković—has espoused here and the practice he has followed as a political figure in Serbia today.

At the beginning of his essay Marković celebrates Macpherson's contributions to our understanding of socialist humanism, democracy, justice, and human rights. He praises Macpherson for unifying theory and practice. Marković explicitly sees himself as sharing this basic project with Macpherson, and with good reason. Marković argued long ago that socialism must respect democracy and human rights. He was penalized severely for taking this stand in Yugoslavia in the early 1960s. Later in his essay, Marković warns forcefully

235

about the dangers that nationalism poses for democracy in Eastern Europe today: "A very undesirable new phenomenon is extreme, and sometimes vicious, nationalism. It turns out that, in addition to appropriate institutions, true democracy also demands a democratic political culture."

How are we to reconcile these admirable thoughts and these principled commitments with the fact that Mihailo Marković served from 1990 until November of 1992 as the vice president of the Serbian Socialist party? This is the governing party in Serbia, the party whose president is Slobodan Milosevic, the political leader of Serbia. Milosevic's regime has promoted precisely the sort of extreme and vicious nationalism that Marković warns us against, a nationalism that has expressed itself through violence and military aggression. While Milosevic does not have complete control of the Serbian parliamentary forces in Bosnia who have carried out most of the ethnic cleansing, he has played a key role in mobilizing, supporting, and supplying them.

Now, Marković is not Milosevic. Marković has not held any official governmental position. Moreover, he has now resigned from the position of vice president of the Serbian Socialist party. He told me that he had originally taken this position in order to fight from the left against the right-wing Chetniki in Yugoslavia who were gaining strength in 1990. Judging that that threat had subsided in late 1992, he said, he no longer wanted to play such an active role in politics and so resigned. All these factors provide reasons for caution in criticizing Marković.

On the other hand, Marković was the vice *president of Milosevic's party, not just an ordinary member of it. I do not see how a person in such a position can be dissociated from the regime. Nor does Marković seem to seek any such dissociation. When I asked him explicitly whether he had resigned in protest, he answered no. When I suggested that Milosevic and his government bore some significant responsibility for ethnic cleansing, he denied this, saying that it was being done by Bosnian Serbs and that Milosevic had tried to restrain them. He said that the widespread view to the contrary in the West was the result of propaganda and disinformation. So, Marković remains prepared to defend Milosevic's regime. Moreover, there were alternative courses of political action open to him. There are democratic opposition parties and even peace movements in Serbia, and some of Marković's former colleagues in the* Praxis *group have joined them. It is not a sufficient justification for supporting Milosevic that the Chetniki would be even worse. In short, Marković was and still is publicly identified with a regime whose policies and practices are morally indefensible.*

Let me add two points of clarification. First, I do not accept at face value every published report of Serbian atrocities. Some have already been shown to be false. Others will doubtless prove false or exaggerated. But the basic picture of ethnic cleansing by Serbian forces has been supported by many different sources. I regard it as clearly established. Second, nothing that I write in criticism of Serbian actions should be taken as a defense of the other parties in the conflict. By most accounts, there is plenty of blame to go around. But I see no point in trying to apportion shares here. The crimes of Stalin did not justify those of Hitler (or vice versa).

To write a note like this is not a normal thing for an editor to do. In thinking about how to respond to this situation, I felt deeply torn. So, I want to explain to my readers why I did not adopt two other courses that some people recommended and that I found genuinely appealing.

The first alternative was to do nothing at all on the grounds that Marković's essay, which was originally delivered at a conference in the fall of 1989, was not concerned with the current conflict in the former Yugoslavia and that, in any event, I did not know enough to pass judgment.

This view was, in fact, my own initial response in the late fall of 1991 when someone mentioned to me that Marković was playing a prominent role in Serbian politics. But during 1992, one would have to have been willfully blind not to have learned about the horrors of ethnic cleansing and about the heavy responsibility of the Milosevic regime for what was happening in the region. I also learned during this period about Marković's position in the Serbian Socialist party and about his willingness to offer a public defense of the Milosevic regime. (See the article on Marković by Stephen Kinzer in the New York Times, *26 August 1992.)*

At some point I asked myself this question: If this were the late 1930s and I were editing a book on democratic theory and I learned that one of the contributors had served until recently as a high official in the Nazi party, would it be right for me to pass over that fact in silence, on the grounds that it was irrelevant or that I did not know enough about what was going on in Nazi Germany to pass judgment? To me, the answer to this question was clearly no. Under those circumstances, I would feel obliged not to treat the former Nazi official as just another academic contributor.

Having established the Nazi case as a limit to business as usual, I had to ask whether the Serbian case also crossed what I think ought to be a very high threshold of tolerance for political and moral differences in an academic context. Serbia is not Nazi Germany, Milosevic is not Hitler, and ethnic cleansing is not the Holocaust. Nevertheless, I concluded that the similarities were strong enough to warrant and indeed require me to take some action outside normal academic practice. And having decided to do that, I thought that it would not be sufficient to bury my criticism in a sentence or two in my discussion of Marković's essay in the first chapter.

The second alternative emerged in the course of rejecting the first: exclude Marković's essay from the volume. This might be justified as a way of carrying out the spirit of the United Nations sanctions against Serbia and as a way of denying Marković the ongoing legitimation of his work as an academic that comes from publishing scholarly articles. Some people suggested that the other contributors and I might simply not want to be associated with Marković.

Having decided to do something, I was at first attracted to this option. Initially I thought of exclusion as a form of sanction and dissociation rather than censorship, in part because my inclination to exclude the essay was not motivated by any deep objection to its contents (with one exception to which I will return). But a few conversations and further reflection convinced me that exclusion would be wrong. For one thing, excluding the article would be perceived as a form of censorship, regardless of my motivations, and I did not want the focus to switch from Serbia to free speech. More fundamentally, I was persuaded that those who care about freedom of thought and expression, as I do, should not be in the business of suppressing academic publications. I had judged Marković's article worthy of inclusion in the volume at the time of the conference and the external referees for SUNY Press had subsequently agreed. His conduct after the conference did not alter the academic merits of the article. As I was thinking through the issue, another analogy from Nazi Germany proved helpful. Would I have published an article by Heidegger? My answer to that was yes. Now, Marković is not Heidegger, but I do not think that philosophical eminence should be a relevant consideration in deciding whether to exclude on moral grounds. Once I saw the issue in that light, my course was clear: publish and criticize, don't exclude.

The final version of Marković's article (submitted in January 1992) presented a further problem. Overall, Marković's article offers a critique of capitalist property and a defense of democratic, self-managed socialism. But it also contains an updated discussion of recent developments in Eastern Europe, including one paragraph on Yugoslavia. That paragraph presents an account of the Yugoslav federal army's role in the conflict that is, to say the least, benign and one-sided. The last part of the paragraph describes Serbia and Montenegro as "the only area in Eastern Europe where democratic socialism will be tested for its viability in coming years." To characterize Serbia today as a testing ground for democratic socialism seems to me pernicious. The enemies of democratic socialism could hardly have asked for a better test.

I do not think that Marković's theoretical case for democratic, self-managed socialism requires the judgments in this paragraph on Yugoslavia. Nevertheless, I did not ask Marković to revise or delete the paragraph, because I thought that too would be a form of censorship, a way of cleaning up the text so that it suited my perspective. Instead, I have stated my disagreements here, and I will leave it to readers to draw their own conclusions about the piece as Marković himself wrote it.

I discussed the situation and alternative ways of responding to it with many people, including all of the contributors except Marković. I regarded the final decision about what to do as my responsibility alone, but if most of the contributors had urged some alternative course, I would have given that great weight. In fact, most agreed with the idea of keeping the article in the volume and saying something about the situation in a note, although a couple favored doing nothing and a few preferred exclusion. So, I wrote a draft of this note. I then had a preliminary conversation with Marković, revised the note somewhat as a result of that, and then sent it to him so that he could have an opportunity to respond before the volume went to press.

A Reply by Mihailo Marković

I agree with the basic assumption of Joe Carens: while following the principles of academic freedom and publishing the texts of an author, as long as they meet intellectual standards, one must be free to criticize the practical activities of that author if they violate certain norms of morality and human decency. As a member of the Yugoslav Praxis group I should be the first to accept the requirement of the unity of theory and praxis.

The problem is, however, that we don't always have reliable information about those practical activities. It is one thing to establish what Nazi Germany was and what Heidegger did as the first Nazi rector of Freiburg University in 1933. It is another thing to establish the truth about present-day Serbia, its role in Bosnia and Hercegovina, and my role in Serbia. There is a nasty media war in which disinformation is produced on a large scale daily.

Does one Canadian really have reliable evidence about events in the distant Balkans? If ordinary citizens are helpless against manipulation by the mass media, at least social scholars are normally expected to have a critical distance and at least try to hear the other side. As early as the thirties the Frankfurt Institute for social research established that an entirely new factor in social reality is the tremendous power of the mass media in molding public opinion.

There are sufficient reasons to be very cautious in one's judgments concerning the tragic war in Bosnia and Hercegovina. Several false horror stories widely circulated in the West prove beyond any doubt that the mass media are extremely biased in this case.

The entire world was shocked by dreadful pictures of people killed by explosions while they were waiting for bread in Vase Miskina street in Sarajevo in late May 1992. The crime was attributed to Serbs. This was the immediate reason for the UN Security Council introducing sanctions against Yugoslavia on 31 May 1992. The truth about the event was revealed with considerable delay owing to the report of the Canadian general Mackenzie who, at that moment, was the commander of the UN peace forces in Sarajevo. And the truth is that it was Bosnian Muslims who set the mines that killed all those innocent people, including a number of Muslims. They did it deliberately in order to put the blame on Serbs and have them satanized in front of the entire world.

A little later came the story about detention camps in which Serbs were allegedly keeping dozens of thousands of Bosnian Muslim civilians, women and

MIHAILO MARKOVIĆ

children. Dozens of delegations, journalists and human rights defenders tried to substantiate those charges—without any success. There are no such camps, nothing except a few centers for prisoners of war, which are in much better shape than those camps in which Muslims and Croats detain Serbs.

The next story, to which Joe Carens refers in the beginning of his note, was the one describing the systematic raping of Muslim women by Bosnian Serbs. The numbers given of such victims grew from day to day: from twenty thousand to one hundred thousand. No one mentions any numbers any more. The entire story was based on hearsay. No one ever provided any evidence. This is not to deny that there were cases of rapes. There are 3-5 percent pathological individuals in any community and an ugly civil war offers excellent opportunities for them. What I firmly deny is that there was any deliberate systematic activity of this kind. One of the absurdities of the story is the accusation that General Mackenzie also took part in alleged rapings. Those who accused him of being pro-Serbian tried to punish him in this way.

Obviously all that newspapers publish need not be true. What they say about the war in Bosnia and Hercegovina is hardly ever true. This also holds for the view produced by the mass media in the West that the war in Bosnia and Hercegovina was produced by Serbian aggression. The fact, however, is that the war was caused by the act of unilateral and violent secession of Bosnian Muslims and Croats. People who live on the American continent are supposed to know well what secession means. In the American Civil War it cost six hundred thousand lives. Only those who blame Lincoln for the atrocities of General Sherman (who burnt Atlanta and everything between Atlanta and Savannah in November 1864) could consider blaming me as a leading socialist of Serbia (until 1992) for the unfortunate events in another country, which I personally condemned several times.

Anyway, the civil war in Bosnia would not have broken out without an obvious foreign interference. The fact is that the Lisbon conference in March 1992 reached a peaceful solution; an agreement quite similar to the Vance-Owen plan was already signed by the leaders of the three constitutive nations in Bosnia (Izetbegovic, Boban, Karadzic). The surprising recognition of Bosnia and Hercegovina as a sovereign state by the U.S.A. on 6 April 1992 induced Izetbegovic to withdraw his signature and prepare for war.

Establishing similarities between Serbia and Nazi Germany means adding insult to injury. During the Second World War the Serbian people were brutally occupied by Nazi Germany and lost nearly one million people in their struggle for liberation. In its entire modern history Serbia never attacked or occupied any other country. In Serbia today there are freedom of the press, a multiparty system, and free elections. In Serbia there is no ethnic cleansing of any of its numerous minorities. Serbia has not committed any aggression against its neighbors. It only defends the equal right to self-determination of all three Bosnian peoples: Serbs, Muslims, and Croats. It is therefore wrong both to identify me with the policies of Bosnian Serbs and to say that those policies and practices are "morally indefensible."

I should prefer to stand by the paragraph in my article describing Serbia and Montenegro as "the only area in Eastern Europe where democratic socialism will be tested for its viability in coming years." There is complete political freedom in present-day Yugoslavia with free elections and a multiparty representative democracy. There is a regulated mixed economy with both social and private property. And there is a reasonable level of social solidarity even under very difficult conditions of economic blockade. Yugoslavia is at peace and its only crime is its concern over the destiny of the Serbian people in Croatia and in Bosnia and Hercegovina who have already suffered a terrible genocide during the Second World War. Consequently there is nothing in the notion of democratic socialism that would justify the exclusion of Yugoslavia from it.

The question, of course, is: Does not the fact that Serbia and Montenegro stayed socialist alone in Eastern Europe at least partly account for the launching of such a vicious media war and for the imposing of such cruel sanctions on its people?

Those who compare Serbia with Nazi Germany and Serbian socialists with officials of the Nazi party will be ashamed one day when the full truth about the complex events in the Balkans finally emerges.

Property and Democracy

The relation between property and democracy was one of the focal points of all of the writings of C. B. Macpherson. He opened a problem that, for many liberal-democratic theorists, seemed to be closed, and he lucidly and convincingly showed that it required an entirely new thematization. In contrast to Western mainstream political theory, which tended to reduce property to private property in a capitalist market economy,[1] and democracy to market-like pluralistic liberal democracy, C. B. Macpherson offered a very rich analysis of both with a variety of conceptual meanings and institutional forms.

This philosophical framework incorporated some of the best elements of the analytical method and liberal political philosophy, but also of a critical method and socialist humanist tradition. When he examined distinctions between various types of democracy, property, power, or social justice, that was conceptual clarification at its best. But he was much more than an excellent theoretical analyst.

He succeeded in unifying theory and practice. He examined both ideas and the institutions in which they were practically implemented,

241

and he not only studied how the concepts may be broadened, enriched, and revised, but also how corresponding institutions could be practically transcended and further developed. He stated his theoretical purpose explicitly as "a retrieval of a genuine democratic theory," but he also asked about the historical conditions under which "we can move from a society that has necessarily diminished our humanity by defining it as a possession, to a society which will reinstate humanity as a creative activity."[2]

In his *Political Theory of Possessive Individualism* (1962) and *The Real World of Democracy* (1966), he developed a philosophy of *praxis* just at the time when a group of younger Yugoslav philosophers started their journal *Praxis* (with the first issue of the international edition in 1965) and the Summer School of Korchula (in 1963). In both cases, there was an almost identical critique of the false image "of man as infinite consumer" and "infinite appropriator."[3] The essence of man was defined by both as "free and creative activity in pursuit of a rational conscious purpose."[4] The ultimate human goal in each case was to provide conditions for the full and free development of essential human capacities—equally for all members of society,[5] or in other words, "maximizing man's developmental powers."[6]

At that time, the *Praxis* group was still under the influence of Hegelian and Marxian essentialism and debated extensively philosophical anthropological issues—such as human capacities and needs, alienation, and universal human emancipation—whereas Macpherson had already arrived at the conclusion that a practically committed philosophy did not need so much a humanist ontology but rather axiology and ethics. Therefore, while we still debated whether ethics was possible at all within a philosophical tradition that did not distinguish between the factual and the normative but smuggled values into "essences," Macpherson very clearly and consistently insisted on the need for a concept of justice in general and economic justice in particular, and made it clear that the concept of economic justice was a value-laden concept that presupposed some ethical principle deduced from natural law or from a supposed social nature of man.[7]

Like Macpherson, we in Yugoslavia concentrated on the issue of further political democratization and, in contrast to the Leninist-Stalinist condemnation of bourgeois democracy for being abstract "and purely formal," believed that existing liberal democracy was the elementary ground of any more radical and more participatory form of democracy. The difference, however, consisted in the fact that Macpherson lived in and directly experienced a system of liberal democracy with all its vast intellectual tradition, whereas we learned from the experience of an essentially bureaucratic political system, which, however, passed through an extraordinarily important experiment with direct, industrial democracy or self-management.

We had articulated philosophical underpinnings (philosophical anthropology—in particular, a normative theory of human nature and a critique of economic or political alienation) and we had developed a critique of the bureaucratic state and a vision of a full-scale self-governing socialism. What we were missing was a sophisticated critical theory of liberal democracy that would make it possible to build bridges between existing limited democratic forms and genuine democracy in Macpherson's sense. We had those limited democratic institutions only in Serbia—of all Yugoslavian countries—at the end of the nineteenth and the beginning of the twentieth century. The time has now come for building those bridges—and not only in Yugoslavia, but in the former parts of the U.S.S.R. and all of Eastern Europe.

However, in the absence of a critical theory of liberal democracy in those countries, the pendulum is likely to move from one extreme to the other, from a complete disillusionment with an authoritarian rule—which attempted to legitimate itself ideologically as "socialist democracy," "democracy of Soviets," "self-governing socialism," and the like—to a completely uncritical reception of the Western political system as the only possible form of democracy. What was and is badly missing has, in fact, been admirably achieved by C. B. Macpherson. That is why his work in political theory will grow in both theoretical and practical importance in coming years. That will happen not only in the West— where people will begin to understand that it is impossible to arrest the historical development of political institutions and that existing forms of democracy, far from being perfect, can be greatly improved—but also in the East, where the very existence of social property will preclude simple copying of market-like, private property-grounded institutions of democracy.

In this chapter I (1) follow Macpherson in examining the connection between capitalist property and liberal democracy; (2) indicate present-day changes in the concepts of property and democracy; (3) examine the concept of social property in socialist countries; (4) analyze the emerging elements of democracy in those countries; and (5) project future possibilities of a specifically socialist form of democracy based on a predominantly public sector of social production.

Mihailo Marković

CAPITALIST PROPERTY AND LIBERAL DEMOCRACY

In a very illuminating essay entitled "Human Rights as Property Rights,"[8] Macpherson explained the changes that occurred in the concept of property between the seventeenth century and our time. The meaning of the term was narrowed in four different senses.

1. At the time of Hobbes and Locke, the word *property* included ownership of one's life, body, capacities, members of one's family, liberties, and estates.[9] In modern market society, its meaning was reduced to property in material things and revenues.

2. The concept of material property was further reduced. From Aristotle to the seventeenth century, property involved two individual rights: the right to exclude others from the use or enjoyment of something, and the right not to be excluded from the use or enjoyment of common things such lands, parks, roads, and waters.

3. Property was once a right merely to use and enjoy something. Now in a society in which everything is marketable, it is the right to use and dispose of a thing (to sell it, to alienate it).

4. From a right to a revenue, property changed to a right to things.

The result of those changes is the reduction of property to private property. The right not to be excluded from the use of things for common use has vanished. Thus, the concept of common, public, or social property has become almost meaningless.

Different limited rights in the same piece of land were replaced by one unlimited right of the owner. The thing itself became the object of right in capitalist market economy, and it was justified by labor. Land or capital belong to an individual allegedly on the ground of his labor. One's property was the fruit of one's own labor.

Macpherson showed how this reduced capitalist notion of private property contradicts basic principles of both democracy and individual property itself.

Democracy is taken here in a normative sense, as a society that maintains equal opportunity for each individual to use, develop, and enjoy whatever capacities each person has.[10] Private property, in the sense of an exclusive right to use and dispose of material things, leads necessarily, in any market society, to an inequality of wealth and power that denies many people access to the means of work and, therefore, also the very possibility of a reasonably human life.[11]

Property has been justified since the time of Aristotle on the ground that it was a necessary condition for the use of one's natural powers and for the satisfaction of human needs. If it is so, each individual needs property at least in the sense of not being excluded from the use of certain things, which, among other things, would permit free access to the means of work and give the individual a necessary amount of independence and autonomy. This is exactly what is excluded by capitalist private property. This type of property denies the very ground for the justification of individual property.

By putting liberal democracy into this historical context, Macpherson demystifies it. Far from being the ideal institutional framework of any conceivable free society, it is just a fairly late product of the market society, and it is "a double system of power."[12] First, as in every other state, it uses power to enforce certain necessary social rules. Second, more specifically, it uses power in order to maintain legal institutions and private property, and to protect and enforce the transfer of power from those who have no access to means of work to those who enjoy a monopoly of those means.[13]

This political system permits a reasonably high level of individual political freedom. It guarantees civil rights. It is based on choices and on competition between political parties. It permits constitutional channels of popular pressure. It also eventually introduced the general franchise which, in the nineteenth century, scared even such sincere liberals as John Stuart Mill. As long as the capitalist economy stays stable and viable, liberal democracy remains the most successful existing political system. But it is not the ideal, the perfect, the only possible, or the everlasting form of democracy. It is the most adequate system for "an unequal society of conflicting consumers and appropriators. Indeed, nothing but that system with its competing political elites and voter apathy, seems competent to hold such a society together."[14]

PRESENT-DAY CHANGES IN THE CONCEPTS OF PROPERTY AND DEMOCRACY

When in the 1960s and 1970s Macpherson spoke about the changes in the Western economic and political system, he referred partly to actual modifications, and partly to what he thought were possible developments. Now the picture is more complete. In capitalist economies, there is a clear tendency toward the steady increase of state regulation and ownership. This is especially obvious in Western Europe. The state increasingly interferes in the economy. In Sweden, for example, it imposes full-scale planning on private enterprises. The state acquires control over banks, transportation systems, and defense industries. In fact, the process of nationalization has gone rather far in France and in other countries in which Socialist or Social Democratic parties have come to power. Heavy progressive taxation of corporations is a fact of life today, especially in Sweden, Germany, and Northern Europe in general. This tendency is far less present in the United States, where the neo-conservatism of the Reagan administration managed to reverse temporarily some of the state-capitalist trends. Yet, a large part of industry living on military investments is effectively outside the market economy. Agriculture is heavily subsidized, and losses are covered by the state, quite analogously to what happens in socialist industries. Fiscal policy is still not only a source of revenues but also an instrument of economic regulation (with taxes for various branches varying from nothing to 30 percent). The government, more and more often, bails banks and other enterprises out of bankruptcy. One example was Chrysler just a few years ago.

Here the question arises whether this growing role of the state in the economy and the reemergence of state ownership brings about a promising change in the character of property. Is this, indeed, a change toward social property? Macpherson spoke about a shift from property over things to property of revenue, and from the right to exclude others from the use of things to the right not to be excluded from such use. It seems that here a form of property arises that is not private, but that is not common, collective, or social either. It is statist bureaucratic property which gives all the decision-making power to the elite of professional politicians, still excluding citizens from its control or use. Such a process does not strengthen either what Macpherson called "developmental" or "participatory" democracy. In fact, it reinforces the equilibrium model introduced after World War II.[15] This model saves the system from major crises comparable to that of the 1930s, but the social price paid for it is a low level of citizen participation and a decrease of governmental responsibility. If only the experts can save the system and give it the necessary stability, the political decision-making policy remains almost entirely in the hands of a bureaucratic-technocratic elite. The original meaning of democracy—rule by the people—is reduced to the right of approval or disapproval of the rule by competing aristocratic elites of a new type.

The nature of this basic change becomes clearer when one takes into account several other parallel changes in the economy and in politics. One of them is the expansion of the middle class. While the distance between upper and lower classes decreases in Europe and continues to increase in the United States, middle classes are growing in both. That is partly the result of the welfare state and improvements in the overall condition of the working class, partly the fruit of a merciless exploitation of the Third World, and partly the consequence of saving and stockholding.

With the poor and ethnic minorities apathetic and silenced, with the labor movement substantially weakened, and with the fabulously rich upper-upper class engaged in multinational corporations and interested more in international than national politics, the decisive voice in the electorate is now that of the central section of the middle classes. This is the 5 percent of the electoral vote that now decides all elections, and the primary interest of that social segment is stability, maintaining the status quo.

Another important dimension is the transformation of a truly competitive, unpredictable market, in both economy and politics, into a controlled, predictable market that Macpherson sometimes referred to as a "quasi-market." It has to do with the overwhelming power of big mass media. In the same way in which they create consumers' false, artificial needs and demands on the economic market, they mold voters' beliefs and preferences on the political market. The process of getting consensus is far more manipulative than it ever was, and building any radical opposition turns out to be nearly impossible.

That is at least so in times of stability and while the system continues to deliver its economic and political goods. In *The Life and Times of Liberal Democracy,* Macpherson saw two prerequisites for the realization of an alternative participatory model of democracy. One was a change in people's consciousness toward a greater sense of community and a greater concern with the development of one's capacities than with consumption. Another was a great reduction of existing social and economic inequality. Macpherson saw a vicious circle in the fact that those changes presuppose a prior increase in democratic participation. Yet he noticed already in 1977 that "capitalism in each of the Western nations in the 1970s is experiencing economic difficulties of near-crisis

247

proportions" of which "there is no end in sight."[15] People were beginning to realize some of the actual costs of continuing capitalist expansion: pollution, extravagant depletion of natural resources, the likelihood of irreversible ecological damage, and the decline in the quality of life. At the end of the 1980s, one could add to this list a serious discrepancy between production and consumption, and between exports and imports, which leads to a suicidal growth of the national debt. Possessive individualism and the drive toward maximization of utilities have ultimately produced a pathological situation in which the equilibrium model of democracy may no longer be able to function.

SOCIAL PROPERTY IN SOCIALIST COUNTRIES

Whatever else we may wish to say about countries known until recently as socialist ones, one thing is certain—they have not emerged from a crisis of liberal democracy as a higher form of political or economic organization. Marx was very clear in specifying the historical conditions under which a revolutionary emancipation could take place. It was possible only on the grounds of an already developed capitalist society in which civil rights and liberties were guaranteed and institutionalized. Only then could a new society emerge in which associated producers themselves regulate production, and "the free development of each citizen becomes the condition of free development of all."[17]

Predominantly rural societies in Eastern Europe, which passed through a process of revolutionary transformation after 1917 and after 1945, did not and could not develop postcapitalist economic and political structures. Instead, they developed an alternative form of modern society. Liberal capitalism in the West was grounded on the principle of liberty—both economic and political. As Macpherson has shown, this system was throughout the nineteenth century liberal, but not yet democratic, and it completely neglected the other principles of the great anti-feudal revolutions—that is, equality and fraternity. It turned out that total disregard for them (or what we today characterize as socioeconomic rights) led to social conflicts and to a series of economic crises. Stability was restored only with the introduction of social welfare and some degree of distributive justice.

In the meantime, in Eastern Europe a society emerged that was grounded on the principle of equality, in the sense of the abolition of private property and of class differences. It completely neglected political liberty. In many respects, it did not really follow the Marxian but the Jacobin tradition. For example, the Leninist party had nothing to do with the Marxian concept of a broad pluralist democratic movement of various different segments of the working class, in which communists would be nothing but a vanguard of consciousness.[18] Such a society is an alternative type of modern society in the sense that, like Western capitalism, it also tends toward accelerated industrialization and urbanization, and is committed to the same paradigm of exponential material progress.

Abolition of private property in this society did not take the form of a true socialization. Expropriated private property was not turned into common property from the use and enjoyment of which no one could be excluded, as Macpherson would put it, and which would be directly or indirectly managed by all citizens. On the contrary, all nationalized property became state-owned and the entire economy turned out to be one big centralized state-controlled system. Rather than being the cause—in accordance with the historical-materialist scheme—state property was the consequence of a rigid centralistic and authoritarian political system. Once political power was seized from the bourgeoisie, it was concentrated in the hands of the leadership of the Communist party, which (often even physically) coincided with the leadership of the state.

To the extent to which intraparty democracy disappeared after the Tenth Congress of the Bolshevik party in 1921—which condemned the Worker's opposition and banned any factions in the party—the Vanguard turned into a bureaucratic elite that became the exclusive subject of all nationalized property. Most ownership rights were in its hands, including:

- the right to decide about its use
- the right to exclude whoever bureaucracy wanted from the use of state property
- the right to dispose of the products and revenues earned by using state property
- the right to alienate property (short of inheritance rights)

Major decisions about the use of state property were taken by the political leadership itself. These decisions would be operationalized and implemented through the Central State Planning Committee. Planning went into the smallest details, leaving very little decision-making power to the managers of the state enterprises. Soviets were completely excluded and became only an ideological facade of the system. Soviet bureaucracy relentlessly used its unlimited powers to exclude disloyal and undisciplined citizens from prestigious positions, from any jobs, from their homes, from any freedom of movement, and from life altogether. With the partial exception of cooperative farmers (*kolkhos-niks*), the percentage of whom was reduced from 47.2 percent in 1939 to 12.4 percent in 1985,[19] all salaries and wages were fixed by the bureaucracy. Large material privileges of the functionaries highly placed in the system of *nomenklatura* were the new form of exploitation—appropriation of workers' surplus value—invented by bureaucracy. It is true that their right to alienate property was limited in one sense: they could not leave their power and all the objects they enjoyed to their children and relatives as an inheritance. However, they were able to grant them high rank and prestigious jobs, and they enjoyed unlimited power to grant other countries and their leaders priceless gifts, favorable loans, and free armaments and equipment.

After the conflict with Stalin in 1948, Yugoslavia changed the nature of state property. According to official ideology, it was turned into genuine social property. What really happened was that the functions of the state were substantially reduced in economy and culture. State planning was dismantled. In the first phase, in the 1950s, a step was made from rigid administrative orders telling enterprises what they must do in the smallest detail to an overall coordination of the economy, with the purpose of attaining some principal targets and with the purpose of maintaining the major proportions. The second step was made with the 1965 economic reform, which introduced market regulation and reduced planning to a projection of basic desirable trends of development without any instruments to enforce those trends. Soon it was realized that such arbitrary and nonobligatory projects did not make any sense. After the outbreak of a serious economic crisis in 1980, the federal government came up with yearly declarations of intended policies, which also lost any sense since those intentions lacked effective instruments to bring them to life.

If the state was no longer the subject of ownership, who else was? The official answer was that social property does not have any specific subject of ownership rights. Furthermore, it is no longer property in the usual sense of the word. Thus, there were dozens of billions of dollars of past objectified labor of several generations of Yugoslavs invested in buildings, machines, mines, means of transportation, and the economy's infrastructure—and they were at the disposal of workers' collectives but were not the property of any of those collectives. This total confusion about the nature of social property had grave practical consequences. First, if there was no subject of all that property, no one was responsible for its overall rational use. Second, if all that wealth was no property at all, it did not have any price for its use, which is the case with capital in any market economy. Third, it took a short time before citizens understood that, if that wealth belonged to all of them, each of them was free to appropriate what he could. Each one of these factors alone would be sufficient to bring about an economic crisis.

Because no one was in charge, social capital was used in all types of chaotic irrational ways. Because this most scarce of all goods in developing countries had no price, it was used irresponsibly and wastefully. Because it was not protected against usurpation, it was up for grabs. Citizens were lured into corruption and plundering. For example, with inflation anywhere between 30 percent and 900 percent and the possibility of easily getting credit for building private houses with an interest rate of 5 percent or less, a good deal of social property was transferred to private property. In the case of important comrades who took any number of loans with a specially low interest rate of 1 percent for fifty years in order to build luxurious villas on the Adriatic coast, the "no property" formula was a rationalization of downright stealing from society.

Now, when the criminal stupidity of that approach has become obvious, the pendulum tends to swing to the other extreme. Because, apparently, there is no such thing as social property, all social wealth should be reprivatized. It is not only Hungarian, Polish, and Baltic intellectuals who advocate this as a part of the project of a return to the West where they believe they belong. It is also the view expressed at a Beijing Congress in 1988, and the conviction of many Yugoslav economists and politicians.

We shall, of course, see mixed economies in all socialist countries in the coming decades. One-quarter or one-third of the entire economy will consist of private or cooperative business or joint venture enterprises. Nevertheless, social property will inevitably remain as the dominant sector of the economy. All the savings of individuals are only a fraction of this accumulated objectified work of several generations of the entire working class in those countries. Thus, even if an Eastern European government wanted to privatize its economy, it would be able to sell only a small part of it to its own citizens. It could sell another limited part to multinational corporations, if they would be willing to take the risk and invest their capital under such unstable conditions. No government can, however, sell off its entire economy to foreign capital. That would be the end of its sovereignty and political independence, and that would indeed be an act of ultimate disloyalty to one's country, an act of high treason.

There is, of course, a much more reasonable alternative. Social property becomes a viable institution under the following conditions:

1. In a genuine democracy the subject of social property is the supreme representative organ of the political system.

2. In a market economy any objectified labor has its exchange value and its price at the market.

3. In the same way in which every other property must be protected by law, adequate legislation is necessary to protect social property from abuse and from usurpation.

Once this issue is settled, it is easy to understand that a social enterprise can be at least as efficient as a private firm. Both need able managers. A long time ago, Galbraith established that there is not much difference between what he called the "technostructure" (operative management) in a Western and in a Soviet firm.[20] In the former, the manager is responsible to a board of directors composed of the representatives of stockholders. In the latter, he is responsible to a council composed of elected representatives of employees. Both exert an overall control and expect from management efficiency and a satisfactory level of revenues, from which the owners will get their profits and the employees their salaries and bonuses. In a true socialist model it is essential that management stay independent from both arbitrary bureaucratic state interventions and the interference of local party committees. On the other hand, both in socialism and capitalism—and indeed in any modern economy—government's economic policy, enforced by economic instruments, will determine the basic framework of market competition and of all economic activity.

The difference between capitalism with social welfare and socialism with mixed property and market competition will in the future consist in the fact that, in the former, private initiative will prevail, and in the latter, social coordination will prevail.

CHANGES IN THE POLITICAL SYSTEM
OF FORMER SOCIALIST COUNTRIES

An amazing, totally unpredictable process of political change took place in former socialist countries after 1989.

It started in the Soviet Union with Gorbachev's policy of *glasnost* for greater freedom of speech, the press, organization, and movement. The one-party system was not challenged in the beginning, but elections were freer than in the past, and a number of dissidents, independent intellectuals, and politicians out of favor with the Party leadership were elected to the Supreme Soviet and its presidency. A political opposition was formed without previously organizing any political parties.

Two trends of developments proved to be fatal for the very survival of the Soviet Union. One was the complete failure of the economic reform. What Gorbachev called *perestroika* was, among other things, a project of dismantling former bureaucratic command over the entire economy. However, a viable new model of the economy was lacking. The leadership obviously did not know what to substitute for the totally inefficient *kolkhozy* system of agriculture. There were no managers able to reorganize state enterprises in accordance with the requirements of a market economy. Commercial and banking networks were nonexistent. As a consequence, a huge grey economy emerged. In contrast to the nearly empty shelves of the state department stores, black markets flourished with prices a dozen times higher than the official ones. Yet, the government did not dare to raise official prices and permit free market regulation for fear of social unrest. Time passed without any solution on the horizon, and the mass support for Gorbachev's leadership eroded quickly.

Another detrimental trend was the disintegration of the federal state. First, there were strong nationalist and secessionist movements in the Baltic states, then in Ukraine, Georgia, Armenia, Moldavia, Azerbaijan, and Russia itself. Once Russia under Yeltsin turned against the federal state, the fate of the latter was sealed. The August putsch was a weak attempt both to stop the dissolution of the union and to try to push through the exceedingly unpopular economic measures (especially economic prices for basic goods and services). Its failure accelerated the course of events. The Soviet Union does not exist any more. Yet the aspirations of people to achieve democracy and a better life have not been realized. Regimes in particular republics are rather authoritarian, and basic political and economic problems remain unsolved.

There was more discontinuity in East Germany, Poland, Czechoslovakia, Hungary, and Bulgaria. The governments in those Eastern European countries rejected Gorbachev's policy of *perestroika* more or less openly. For that reason, they lost the political and military support of the Soviet Union during the decisive year of 1989. Then, they lost their own self-confidence and unexpectedly surrendered to populist movements in their countries, almost without any resistance. The exception was Romania, which had a special status in the Warsaw Pact and did not depend for the survival of its ruling regime on the presence of Soviet troops. After the overthrow of the one-party system and the introduction of political pluralism in Eastern Europe, free elections took place, and new Western-like liberal political institutions were created. Those countries are now on the road to democracy. However, much of the old political style—characterized by the spirit of intolerance and ideological militancy—has survived. A very undesirable new phenomenon is extreme, and sometimes vicious, nationalism. It turns out that, in addition to appropriate institutions, true democracy also demands a democratic political culture.

Yugoslavia is a unique case in many respects. It was the first to liberate itself from Soviet domination. In the 1950s it relaxed its control over the mass media, opened channels of freer communication and debate, and reestablished the links with the West. Yugoslavia was the first to explore the market economy and open itself to the world markets. Unfortunately, it went too far in its decentralization, and by the beginning of the 1970s permitted the creation of six sovereign national republics and six national economies. As a consequence, strong separatist economies developed, especially in Slovenia, Croatia, and Kosovo. Under the conditions of a grave economic and political crisis those movements grew stronger and eventually led to the secession of Slovenia and Croatia in June 1991, and the civil war in subsequent months. The main cause of the war was the ambiguous and inconsistent application of the right of self-determination. Croats and their allies interpreted it as the right of republics. Serbs, who have lived in the territory of Croatia since the fifteenth century, understood it as the right of nations. Thus, when Croats decided to secede from Yugoslavia along with the entire territory of their republics, Serbs in Croatia decided to secede from Croatia and stay in Yugoslavia. Croatian secessionist authorities tried to discipline them by force. The Yugoslav federal army stepped in to protect them, and the war erupted—the first war on the European continent since the end of World War II. This conflict has, to some extent, slowed down a process of democratization of political life in all the Yugoslav republics. A multiparty system was introduced and free elections were held in 1990. Nationalist parties won in the four republics that decided to secede from Yugoslavia. In the remaining two—Serbia and Montenegro—socialists prevailed with programs combining political democracy with a mixed economy and social security. At the moment, this is the only area in Eastern Europe where democratic socialism will be tested for its viability in the coming years.

Outside of Europe, and especially in China, some forms of socialism have survived without a clear indication of development toward democracy.

MODELS OF DEMOCRACY FOR SOCIALIST SOCIETIES

In *The Real World of Democracy,* Macpherson allowed the possibility of a "communist variant of non-liberal democracy." The distinction between the liberal state and democracy is, of course, essential. Macpherson reminded people who forgot that, in its original sense, "democracy was a class affair and meant" rule by or in the interests of the hitherto oppressed class.[21]

Macpherson made a mistake when he allowed for the possibility that, under certain conditions (which, he rightly said, were not met), a one-party system could be considered democratic in either a narrow or a broad sense.[22] There is now almost complete consensus among serious scholars in socialist countries that, under one-party rule, one can, at best, start a process of liberalization and make steps toward democracy, but not bring to life any model that deserves to be characterized as democratic. The reason is that, even with a high level of intraparty democracy (which was the basic condition of Macpherson) a vanguard party remains essentially oligarchic. Only free elections could prove that it really rules in the interest of the people, and free elections presuppose a plurality of candidates proposed by a plurality of free organizations, all of which are incompatible with one-party rule. Thus, the precondition of any democracy in former socialist countries is the abolition of the monopoly of power of the Communist party. That means that neither the constitution nor any specific law should grant the Party any privilege, nor prescribe that Party membership or loyalty to the Party and agreement with its policies are a condition for occupying important social positions. All elections—including those in the economy and in culture—have to be free and direct, with an unlimited opportunity to propose candidates and maintain effective control over them if they are elected.

If there is full consensus that political pluralism is a necessary condition for any democracy, there is less agreement about what form pluralism should actually take. The customary pro-Western view is that it must take the shape of a multiparty rule. This view is widely accepted, not only by those who have struggled for a full-scale restoration of a Western-type society (capitalism *cum* parliamentarism), but also by those who are tired of "experiments" and who think in a customary dichotomous way: If there are only two alternatives, and one failed, then there is not much to choose but to accept the other.

Yet this view may be challenged for several reasons.

First, the concept of rule by any party should be given up as a traditional liberal concept. Modern political life with its new movements—ecological, feminist, antimilitarist, and so on—with already existing forms of participatory democracy, and with a need for a more effective control of citizens over the elected representatives (including the right of recall) is too complex to be embraced by the old model of party politics.

Besides, the party in itself has never been a very democratic form of political organization. Because its basic purpose is to win and maintain power, power relations completely determine its entire inner structure. Each party is hierarchical and governed by an oligarchy of professional politicians. Its decision making has an authoritarian character from the top to the bottom of the pyramid of power. Each party needs an ideology in order to rationalize and legitimize particular interests that it represents, and it uses ideological manipulation of the electorate as a means to win votes. These are some of the reasons that so many citizens in the West resent party politics and refuse to take part in elections. Parties have played a progressive role in the struggle against any absolute rule, and their existence must be permitted in any democracy. However, it does not follow that any party should be permitted even a temporary monopoly of power. This is exactly what happens in a parliamentary system, which many Eastern Europeans today consider the most perfect conceivable political system. The party that wins the election not only controls the parliament, in which it enjoys the majority, but also forms the government and seizes control over the entire executive apparatus. Elected members of the parliament must not vote according to their own convictions or even according to the preferences of their constituency, but according to the orders of the party leadership, enforced by the party whips. This is the rule of a power elite that can be maintained with the support of little more than one-quarter of the citizens (as results of British elections during the 1980s clearly indicate).

Another argument against party rule is grounded on the new property structure and the need for self-management in the economy. Even in the conditions of a mixed economy in socialist countries, the predominant form of property will not be private. If the state bureaucracy is the effective subject of ownership, the political system will be a mixture of liberalism and bureaucratism, which was seen in the West, for example, after the Labour government in Great Britain nationalized a major sector of the economy. Elected political leaders appoint bureaucrats and technocrats who have a monopoly of decision making about state property. The only democratic alternative is integral self-government for the entire sector of the socialized economy. Workers' councils, which would have the right of overall political control over the management, would send their representatives to higher-level self-managing organs that would regulate and coordinate work in their branches. All branches would be represented in a chamber of work, which would be responsible for basic decision making in the entire socialized economy. In such a way, property would have a definite subject of ownership rights, and the entire decision-making process about the use of this property and distribution of revenue from it would have a truly democratic character.

It is essential to note that the distinction between government and self-government consists in the fact that the members of self-governing bodies are not professional politicians, that they rotate regularly, that they are directly responsible to their electorate and subject to recall, and that they do not enjoy any material privileges. From the preceding analysis, it follows that there are two basic criteria for distinguishing among possible models of democracy in socialism.

One is the nature of public collective property. In all those models, the economy is mixed with an unlimited number of small private and cooperative businesses and a limited import of foreign capital in joint venture enterprises of any size. The dominant sector is, nevertheless, based on public property. If the subject of ownership rights is the state, decision making about its use is in the hands of managers appointed by and responsible to the bureaucratic technocratic apparatus of the state. If this property is truly social, that implies that there must exist a self-governing structure that elects and controls managers.

The other criterion is the nature of political pluralism. There is no

257

MIHAILO MARKOVIĆ

democracy without freedom of speech, of the press, of organization, and
of the existence of legal opposition to the government. However, two
different pluralistic political systems are possible. One resembles parliamentary systems—several parties struggle for power and the one which
wins the election controls (alone or in coalition) both legislative and
executive power for the duration of its mandate. Another system resembles, to some extent, the congressional system of the United States.
Parties promote their candidates, but once they are elected their primary
responsibility is to their constituencies. In contrast to the two-party
system in the United States, there could be any plurality of organizations,
movements, and groups of citizens who propose candidates, and the
opposition could be constituted in a number of possible ways. A good
example is the emergence of the opposition in Poland through the trade
union movement called Solidarity.

Those two criteria permit projection of the following four possible
models of democracy in socialism.

Multiparty System with State Property

This is a model that is very similar to liberal democracy in those Western
countries where the state sector in economy is very strong, as in Northern Europe and England under the Labour government in the first postwar decades. Hungary and Poland are obviously headed in this direction.
If state capital were sufficiently reprivatized, those societies would no
longer be distinguishable from Western European societies.

Multiparty System with Social Property

If managers of enterprises are elected and supervised by workers' councils, and the state apparatus has no decision-making power over any
property, the capital that is invested in the major part of the economy is
obviously not state property. On the other hand, a multiparty system is
incompatible with economic self-government at the level of society as
a whole. The traditional parliament has no room for another chamber
of associated labor or, as Marx has put it, of "associated producers." Self-
management in the economy remains effective only at the level of social
microstructures—that is, at the local, regional, or intrabranch level. Thus,
social property assumes the form of group property. This involves enormous injustices. A huge amount of work of the entire nation invested
into a particular enterprise that in some cases need not even employ a

large number of workers (e.g., a hydroelectric power plant, a highly auto-mated enterprise) becomes for all practical purposes the property of a small collective. However, problems of that kind have no solution within the framework of classical liberal democracy built for the purposes of capitalist society.

A Pluralist Political System without Party Rule that Maintains State Property

In this model the structure of property will not change much with the existing market-oriented reforms. However, separation of the state from the Party, increasingly free elections, plurality of candidates in addition to Party members, a strong voice of the opposition in governing institu-tions—all that undermines the monopoly of power of the Communist party and leads to a structure in which free public opinion becomes the most powerful determinant of political decision making. If this develop-ment were realized—for example, in China—it would be possible to speak about the democratization of a Soviet-type system. Until then, it is proper to speak only about a liberalization.

Self-governing Democracy with Truly Social Property

In contrast to the second model, self-government here exists also at the macro level of the social structure. In addition to the customary two chambers of a federal assembly—one comparable to the House of Repre-sentatives, representing individual citizens, and the other comparable to the Senate, representing federal units—there must exist a third one representing the branches of economic activity, and carrying on the ownership functions of social property.

The advantage of this model is that it expands democracy from politics to all of economic and cultural life, and that it combines repre-sentative with participatory democracy. This model makes ample room for the effective role of social movements and citizen initiatives. It also makes use of referendums for making decisions on crucial problems of general interest, and permits recall of elected representatives by their constituencies. For all those reasons, rule by any party is hardly conceiv-able. Parties may exist, but they have more limited roles to politically educate, to mobilize support for their problems, to select able activists and propose them as candidates for political positions.

This model best expresses the original utopian vision of Marx under present-day historical conditions. In spite of all the disillusionment and confusion in the present-day world, social property and a self-governing form of democracy remain the two most reliable pillars on which conceivably more free and more just forms of future society can be built.

NOTES

1. Most Yugoslav economists follow the leading Yugoslav politician Edward Kardelj in his views that social property is no property at all, and that it has no definite subject entitled to property rights. One of the basic causes of the present-day economic crises of socialist societies is seen in the lack of responsibility for social property and the possibility of its easy usurpation. This approach turns out to be quite shallow against the background of Macpherson's analysis.

2. C. B. Macpherson, *The Political Theory of Possessive Individualism: Hobbes to Locke* (Oxford: Oxford University Press, 1962). C. B. Macpherson, *The Real World of Democracy* (Oxford: Oxford University Pres, 1966); hereafter referred to as *RWD.*

3. C. B. Macpherson, *Democratic Theory* (Oxford: Clarendon Press, 1973); hereafter referred to as *DT.*

4. Macpherson, *RWD,* 54.

5. Ibid., 37.

6. Macpherson, *DT,* 120.

7. C. B. Macpherson, *The Rise and Fall of Economic Justice and Other Papers* (Oxford: Oxford University Press, 1985), 2-3. Hereafter referred to as *RFEJ.*

8. The essay was first published in the journal *Dissent* (Winter 1977) and reprinted in Macpherson, *RFEJ,* 76-86.

9. See Hobbes, *Leviathan,* ed. C. B. Macpherson (London: Penguin Books, 1968), chap. 30, pp. 382-83.

10. Macpherson, *RFEJ,* 79.

11. Ibid., 78.

12. Macpherson, *RWD,* 35.

13. Ibid., 39-43.

14. C. B. Macpherson, *The Life and Times of Liberal Democracy* (Oxford: Oxford University Press, 1977), 99.

15. Ibid., chaps. 3, 4, and 5, pp. 44-116.

16. Ibid., 106.

17. Karl Marx, *Communist Manifesto* (Arlington Heights, N.J.: Croth Classics, 1955), 32.

18. "The Communists do not form a separate party opposed to other working class parties . . . The Communists are distinguished from other working class parties by this only: (1) In the national struggles of the proletarians of the different

countries, they point out and bring to the front the common interests of the entire proletariat, independently of all nationality; (2) In the various stages of development which the struggle of the working class against the bourgeoisie has to pass through, they always and everywhere represent the interests of the movement as a whole." Ibid., 23.

19. A. Pollard, ed., *USSR Facts and Figures Annual* (Gulf Breeze, Fla.: Academic International Press, 1981), 12:102.

20. John Kenneth Galbraith, *The New Industrial State* (Boston: Houghton Mifflin, 1967).

21. Macpherson, *RWD,* 12.

22. Ibid., 21-22.

Chapter 12
The End of History and Its Beginning Again;
or, The Not-Quite-Yet-Human Stage
of Human History

William Leiss

Brough Macpherson formed the core of his intellectual vision in the early 1930s. That core consisted in a firm conception of the unfolding world-historical drama in which he lived—a conception defined by the opposition between capitalism and socialism. Not a new idea, as he would have admitted readily, but one that was sufficient to frame for him the decisive issues in political theory and political practice that would occupy him for the rest of his life. In accepting the demand (originating, in its most influential modern form, in Hegel's philosophy of history) that events be understood as episodes in a developmental process unfolding on a world scale, Macpherson and a relatively few other academics in his time—notably the Frankfurt School—stood apart from the dominant orthodoxies of their profession.

I, too, accept this demand. I will show that, if we return to this essential core of Macpherson's thought, taking up its challenge again at the point where he began and reflecting on its meaning in our own time, we will arrive, not at his own response to this demand (which is understandable), but rather at the threshold of a new world-historical epoch.

The route for this exercise is marked out in Ernesto Laclau's paper in this volume (chapter 10), which opens by returning to Macpherson's three-part typology of twentieth-century democracy—the Western liberal, socialist, and national liberation variants.[1] Both in themselves and as a group, the three express the dominant political forms of the world-scale opposition between the social systems shaped by capitalism and socialism. Their fate, in our own time, signifies the final exhaustion of the historical dialectic on which they are based. The exhaustion of political forms—that is, their inability to recognize and express the work of qualitatively new dimensions of existence—marks the end of one epoch and the dawn of another.[2]

A TRIO OF ILLUSIONS

Each of the three political forms incorporated what may be called a foundational idealism, a key element of which was the conviction that it had a universal significance—specially, that it was destined to sweep the world. To enliven this account, I will describe them roughly as I experienced them myself in their expressions as political ideologies in the period after the close of World War II.

First, Western liberal democracy. Having grown up in the United States during the 1950s, I can still recall the degree of genuinely popular emotion that was attached to democracy as a morally superior political system. To be sure, this was achieved in part through a contrast with the feared "Communist bloc," and it also sustained McCarthyism and the ideology of the cold war. But undeniably there was a powerful and positive element of idealism in it. For this was the time when the spread of material affluence based on rising real incomes had begun to make itself felt widely among the population in North America, giving rise to the belief that these benefits could be shared by everyone—first, within the nation, and then in all foreign lands, provided that they adopted the "American way." Shortly thereafter, the civil rights movement appeared to promise that such benefits would be extended soon to the sizable and visible minority in the United States who had been locked out of the political system.

Second, socialist democracy. A few years of study in U.S. labor history with Herbert Gutman introduced me to the idealism and courage exhibited in the working-class struggle against predatory capitalism in the nineteenth and twentieth centuries. Whether this struggle was carried out in the trade union movement, in the effort to found social democratic parties, or in revolutionary cells, its mostly nameless protagonists risked injury, deprivation, and death in the hope of ending exploitation and despotic rule for future generations. This idealism was carried over into the founding rhetoric of regimes which, upon the military victory of revolutionary parties, proclaimed their official dedication to the goals of achieving socialism and communism.

Third, national liberation struggles. During the 1960s, especially for those involved in the student movement, attention shifted to the rebirth of revolutionary idealism manifested in the guerrilla-warfare uprisings in the Third World against the imperialist order established by capitalism. This is the era that began with Fidel Castro and Che Guevara, and continued in the Algerian revolution, in the Congo with the now-forgotten Patrice Lumumba, in Vietnam with Ho Chi Minh and the Vietcong, and in Ethiopia, Cambodia, and elsewhere. Its dominant motif—as experienced vicariously in the student movement—was the selfless idealism of the revolutionary warrior who risked death for the sake of the "wretched of the earth." The idea was mooted by Marcuse and other theorists of revolution that the cleansing force of this revolutionary idealism might sweep through both the capitalist world and the sclerotic regimes of state socialism.[3]

Two points can be made about these political regimes and about some illusions concerning the political orders on which they were based. First, the element of idealism was cast in terms of a clarity of vision about the opposition between capitalism and socialism on a world scale. In other words, it was the absolute conviction that this opposition was the determining historical reality of the age, that the fate of civilization hung in the balance, and that a person must choose one side or the other in this contest, upon which the sense of idealism was (and still is) based. Second, each of the three illusions was impelled by the prospect of a "complete" victory on a world scale—that is, by the vision of the final collapse of the opposition between capitalism and socialism through a definitive victory of one side over the other. For a long time this self-serving version of the "end of history" has nourished the true believers in both ideological camps.

THE DISINTEGRATION OF THE THREE VARIANTS OF DEMOCRACY

These illusions have now been unmasked. Let us consider them in reverse order, the Third World variant first. In the wake of the national liberation movements, we find neither democracy, nor social justice, nor much material betterment for the masses—nor, in most cases, any reasonable hope of attaining the same. All the fond dreams have been smashed by some combination of elite corruption and mismanagement, political tyranny, foreign debt and dependence, environmental degradation, ethnic division and protracted civil war, and so on. All idealism has vanished and, indeed, was turned into madness under the revolutionary genius of Pol Pot, for whom the communist ideal was expressed as a people's auto-genocide.

For many of the best-educated and best-motivated persons in the Third World, in Africa, Asia, Latin America and elsewhere, despair over these blasted hopes for a political order based on principled action, democracy, and human rights has turned into the search for a private solution—namely, escape to the West. For example, it appears that nearly the entire group of more than twenty thousand Chinese intellectuals studying in Western Europe and North America at the time of the Tiananmen massacre in June 1989 has applied for permission to remain permanently in foreign countries.

In the Second World of nations with official socialist ideologies (primary Eastern Europe and the Soviet Union), we have witnessed recently the truly astonishing collapse of the entire edifice of political legitimacy that had sustained those regimes. In the case of Romania, this sudden disintegration revealed to the world the bizarre mixture of corruption, terror, and lunatic economics which had been outfitted with a thin coating of Communist ideology. Moreover, in some of those countries, as soon as free exchange of opinion was permitted, we have heard many people instantly express their hatred for the very words *socialism* and *communism*—those words that had represented selfless devotion and sacred ideals to earlier generations of social democrats and revolutionaries. Among such persons there is no question of attempting to purge the institutions of the layers of lies and corruption surrounding them. They have rejected those structures root and branch, together with the ideals themselves. The swift and permanent collapse of established political legitimacy in the Soviet Union, following the failed coup d'etat of August 1991, was just the public acknowledgment of what had already occurred in the hearts and minds of most citizens there.

There is an immense labor of social reconstruction awaiting the peoples of those countries, including attempts to replace an economy that simply does not work, and to repair a blasted natural environment that was sacrificed to the demands of a woefully inefficient industrial apparatus.[5] One hopes that, in the future, a skilled theorist will be able to explain why regimes devoted to the realization of the noblest communitarian sentiments considered it acceptable to turn the environment into a pigsty.

Finally, in those parts of the First World where, over the course of the last two centuries, a crusading imperialism had been linked to a native democratic order, and where the rhetoric of capitalist ideology endures today in its purest form—in Great Britain and the United States—the idealism of democracy seems finally to have exhausted itself. Under Thatcher and Reagan-Bush during the decade of the 1980s, there occurred a radical privatization of what were formerly public interests. Here we observed an already highly privileged segment of the democratically empowered populace—namely, the middle and upper-middle classes—asserting aggressively a claim to an even larger share of the national wealth, and remaining indifferent to the fate of other groups (such as blacks in the United States) or particular regions (such as Scotland) that were being consigned to perpetual backwardness.

Much of continental Europe and other nations such as Canada have achieved in varying degrees a democratic order based upon a compromise in political economy between roughly equal parts of capitalist and socialist institutions—a "quasi-market" society.[6] However, where the ideological polarization persists, especially in Britain and the United States, the dominant social and economic interests have effectively withdrawn political legitimacy from the hope of realizing the earlier promises of universality, equality, and social justice under the force of the democratic ideal. In that political order, we are left only with the degrading spectacle of special-interest groups, representing the privileged interests, bargaining for new favors in the corridors of government buildings: the public form of a privatized politics.

TWILIGHT AND DAWN

In most parts of the world, the collapse of the traditional political legitimacy and idealism associated with the three different variants of democracy is not the result of accidental phenomena such as bad luck, bad people, or whatever. Nor, I submit, are we likely to see a revival of that idealism. Rather, what we are witnessing are the signs of something essential and definitive—namely, the exhaustion of the "spirit" that defined the character of a world-historical epoch, the epoch whose history was shaped by the opposition between capitalism and socialism on a world scale. More specifically, that exhaustion is reflected in the fact that this opposition is no longer capable of generating creative political solutions to practical problems in our era.

In part, this exhaustion of creativity is a sign of success, representing the resolution of great contending global forces. The opposition between capitalism and socialism on a world scale resulted in a historical compromise, in a hybrid form of political economy that has some important features of both systems and that is, therefore, beyond capitalism and socialism. This hybrid is what I have called (using Macpherson's phrase) the "quasi-market" society, a social form in which fully developed market relations in the economic sphere coexist with a state apparatus that oversees the national economy and takes responsibility for major social programs through transfer payments. All societies in the First World already have this character, albeit in some cases in severely stunted form. The recent upheavals in the Second World will propel those nations toward it as well. Moreover, even many regimes in the Third World now recognize it as an objective toward which they must strive. The historical victory of socialist forces was not to be, as the nineteenth-century visionaries thought, the replacement of capitalism root and branch by an entirely different social form, but rather their ability to require capitalism to transcend its predatory phase and to accept a welfare state apparatus as the price of its own survival in a hybrid political economy.[7]

It is twilight, dusk. The owl of Minerva has taken flight. What we may call the "spirit"—the driving force, the spark of creativity—has gone out of the dialectical opposition (capitalism *versus* socialism) that formed a historical epoch. *And now we may understand it.* When a decisive historical form is still infused with energy, attracting adherents to one side or another of the dialectical opposition that defines it, no calm and "objective" assessment is possible, because the human actors are blinded by the passion of their commitment to the realization of particular goals. It is just when the spirit goes out of a historical form, Hegel says, that philosophy (reflection) arrives to paint its "gray in gray," its poor attempt to grasp the vanishing substance of an exhausted historical form.[8]

This is not quite as outrageous as it sounds. We must remember *Aufhebung,* the process of simultaneous preservation and cancellation. First, this exhaustion does not mean that what has occurred during the past two centuries, or what is now occurring, is meaningless so far as our future is concerned. Quite the contrary. Specifically, the struggle for democracy and political freedom remains an absolute necessity, a precondition for any form of the good society. Likewise the effort to define an adequate form for what Mihailo Marković calls in chapter 11 of this volume "social property"; likewise the struggle for distributional justice in international relations. In the second place, this notion of exhaustion does not mean that conservative political thought, which fielded a different conception of the problematic of the modern era, was right instead. That way of thinking was always irrelevant, and remains so. This is because conservative thought has remained bound to the idea of caste, in one form or another, and rejects what Hegel called the "definitive idea of the modern age"—the idea that "all are free."

It is for this same reason that we can understand the dialectic of capitalism and socialism as the "true" self-understanding of the modern age, for at the core of that dialectical relation was the attempt to actualize the idea that all are free. In its early (protocapitalist) form, expressed as the ideology of a social order permeated by generalized market exchanges, we find the attempt to realize the idea of universal freedom as a celebration of unlimited desire and the Macphersonian "maximization of utilities." In its later form—originating in socialist ideology and then adopted by a reformed capitalism—this attempt is cast in the form of material abundance, the prospect of a transition from the realm of necessity to the realm of freedom, with the latter understood as being based on the complete satisfaction of wants. And this prospect itself is based firmly on humanity's technological mastery over nature.

With these points in mind, we can return to the contemplation of Minerva's owl. What the onset of twilight does mean is that a particular world-historical dialectical movement—the opposition between capitalism and socialism—has lost its creative capacity to generate political forms that are adequate for the coming epoch and its new challenges. For example, I have acknowledged that the struggle for democracy in the formerly socialist and Communist nations is an unavoidable task. However, we already know, more or less, what specific political institutions are available for that purpose: various forms of representative government, electoral and multiparty systems, and so on. Although the journey will be long and arduous, there will be few surprises along the turnings in the road.

Let us be very clear on this point. Democratic institutions are not easy to achieve or to maintain in good working order, and there are those who continue to risk death or long imprisonment on their behalf.[9]

WILLIAM LEISS

Yet the basic forms for those institutions have been created already, and there simply will not be very many new options permitted to the participants as this endeavor unfolds. What the flight of Minerva's owl means, therefore, is that the historical spirit—the striving toward a fuller, more universal synthesis—has gone from the form we know (capitalism versus socialism) and is already now at work elsewhere, so to speak.

If one takes this perspective seriously (and I do), it is impossible to claim to know "objectively" what the new dawn will bring. Remember that understanding—philosophy's comprehension of a historical epoch—can occur only after the spark of creativity has vanished from that epoch. At this point we must also refer to another notorious Hegelian expression: the "cunning of reason." This audacious notion suggests that the working out of humanity's essence in history is impossible on the presumption that human agents can comprehend the nature of a historical epoch as they are experiencing its creative moment. The "movement of the Idea" occurs behind their backs. (Of course, Marx had sought to dissolve this apparent paradox with his concept of the proletariat as the first fully self-conscious historical agent. The enormous motivational force of this concept cannot conceal its ultimate failure, however.)

In the epoch defined by the opposition between capitalism and socialism, many of the human actors in this drama (both individuals and social classes) understood it, necessarily, from a particular perspective. To use Macpherson's terminology, they understood it as two radically different—indeed, antagonistic—views of the relation between property and democracy. Again I must emphasize that I am not suggesting that such an understanding was (and is) "false." On the contrary, it was precisely what was appropriate to that epoch during the time when it was suffused with the historical spirit as a creative force.

But now that epoch is closed. And the understanding that had been appropriate to it is *aufgehoben*—preserved and canceled. A new orientation is needed to prepare us for the dawn, so that we may begin to act creatively in the face of the challenges that will present themselves to us. Now, standing in the twilight, we can comprehend the epoch just drawing to a close, not as it showed itself to social actors throughout the last two centuries, but quite differently—namely, as humanity's attempt to assert finally its technological mastery over nature, to render nature, in Francis Bacon's memorable phrase, the "slave of mankind."

In other words, at the end of the epoch defined by the opposition between capitalism and socialism, when the ideological aspect of that opposition has exhausted itself completely, the concrete result of that opposition shows itself as the attempt to assert humanity's unchallenge-able mastery over nature. Mastery over nature means the intention to extract resources from the natural environment and to turn them into commodities for the satisfaction of needs, without apparent limit and without any regard for the appropriateness of those needs or for the means chosen to satisfy them, judged by some criteria for a truly human existence. In short: To get what we want (or what we think we need in order to be happy) by transforming the planet into nothing but a supplier of our wants for, in common parlance, an abundant, unlimited, never-ending variety of goods.[10]

This program was first envisaged when the predatory phase of capitalism was curtailed and the welfare-state apparatus and the ideol-ogy of managed capitalism promised abundance to all citizens and sought to cement their allegiance to the economic system by demonstrat-ing that a steady rise in everyone's standard of living could be achieved. Before too long, many socialist ideologies took up the challenge. For example, the pathetic boasts of Nikita Khrushchev promised to bury capitalism by outproducing it. Here, too, the promise of an abundance of goods was to be the means for securing the population's allegiance to the regime. The route was the same—namely, industrialization and the intensified extraction of natural resources. And the end result was the same in both cases: the original ideological patina faded, and the social systems came to be judged on the literal truth of their promises. Both have been found wanting in different respects, but so far the course is unchanged. Moreover, that course heading is also accepted by most regimes in the economically underdeveloped world, who are determined to achieve the same ends (abundance of goods for all citizens) by the same means (industrialization and exploitation of natural resources).

It cannot succeed. In trying to deliver the goods, first the industrial-ized world, and then the Second and Third World nations, have threatened the continued viability of the planetary biosphere. There is simply no real possibility that the entire world's population, at any time in the future, can arrive at the material standard of living now possessed by the majority of inhabitants in industrialized nations. The attempt to achieve this goal by means of humanity's technological mastery over nature will fail.

The new epoch will show itself to us, in the coming years, as a century of global environmental crisis. In other words, catastrophic environmental degradation will present this crisis to us as an inescapable fate—necessity. When we grasp this fate conceptually as historical actors, we will begin by rejecting the idea of mastery over nature which we have inherited from the preceding epoch. In doing so, we shall also grasp the task at hand—but not the solution, not yet—to find adequate political forms to yield an appropriate representation of the relation between humanity and nature.

NOTES

1. C. B. Macpherson, *The Real World of Democracy* (Toronto: CBC Publications, 1965).

2. To be sure, there are other significant political forms, such as the Islamic regimes, that do not arise directly out of this opposition; but these may be regarded as revivals of a premodern historical dialectic.

3. Herbert Marcuse, *An Essay on Liberation* (Boston: Beacon Press, 1969), 85.

4. Abraham Blumberg, "Moscow: The Struggle for Reform," *New York Review of Books* 36 (30 March 1989): 37–42; Timothy Garton Ash, "Springtime of Two Nations," *New York Review of Books* 36 (15 June 1989): 3–10 (on Poland and Hungary).

5. For example, see John Gray's article on Krakow, Poland, in the *Globe and Mail* (Toronto), 12 October 1989; Christian Tyler's account of the devastated Aral Sea region in the Soviet Union, in the *Financial Post* (Toronto), 7 August 1989; and Paul Koring's article on northern Bohemia (Czechoslovakia), in the *Globe and Mail,* 9 January 1990.

6. See William Leiss, *C. B. Macpherson: Dilemmas of Liberalism and Socialism* (Montreal: New World Perspectives, 1988), chap. 4.

7. For a fuller discussion, see ibid., 119–23.

8. *Hegel's Philosophy of Right,* trans. T. M. Knox (Oxford: Clarendon Press, 1942), 12–13. See generally Charles Taylor, *Hegel* (Cambridge: Cambridge University Press, 1985), chap. 15.

9. I had chosen the approach for this chapter as a whole—that is, as an exercise in Hegelian philosophical history—before I became aware of the wide currency, indeed notoriety, that Francis Fukuyama's piece "The End of History" (*The National Interest* 16 [Summer 1989]: 3–18) had attained for a short while. Fukuyama sees in recent events the sign that our century is ending with an "unabashed victory" for the "Western idea" (namely, economic and political liberalism), based on "the total exhaustion of viable systematic alternatives to Western liberalism." According to Fukuyama, in a Hegelian perspective, the liberal idea triumphed with Napoleon's victory at the battle of Jena (1806) and, thereafter, the essential task was to actualize the principles of democracy and freedom—

abolishing slavery, extending the voting franchise to women, blacks, and others; and, above all, extending these principles around the world.

I trust that what already has been said in this chapter about the dialectical relation between capitalism and socialism is sufficient to distinguish my own views from those of Fukuyama. Above all, there is not (and cannot be) any final victory in human history. If the actual history of the twentieth century has taught us anything, that lesson is how fragile are the foundations of modern liberalism, and how they must be secured anew by each generation. However, there are a number of other points in what Stanley Hoffman has called Fukuyama's "sophomoric essay" (*New York Review of Books* 36 [23 November 1989]: 17) that merit comment.

In the first place, Fukuyama appears to make a simple error common to all second-rate Hegelians (as well as most Marxists, including Marx himself at times): namely, to confuse philosophical history with actual history. This can be a terrible—indeed, fatal—mistake. Witness the suicidal complacency of European communist parties in the 1920s and 1930s, which were so sure that the historical dialectic was working in their favor that they could dismiss the rising tide of fascism as a momentary aberration.

One can adopt the stance of philosophical history for various reasons. I have done so here because I think that Brough Macpherson cast his own thought in those terms, even when he was laboring away on empirical detail in the history of political thought. Philosophical history can yield the requisite clarity of vision on which human action depends—especially that action that risks loss and sometimes death. In the end, however, it is only a perspective on events whereby such action attempts to justify itself for the crimes it must perpetrate in the name of ideals.

And there are plenty of such crimes. Thus, it is amusing to find Fukuyama referring to the past struggles of liberalism against opposing practices—the battle against slavery, against the denial of suffrage to women, and so on—but not to current issues. We see no mention by this functionary of the government of the United States of his employer's fondness for extending liberalism around the world by propping up murderous dictatorships ("good" dictatorships, according to one of his sophistical predecessors). Such practitioners of philosophical history are a bit like teenagers at a party who are consuming alcohol for the first time. Perhaps they were never told by their teachers that Hegel described the dialectic as a "bacchanalian whirl in which no concept remains sober." After all, every tyrant since the ancient Egyptian theocrats has proclaimed that his reign marks the end of history.

It is also amusing that Fukuyama tells us so much in his essay about Kojève's reintroduction of Hegel's philosophical history, but not how Kojève ended his reflections on the matter. Yet, one would think that for someone in Fukuyama's position this is the most poignant and appropriate part of the story. Kojève thought that it was the Japanese who had arrived first at the "end of history"! He said that he realized in 1959 "that the recently begun interaction between Japan and the Western World will finally lead not to a rebarbarization of the Japanese but to a 'Japanization' of the Westerners (including the Russians)" (Kojève, *Introduction to the Reading of Hegel,* ed. Allan Bloom [New York: Basic Books, 1969], footnote to pages 158–62). Such are the unforeseen perils of philosophical history.

10. See, further, William Leiss, *The Limits to Satisfaction* (Montreal: McGill-Queen's University Press, 1988).

Selected Bibliography

Arblaster, Anthony. *The Rise and Decline of Western Liberalism.* Oxford: Oxford University Press, 1984.

Ashcraft, Richard. *Revolutionary Politics and Locke's Two Treatises of Government.* Princeton: Princeton University Press, 1986.

Bachrach, Peter, and Morton Baratz. "Decisions and non-decisions: An analytical framework." *American Political Science Review* 57 (1963): 632–42.

Baier, Annette. "Trust and anti-trust." *Ethics* 96 (1986): 231–60.

Barber, Benjamin. *Strong Democracy.* Berkeley: University of California Press, 1984.

Bartky, Sandra. *Femininity and Domination: Studies in the Phenomenology of Oppression.* London: Routledge, 1990.

Baumgold, Deborah. *Hobbes's Political Theory.* Cambridge: Cambridge University Press, 1987.

Berlin, Isaiah. *Four Essays on Liberty.* Oxford: Oxford University Press, 1969.

Blits, Jan H. "Hobbesian fear." *Political Theory* 17 (1989): 417–31.

Blum, Carol. *Rousseau and the Republic of Virtue.* Chicago: University of Chicago Press, 1986.

Bobbio, Norberto. *The Future of Democracy.* Oxford: Oxford University Press, 1987.

275

Buckle, Stephen. *The Natural History of Property.* Oxford: Basil Blackwell, 1990.

Cell, Howard R., and James I. MacAdam, eds. *Rousseau's Response to Hobbes.* New York: Lang, 1988.

Cohen, G. A. "Socialist equality and capitalist freedom." In *Work, Markets, and Social Justice,* edited by Jon Elster. Oxford: Oxford University Press, 1986.

Cohen, Joshua. "Deliberation and democratic legitimacy." In *The Good Polity,* edited by Alan Hamlin and Phillip Pettit. Oxford: Basil Blackwell, 1989.

Coleman, John, ed. *Revisions in Mercantilism.* London: Methuen, 1969.

Connelly, William, ed. *The Bias of Pluralism.* New York: Atherton Press, 1969.

———. *The Terms of Political Discourse.* Lexington, Mass.: D. C. Heath, 1974.

———. *The Politics of Ambiguity.* Madison: University of Wisconsin Press, 1987.

Cronon, William. *Changes in the Land.* New York: Hill and Wang, 1983.

Dahl, Robert A. *Dilemmas of Pluralist Democracy: Autonomy versus Control.* New Haven: Yale University Press, 1982.

Di Stefano, Christine. "Masculinity as ideology in political theory: Hobbesian man considered." *Women's Studies International Forum* (special issue: *Hypatia*) 6, no. 6 (1983): 633–44.

Dunn, John. *The Political Thought of John Locke.* Cambridge: Cambridge University Press, 1969.

———. "The future of political philosophy in the West." In *Rethinking Modern Political Theory.* Cambridge: Cambridge University Press, 1985.

Emmett, Dorothy. "The concept of power." *Proceedings of the Aristotelian Society* 54 (1953–54): 1–26.

Ferguson, Ann. "On conceiving motherhood and sexuality." In *Mothering: Essays in Feminist Theory,* edited by Joyce Trebilcot. Totowa, N.J.: Rowman & Allanheld, 1984.

Ferguson, Ann, and Nancy Folbre. "The unhappy marriage of patriarchy and capitalism." In *Women and Revolution,* edited by Lydia Sargent. Boston: South End, 1981.

Follett, Mary Parker. *Dynamic Administration.* New York: Harper, 1940.

Foucault, Michel. *Surveiller et punir.* Paris: Éditions Gallimard, 1975.

———. "Governmentality." *Theoretical Practice,* Summer 1979, 5–20.

———. "The political technology of individuals." In *Technologies of the Self,* edited by Luther Martin et al. Amherst: University of Massachusetts Press, 1988.

———. *Résumé des cours 1970–1982.* Paris: Juliard, 1989.

Franklin, Julian. *John Locke and the Theory of Sovereignty.* Cambridge: Cambridge University Press, 1978.

Franzwa, Gegg. "The paradox of equality in the worlds of Hobbes and Locke." *Southwestern Philosophical Review* 5 (1989): 33–37.

Fukuyama, Francis. "The end of history." *The National Interest* 16 (Summer 1989): 3-18.

Galbraith, John Kenneth. *The New Industrial State.* Boston: Houghton Mifflin, 1967.

Gilligan, Carol. *In a Different Voice.* Cambridge: Harvard University Press, 1988.

Goldie, Mark. "The roots of true Whiggism: 1688-1694." *History of Political Thought* 1, no. 2 (1980): 195-236.

Grunebaum, James. *Private Ownership.* London: Routledge and Kegan Paul, 1987.

Haakonseen, Knud. "Hugo Grotius and the history of political thought." *Political Theory* 13 (1985): 239-65.

Haitsma-Mulier, Eco. *The Myth of Venice and Dutch Republican Thought.* Assen, The Netherlands: Van Gorcum, 1980.

Hardin, Russell. *Collective Action.* Baltimore: Johns Hopkins University Press, 1982.

Harris, Adrienne, and Ynestra King, eds. *Rocking the Ship of State. Toward a Feminist Peace Politics.* Boulder, Colo.: Westview Press, 1989.

Harrison, Ross. *Bentham.* London: Routledge and Kegan Paul, 1985.

Hartsock, Nancy. *Money, Sex, and Power.* New York: Longman, 1983.

Heckscher, Eli. *Mercantilism,* translated by M. Shapiro. 2d ed. 2 vols. London: Allen and Unwin, 1955.

Held, Virginia. "Non-contractual society: A feminist view." In *Science, Morality, and Feminist Theory,* edited by Marsha Hanen and Kai Nielsen. Calgary: University of Calgary Press, 1987.

———. "Access, enablement, and the First Amendment." In *Philosophical Dimensions of the Constitution,* edited by D. Meyers and K. Kipnis. Boulder, Colo.: Westview Press, 1988.

———. "Culture of commerce: On the liberation of expression." *Philosophical Exchange* (1988-89).

———. *Rights and Goods: Justifying Social Action.* Chicago: University of Chicago Press, 1989.

———. "Feminist transformations in moral theory." *Philosophy and Phenomenological Research 1, Suppl.* (Fall 1990).

Herbert, Gary B. *Thomas Hobbes: The Unity of Scientific and Moral Wisdom.* Vancouver: University of British Columbia Press, 1989.

Hinsley, F. H. *Power and the Pursuit of Peace.* 2d ed. Cambridge: Cambridge University Press, 1985.

Hoenig, Bonnie. "Declarations of independence: Arendt and Derrida on the problem of founding a republic." *American Political Science Review* 85 (1991): 97-114.

Hont, Istvan, and Michael Ignatieff, eds. *Weath and Virtue.* Cambridge: Cambridge University Press, 1983.

Hume, L. J. *Bentham and Bureaucracy.* Cambridge: Cambridge University Press, 1981.

Ignatieff, Michael. *A Just Measure of Pain.* New York: Pantheon, 1978.

Jagger, Alison M. *Feminist Politics and Human Nature.* Totowa, N.J.: Rowman & Allanheld, 1983.

————. "Feminist ethics: Some issues for the nineties." *Journal of Social Philosophy* 20, nos. 1 and 2 (Spring/Fall 1989).

Johnson, David. *The Rhetoric of Leviathan.* Princeton: Princeton University Press, 1986.

Keane, John. "Power, legitimacy, and the fate of liberal contract theory." *Praxis International* 2, no. 3 (October 1982): 284-96.

————. "Democracy and the theory of ideology." In *Power/Ideology,* edited by John Keane. Special issue of the *Canadian Journal of Political and Social Theory* 7, nos. 1-2 (Hiver/Printemps, 1983): 5-17.

————. *Public Life and Late Capitalism.* Cambridge: Cambridge University Press, 1984.

————. "The modern democratic revolution: Reflections on Jean-François Lyotard's *La condition postmoderne.*" *Chicago Review* 35, no. 4 (1987): 4-19.

————. *Democracy and Civil Society.* London and New York: Verso, 1988.

————. "More theses on the philosophy of history." In *Meaning and Context: Quentin Skinner and His Critics,* edited by James Tully. Cambridge: Cambridge University Press.

————. "Democracy and the decline of the left." In *Dictatorship and Democracy,* edited by Norberto Bobbio. Cambridge: Cambridge University Press, 1989.

Keohane, Nannerl. *Philosophy and the State in France.* Princeton: Princeton University Press, 1980.

Landes, Joan. *Women and the Public Sphere in the Age of the French Revolution.* Ithaca, N.Y.: Cornell University Press, 1988.

Larmore, Charles. *Patterns of Moral Complexity.* Cambridge: Cambridge University Press, 1987.

Laski, Harold. *The Rise of European Liberalism.* London: Penguin, 1962.

Lefort, Claude. *L'invention démocratique.* Paris, 1982.

————. *Essais sur le politique.* Paris, 1986.

Leiss, William. *C. B. Macpherson: Dilemmas of Liberalism and Socialism.* Montreal: New World Perspectives, 1988.

————. *The Limits of Satisfaction.* Montreal: McGill-Queen's University Press, 1988.

Lloyd, S. A. *Mind Over Matter: Hobbes's Political Philosophy.* Cambridge: Cambridge University Press, 1990.

Lukes, Steven. *Individualism.* Oxford: Basil Blackwell, 1973.

———. *Power: A Radical View.* London: Macmillan, 1974.

MacCallum, Gerald. "Negative and positive freedom." *Philosophical Review* 76 (July 1967).

Macpherson, C. B. "The history of political ideas." *Canadian Journal of Economics and Political Science* 7, no. 4 (November 1941): 567-77.

———. "The position of political science." *Culture* 3 (1942).

———. "The meaning of economic democracy." *University of Toronto Quarterly* 9 (1942): 403-20.

———. *Democracy in Alberta: Social Credit and the Party System.* Toronto: University of Toronto Press, 1953.

———. *The Political Theory of Possessive Individualism: Hobbes to Locke.* Oxford: Oxford University Press, 1962.

———. *The Real World of Democracy.* Oxford: Oxford University Press, 1966.

———. *Democratic Theory: Essays in Retrieval.* Oxford: Oxford University Press, 1973.

———. "Humanist democracy and elusive Marxism." *Canadian Journal of Political Science* 9, no. 3 (September 1976).

———. *The Life and Times of Liberal Democracy.* Oxford: Oxford University Press, 1977.

———. "Needs and wants: An ontological or historical problem?" In *Human Needs and Politics,* edited by Ross Fitzgerald. Sydney: Pergamon, 1977.

———. *Property: Mainstream and Critical Positions.* Toronto: University of Toronto Press, 1978.

———. "Second and third thoughts on needs and wants." *Canadian Journal of Political and Social Theory* 3 (1979): 46-49.

———. *Burke.* Oxford: Oxford University Press, 1980.

———. *The Rise and Fall of Economic Justice and Other Papers.* Oxford: Oxford University Press, 1985.

Mansbridge, Jane. *Beyond Adversary Democracy.* Chicago: University of Chicago Press, [1980] 1983.

———. "On the relation of altruism and self-interest." In *Beyond Self-Interest,* edited by Jane Mansbridge. Chicago: University of Chicago Press, 1990.

———. "A deliberative theory of interest representation." In *The Politics of Interests: Interest Groups Transformed,* edited by Mark P. Petracca. Boulder, Colo.: Westview Press, 1992.

———. "On the idea that participation makes better citizens." *Political Theory.* Forthcoming.

Laclau, Ernesto, and Chantal Mouffe. *Hegemony and Socialist Strategy: Towards a Radical Democratic Politics.* London: Verso, 1985.

Laclau, Ernesto. *New Reflections on the Revolution of Our Time.* London: Verso, 1990.

Mancur, Olson. *The Logic of Collective Action.* Cambridge: Harvard University Press, [1965] 1971.

Marcil-Lacoste, Louise. *La thématique contemporaine de l'égalité. Répertoire, résumés, typologie.* Montreal: Presses de l'Université de Montréal, 1984.

———. "Cent quarante manière d'être égaux." *Philosophique* 11, no. 1 (1984): 113-24.

———. *La raison en procès. Essais sur la philosophie et le sexisme.* Montréal: (HMH)/Utrecht (HRS), 1987.

———. "Les dilemmes de l'égalité." In *Les droits de l'homme et le nouvel occidentalisme. L'homme et la société,* 112-25. Nouvelle série, 85-86. Paris: L'Harmattan, 1987.

———. "L'égalité au siècle des lumières: L'importance de l'aequanimités." In *Les lumières du savoir/Broadening Horizon.* Vol. 7: *Man and Nature/L'homme et la Nature,* 117-29. Edmonton: Academic Printing and Publishing, 1988.

———. "L'avenir de l'égalité." In *Doctrines et concepts. Cinquante ans de philosophie de langue française,* edited by ASPLF, 347-61. Paris: Vrin, 1988.

———. "Le général et le spécifique: Logique de l'égalité." In *Ethique et droits fondamentaux/Ethics and Basic Rights,* edited by G. Lafrance, 100-109. Ottawa: Presses de l'Université d'Ottawa, 1989.

———. "Les problèmes contemporains de l'égalité." In *L'univers philosophique. Encyclopédie philosophique universelle.* Paris: Presses Universitaires de France, 1989.

Marcuse, Herbert. *An Essay on Liberation.* Boston: Beacon Press, 1969.

McNeill, William. *The Pursuit of Power.* Chicago: University of Chicago Press, 1982.

Merchant, Carolyn. *The Death of Nature: Women, Ecology, and the Scientific Revolution.* San Francisco: Harper and Row, 1981.

Meyers, Diana, ed. *Women and Moral Theory.* Totowa, N.J.: Rowman & Allanheld, 1987.

Midgley, Mary. *Beast in Man.* Ithaca, N.Y.: Cornell University Press, 1978.

Miller, David. "The Macpherson version." *Political Studies* 30, no. 1 (1982): 120-27.

Miller, Richard. "Methodological individualism and social explanation." *Philosophy of Science* 45 (1978): 387-414.

Nedelsky, Jennifer. *Private Property and the Limits of American Constitutionalism.* Chicago: University of Chicago Press, 1991.

Nerney, Gayne. "The Hobbesian argument for human equality." *Southern Journal of Philosophy* 24 (1986): 561-76.

Nielsen, Kai. "Alienation and self-realization." *Philosophy* 48 (1973): 21-33.

Pagden, Anthony, ed. *The Languages of Political Theory in Early Modern Europe.* Cambridge: Cambridge University Press, 1987.

Pateman, Carole. *Participation in Democratic Theory.* Cambridge: Cambridge University Press, 1970.

Pateman, Carole, and T. Brennan. "Mere auxiliaries to the commonwealth: Women and the origins of liberalism." *Political Studies* 27, no. 2 (1979): 183-200.

Pitkin, Hanna Fesnischel, and Sara M. Shumer. "On participation." *democracy* 2 (1982): 43-54.

Pocock, John. *The Machiavellian Moment.* Princeton: Princeton University Press, 1975.

———. *Virtue, Commerce, and History.* Cambridge: Cambridge University Press, 1985.

Pollard, Sidney. *The Genesis of Scientific Management.* Cambridge: Harvard University Press, 1965.

Popkin, Richard. *The History of Skepticism from Erasmus to Spinoza.* Berkeley: University of California Press, 1979.

Raeff, Marc. *The Well-Ordered Police State.* New Haven: Yale University Press, 1983.

Rand, Ayn. *The Virtue of Selfishness.* New York: New American Library, 1964.

———. "The age of envy," part 1. *The Objectivist* 10, no. 7 (July 1971): 1-13.

———. "The age of envy," part 2. *The Objectivist* 10 (August 1971): 1-11.

Rawls, John. *A Theory of Justice.* Cambridge: Harvard University Press, 1971.

Reeve, Andrew. *Property.* Atlantic Highlands, N.J.: Humanities Press, 1986.

Rorty, Richard. *Philosophy and the Mirror of Nature.* Oxford: Oxford University Press, 1980.

———. *Contingency, Irony, and Solidarity.* Cambridge: Cambridge University Press, 1989.

Rosenblum, Nancy L. *Bentham's Theory of the Modern State.* Cambridge: Harvard University Press, 1978.

———. *Another Liberalism: Romanticism and the Reconstruction of Liberal Thought.* Cambridge: Harvard University Press, 1987.

———. *Liberalism and the Moral Life.* Cambridge: Harvard University Press, 1989.

Ruddick, Sara. *Maternal Thinking: Toward a Politics of Peace.* Boston: Beacon Press, 1989.

Ryan, Alan. *Property.* Minneapolis: University of Minnesota Press, 1987.

Samuelson, Paul A. *The Foundation of Economics.* Cambridge: Harvard University Press, 1955.

Schmitt, Carl. *Verfassungslehre.* Berlin: Ducker and Humbolt, 1928.

———. *The Crisis of Parliamentary Democracy.* Cambridge: M.I.T. Press, 1985.

Schochet, Gordon. "Radical politics and Ashcraft's treatise on Locke." *Journal of the History of Ideas* 50, no. 3 (July-Sept. 1989): 491-510.

Schottky, Richard. "Épistémologie et philosophie politique chez Hobbes, Locke, et Rousseau." *Archives de Philosophie* 31 (1968): 657-63.

Shapiro, Ian. *Political Criticism.* Berkeley: University of California Press, 1990.

Skinner, Quentin. "The ideological context of Hobbes's political thought." *Historical Journal* 9 (1966): 286-317.

——. "The limits of historical explanation." *Philosophy* 41 (1966): 199-215.

——. "Conquest and consent: Thomas Hobbes and the engagement controversy." In *The Interregnum,* edited by G. E. Aylmer, 79-98. London: Macmillan, 1974.

——. *The Foundations of Modern Political Thought.* 2 vols. Cambridge: Cambridge University Press, 1978.

——. "The idea of negative liberty: Historical and philosophical perspectives." In *Philosophy in History,* edited by Richard Rorty, 193-225. Cambridge: Cambridge University Press, 1984.

Slack, Paul. *Poverty and Policy in Tudor and Stuart England.* London: Longman, 1988.

Smith, Steven. *Hegel's Critique of Liberalism.* Chicago: Chicago University Press, 1989.

Sullivan, Timothy. "The negative dialectic of equality and freedom." *Dialogos* 15 (1980): 83-95.

Tannenbaum, Arnold S. *Control in Organizations.* New York: McGraw-Hill, 1968.

Taylor, Charles. *Hegel.* Cambridge: Cambridge University Press, 1985.

——. *Sources of the Self.* Cambridge: Harvard University Press, 1989.

Tempkin, Larry S. "Inequality." *Philosophy and Public Affairs* 15 (1986): 99-121.

Thomas, Keith. "The levellers and the franchise." In *The Interregnum,* edited by G. E. Aylmer. London: Macmillan, 1974.

Tinland, Franck. "Hobbes, Spinoza, Rousseau et la formation de l'idée de démocratie comme mesure de la légitimitée du pouvoir politique." *Revue philosophique de la France et de l'étranger* 175 (1985): 195-222.

Tomaselli, Sylvania. "The enlightenment debate on women." *History Workshop Journal* (1985): 101-23.

Tribe, Keith. *Land, Labour, and Economic Discourse.* London: Routledge and Kegan Paul, 1978.

Tronto, Joan C. "Beyond gender difference to a theory of care." *Signs* 12, no. 4 (Summer 1987): 644-63.

Tuck, Richard. *Natural Rights Theories, Their Origins and Development.* Cambridge: Cambridge University Press, 1979.

——. *Hobbes.* Oxford: Oxford University Press, 1989.

———. *Philosophy and the State in Europe, 1550–1650.* Cambridge: Cambridge University Press, 1992.

Tully, James. *A Discourse on Property.* Cambridge: Cambridge University Press, 1980.

———. Introduction to *On the Duty of Man and Citizen,* by Samuel Pufendorf. Cambridge: Cambridge University Press, 1991.

Viroli, Maurizio. *Jean-Jacques Rousseau and the "Well-Ordered Society."* Cambridge: Cambridge University Press, 1988.

Waldron, Jeremy. *Nonsense upon Stilts.* London: Methuen, 1987.

———. *The Right to Private Property.* Oxford: Clarendon Press, 1989.

Warrender, Howard, ed. *Philosophical Rudiments Concerning Governments and Society.* Oxford: Clarendon Press, 1983.

Wittgenstein, Ludwig. *Philosophical Investigations,* translated by G. E. M. Anscombe. Oxford: Basil Blackwell, 1988.

Wood, Gordon. *The Creation of the American Republic.* Chapel Hill: University of North Carolina Press, 1969.

Wood, Neal. *The Politics of Locke's Philosophy.* Berkeley: University of California Press, 1983.

———. *John Locke and Agrarian Capitalism.* Berkeley: University of California Press, 1986.

Wootton, David, ed. *Divine Right and Democracy.* Harmondsworth: Penguin, 1986.

Zarka, Charles Yves. *La décision métaphysique de Hobbes.* Paris: Vrin, 1987.

Contributors

Joseph H. Carens is Professor of Political Science at the University of Toronto. He is the author of *Equality, Moral Incentives and the Market: An Essay in Utopian Politico-Economic Theory.*

William Connolly is Professor of Political Science at Johns Hopkins University. His latest publications are *Political Theory and Modernity* (2d ed.) and *Identity\Difference: Democratic Negotiations of Political Paradox.*

Virginia Held is Professor of Philosophy at the Graduate School of the City University of New York and at Hunter College. Her works include *Rights and Goods: Justifying Social Action* and *Property, Profits, and Economic Justice* (editor).

John Keane is Professor of Politics at the University of Westminster and Director of the Centre for the Study of Democracy. His recent publications include *Democracy and Civil Society* and *The Media and Democracy.*

Ernesto Laclau is Professor of Political Theory and Director of the Centre for Theoretical Studies in the Humanities and the Social Sciences at Essex University. His works include *Socialist Strategy: Towards a Radical Democratic Politics* (coauthor with Chantal Mouffe) and *New Reflections on the Revolution of our Time.*

William Leiss is Vice President, Research and Professor of Communication at Simon Fraser University. His books include *C. B. Macpherson: Dilemmas of Liberalism and Socialism* and *Under Technology's Thumb.*

Jane Mansbridge is Jane W. Long Professor of the Arts and Sciences in the Department of Political Science and Research Faculty at the Center for Urban Affairs and Policy Research at Northwestern University. She is the author of *Beyond Adversary Democracy* and *Why We Lost the ERA.*

Louise Marcil-Lacoste is Professeur Titulaire in the Département de Philosophie at the Université de Montréal. Her publications include *Claude Buffier and Thomas Reid: Two Common Sense Philosophers* and *La Thématique contemporaine de l'égalité. Répertoire, résumés, typologie.*

Mihailo Marković is a member of the Serbian Academy of Sciences and Arts in Belgrade and Adjunct Professor of Philosophy and Political Science at the University of Pennsylvania. His books include *From Affluence to Praxis* and *The Dialectical Theory of Meaning.*

Chantal Mouffe teaches at the Collège Internationale de Philosophie in Paris. She is coauthor (with Ernesto Laclau) of *Hegemony and Socialist Strategy: Towards a Radical Democratic Politics* and editor of *Dimensions of Radical Democracy, Pluralism, Citizenship, Community.*

Nancy L. Rosenblum is Professor of Political Science at Brown University. Her latest publications are *Another Liberalism: Romanticism and the Reconstruction of Liberal Thought* and her edited volume *Liberalism and the Moral Life.*

James Tully is Professor of Political Science at McGill University. His publications include *A Discourse on Property: John Locke and His Adversaries* and *Meaning and Context: Quentin Skinner and His Critics* (editor).

Index

Liberty, 9, 13, 15, 24, 25, 59, 64, 82, 119, 177, 184, 187-88, 190, 248-49. *See also* freedom.
Lincoln, A., 240
Linguet, 37
Lisbon conference, 240
Locke, J., 4, 6, 22, 24-36, 38, 119, 125, 148, 244
Lockean jurists, 34
Louis XVI, 37
Lowenthal, L., 212
Lumumba, P., 265
Lyotard, 116

MacIntyre, A., 186
MacIver, R., 6, 182, 196
Mackenzie, Gen., 239-40
Macpherson, C. B., on
  abolition of state, 114, 118-24
  abundance, 7
  Bentham, 4, 5, 77, 79, 85, 88, 92-99
  capitalism, 98, 110, 124
  conceptual models, 106, 108-9
  democracy, 7, 11, 12, 16, 99, 105-32, 138-41, 143, 150, 155-68, 175-90, 194-97, 202-5, 208-9, 215, 218, 221-26, 230, 233, 241-44, 246, 254-55, 263-64
  developmental idealists, 6-7
  domination, 7
  empirical realists, 6-7
  equality, 63-64, 122, 195
  ethical pluralism, 114-18
  extractive versus developmental power, 202
  feminism, 144
  freedom, 11, 127, 138, 195
  government, 158
  Harrington, 35
  Hobbes, 5, 29-30, 46
  human development, 11
  human nature, 2-3, 111, 162
  individualism, 98-99, 147
  inequality, 195, 197
  labor, 27-31
  Levellers, 6, 28
  liberal-democracy and liberal-democratic theory/tradition, 12, 16-17, 20-21, 78, 106-13, 137, 158, 175-90, 244

liberalism and liberal tradition, 4, 6, 10-11, 106, 108, 110, 121, 146-47
Locke, 28-30
market (the), 247
mastery of nature, 11, 128-29
means of production, 12
Mill, J. S., 98
natural right and natural law, 4
needs, 127-28
nuclear arms, 122
one-party states, 158
ontology, 149
political participation, 160-63, 195-98
political theory, 5, 9
possessive individualism, 1, 3-4, 6, 10, 19-21, 23, 25-27, 32, 35, 38-39, 64, 92-93, 124
property rights, 112-13, 122, 126, 146, 243-46, 249
Rawls, 157
scarcity, 11, 124-32, 160, 164
self-development, 138-46, 148-51, 160-63
self-proprietorship, 27
social relations, 12
technology, 11, 124-32
utilitarianism, 119-20
Mandeville, 36
Mansbridge, J., 12
Marcil-Lacoste, L., 9
Marcuse, H., 265
Market (the), 8, 21, 37, 39, 64, 77, 95, 110, 119-20, 124, 130, 226, 247
Market capitalism, 9, 92, 118, 161, 195. *See also* Market society, Capitalism, Bourgeois society.
Market economy. *See* Market society.
Market society, 21-22, 25, 33, 35-36, 39, 64-65, 110-12, 119-20, 125, 157, 168, 222, 244-46, 251-54. *See also* Capitalism, Market capitalism, Bourgeois society.
Markets, 15, 20, 121, 198
Markovic, M., 15, 235-39, 269
Marx, K., 30, 39, 78, 110, 119, 123, 126, 127, 148, 160, 163, 203, 222, 248, 258-60, 270